Love Factory

The History of
Holland Dozier Holland

Howard Priestley

NEW HAVEN PUBLISHING LTD

Published 2021
First Edition
New Haven Publishing
www.newhavenpublishingltd.com
newhavenpublishing@gmail.com

Cover art ©Howard Priestley
Cover design ©Pete Cunliffe

newhaven
publishing

ISBN: 978-1-912587-57-5

Content

Holland Dozier Holland

The Motown Sound

Motown (mo'toun') adj [[Mo(tor) Town, nickname for Detroit, Mich]] designating or of style of rhythm and blues characterised by a strong, even beat.
Webster's New World Dictionary of the American Language

Lamont Dozier once described the Motown sound as gospel and classical music merging together and even having a touch of country and western in there. He was raised listening to both the gospel and the classical genres and his grandmother wouldn't allow anything else in the house unless it happened to be Tony Bennett or Nat 'King' Cole. He felt that Motown encapsulated all these elements which could be heard in the intricate patterns that Holland Dozier Holland were weaving in such classics as "Reach Out (I'll Be There), "I Hear A Symphony" or "Stop!" In The Name Of Love". To his mind this type of structure had not been explored to this degree in Popular music up until they started working together. Abdul Fakir of the Four Tops said that they were the greatest writers and tailors of music ever and that he would marvel at their production talents. Dusty Springfield called Holland Dozier Holland the 'motor' in the Motor City whilst General Johnson who would play such an important role in their later work said that Pop/R&B as it became started in Detroit with Holland Dozier Holland which was something that no one else could boast.

This is the story of the three friends, how they came together, built up their own company and how their vision became a nightmare, leaving Detroit a place of broken dreams as well as promises.

Howard Priestley

Reflections of the way things used to be...

For every known history there seems to be an equally fascinating secret history. I love the job of finding that out, looking back, reflecting. This is a book about that. It is also about putting something down on paper that deserves to be read and not because I have written it but because of the subject. The book started way back in late '74, 47 years ago, August of the previous year ABC Records in America announced that they had signed Lamont Dozier to a solo deal. To many people this was no world-shaking news but to loyal fans and people within the music business it was the end of an era. The end of a 10 years' rollercoaster for three joy riders.

I felt disgust and sadness that the news was not greeted with more ceremony and made the point in front of a group of Art Students as part of our General Studies session. After all, this man was partly responsible for bringing to Soul music in the early 60's what Lennon and McCartney had brought to the wider musical field of Popular music. As part of the legendary team of Holland Dozier Holland he had developed and stretched the boundaries of this musical genre further than any creators before them had dared to do. It's 2021 as I write these words and it's a long time since I first sat transfixed by the sound of Freda Payne's "Band Of Gold". I must have been about fourteen when I fell in love with her and I played her track over and over again. I remember playing it at 6 0'clock in the morning to a friend of mine before we went to our Saturday morning jobs. As soon as I got home in the early afternoon, I'd be downtown spending my hard-earned cash, looking for new material on the Invictus or Hot Wax label. During the week I went to the job after school and when I was on my own, scrubbing the floors and cleaning the chopping blocks in the butcher's shop down the road, I would listen to an old radio that we kept for company and sanity. Around 7 o'clock I was able to move the 'wireless' just enough to tune in to 208 on the Medium Wave band and to pick up Radio Luxembourg. This was my introduction to Flaming Ember's "Westbound Number 9" and Glass House's "Stealing Moments from Another Woman's Life" two tracks that had seemed to elude the British national station, Radio 1.

In 1974 I embarked on a career in art and gave my lecture to fellow students about Holland Dozier Holland: by now their glory days had gone, fizzled out, no shock, no horror, no respect. Two years later, whilst studying for my Bachelor of Art Degree I carried on bemoaning the rise and fall of

Holland Dozier Holland, while being the DJ alongside my good friend Ian Craig for the weekly student disco. On cultural visits to other Cities and their art treasures I usually disappeared down some side street or to a market to hunt the second-hand record stores in search of my own treasures: I bumped into Freda Payne, or rather her third album that never got released in England, in one such store and my heart skipped a beat again. The old magic was still there. As my studying drew to a close, I had to present a thesis. I chose the rise and fall of the Invictus label. Why? Music is art, simple explanation. Another explanation was that I wanted to put something down on paper that had never been done before. Holland Dozier Holland's story had yet to be told and I argued that they should be written about and given the amount of respect due to any creative architects of Twentieth Century Popular culture. My lecturers failed to agree, marked my work down and thanked me very much for the wonderful insight and have a nice life.

Around this time, I was building my comic book collection and in the fan mail page of The Flash I came across a very familiar name, Paul Gambaccini. Not only did it give his name, but it also printed his address. So off to the typewriter I went for I was well aware of Paul Gambaccini's knowledge of Popular music and also of the Radio 1 documentary style programmes he had presented. The station had also recently broadcast Hitsville: The Story of Motown, so I thought why not the Invictus Story. I sent him a proposed script and track list and surprisingly he replied. Unfortunately, as he said, although he too was a big fan of the music, he was the wrong guy to ask and suggested that I send it to his producer. I may as well have been writing about Simon & Garfunkel as all I got was the sound of silence.

Let us move on to 1990 now and my becoming a quarter of a very successful local Pop Music quiz team. One of my teammates suggested that I should send off some of my writing to a magazine called Music Collector, I went along with the idea and revised my old thesis to a 3 pages article that was published. That article led on to other ones until Music Collector folded. Four years on and I heard about the Holland Dozier Holland catalogue being re-issued again, this time the company responsible didn't seem too eager to explore the lesser-known material, preferring to stay with the security of Chairmen Of The Board and Freda Payne. Then something wonderful happened. Marcel Visser, Dutch Soul Brother #1, informed me that Deep Beats, part of the Castle Communications group, had secured the rights to the Holland Dozier Holland catalogue. I contacted them, they contacted me and, lo and behold, I started to write sleeve notes for them. Stourbridge Art College was fading further and further into the deepest recesses of my memory and yet for all the artwork I created over my three years it seemed funny that the thing I was suddenly getting noticed for was my forgotten thesis. You know, I have had recurring dreams ever since Invictus and Hot Wax closed their doors. Every so often I am walking into an old back street record shop or looking on a market stall and I come across a box of 45's. I delve deep into it and start coming across songs and singers who I have never heard of but the one thing that remains constant in all of the dreams is that touch of blue with Rodin's Thinker emblazoned in all its power and glory across the label. After I have woke up the vision remains with me for a while then it fades. It would appear that the market stall and back street emporium could well become a dream come true as previously unearthed treasures slowly find their way to the surface instead of remaining buried in the subconscious thoughts of an old anorak wearer.

Just like their music, the book never went away, then a few years ago I started joining the Soulfuldetroit.com forum, sharing my knowledge and gaining some too. I mentioned that I was putting this book together and was happy to fill in some gaps for the forum's members. Then in 2018, one afternoon I was at the local Community Station that I manage when the phone rang. The voice at the other end was American and he asked if he could speak to Howard Priestley. I told him that he was and he introduced himself. I didn't quite catch his name and at first was convinced that someone was winding me up. He asked about the book, had I managed to get it published and had I ever spoken to Eddie and Brian Holland. I answered no to both of these questions, still convinced someone was playing a clever trick on me. Then he dropped the bomb, "They're my uncles." I stopped for a minute and then asked his name again. "Johnny Terry, my father was called Johnny Terry as well, my mother was Carole Holland." That's when it hit me that this was a genuine call and I was suddenly lost for words, especially when he said, "Uncle Eddie is here in Detroit right now, I'll get him to call you." My speech returned and the interview with Eddie Holland was arranged. I had so many questions and when I called him he said, "my nephew told me that it was important to speak to you and if he says that, well it must be." We got on well, I got a rare interview and made a link with the family which I have now kept. When Mary Wilson passed away, I asked if there was any way they would have the time to send me an audio reflecting on their time together with The Supremes. Unfortunately, I had to get a tribute show out and wasn't able to include it but a few days later it arrived and so the next show I did was about the Johnny Terry Holland brothers' connection plus an interview that Johnny's daughter, Mya had done with her great uncles.

Now we are here, at last thanks to Teddie at New Haven for having faith in me. I feel as though I've been writing this almost as long as they've been making music.

In this book I hope to tell the story of the three friends, their meteoric rise to fame and their fall from the heights. How they helped to put Detroit Soul on the map and how time and timing saw the collapse of not only the recognised sound of Detroit but Soul in general as the 70's gave way to a more collective sound away from the diversity of Memphis, Philadelphia, Chicago, Miami and of course Detroit. Along the way there will be theories put forward that may or may not be the truth. I, for one, am not prepared to judge. However, the words will possibly speak for themselves. For example, was Berry Gordy Jr directly or indirectly responsible for the demise of Holland Dozier Holland's operation? Some critics have long argued that he had orchestrated the collapse of other competition in Detroit or bought it out. I will leave it up to you the reader to decide. Much has been written already about Gordy as a businessman. What he achieved deserves all the respect he has had throughout his lifetime and maybe it is true that only the strong survive.

The name of Berry Gordy Jr has survived to remain synonymous with the Motown sound and yet that sound was honed to perfection by three young hopefuls: Brian Holland, Lamont Dozier and Eddie Holland,

Holland Dozier Holland

… Heaven must have sent you.

9

Faded letter, a tear for the girl.

"Darling Baby, love is here and now you're gone. Don't let true love die, don't leave me starving for your love, hanging on to a memory, flashbacks and reruns, reflections. Here comes that feeling again. Bernadette, can you fix it, my broken heart? All I do is think of you , baby I need your loving. Ain't too proud to beg, because I love you. Lonely, lonely man am I. Come on home, back in my arms again. Put yourself in my place, the road we didn't take. Standing at the crossroads of love, nowhere to run, no time for tears, my world is empty without you. Where did you go? Meet me halfway, my weakness is you, loneliness made me realise, it's you that I need. Little darling, I need you, look what we've done to love. Like a nightmare, shake me, wake me when it's over. Remember me, reach out, I'll be there."

Something About You

England has finally caught up with the street violence that we could only look at on the television, or read about in a newspaper, which added to the pot from which Soul was being fermented. We listened to the music from a safe distance and at a time when we could buy novelty stick-on bullet holes from a Shell petrol station over here, you could get the real thing in certain areas of Detroit without even having to buy gas. Soul is full of fallen heroes and Detroit Soul has its own roll call. Mike Hanks shot dead outside of the 20 Grand Club. Tony Hester, victim of a drug related killing. Darrell Banks shot by a policeman over an ex-girlfriend, David Ruffin overdosed, Shorty Long drowned and Marvin Gaye dead at the hands of his own father. What is fascinating is that all the above can be linked in one way or another to Holland Dozier Holland's story. Now this is not to make up facts to suit the story, some of the links are admittedly tenuous but the point is that the story of Motown, the story of Detroit and of its soul plus the story of these three pioneers can never be treated separately.

Taking those above names, let's try the Soul version of 6 degrees of separation, the idea that, if a person is one step away from each person they know and two steps away from each person who is known by one of the people they know, then everyone is an average of six "steps" away from each person on Earth.

Mike Hanks owned the D-Town label where Ronald Dunbar and Melvin Davis wrote and recorded. Ronald Dunbar then wrote and produced for Melvin Davis for Holland Dozier Holland's Invictus label. Melvin Davis also wrote for Darrell Banks and Melvin Davis shared the same group, The Mount Royal Clefs, with David Ruffin who sang lead on many of the Temptations hits co-written by Eddie Holland. Tony Hester briefly stayed at Motown and co-wrote with Brian Holland and Lamont Dozier. Ronald Dunbar also co-wrote for Shorty Long. Holland Dozier Holland wrote for both Shorty Long and Marvin Gaye and the wheels of the Motor City go 'round and 'round.

11

The Motown Years

1963 - 1968

Detroit has a chequered history, one could even say, a checkerboard history. Although the black and white components have sometimes stood uncomfortably side by side. Still, the Seal of the City of Detroit speaks of hope with its twin mottoes of: "Speramus meliora" (We hope for better things) and "Resurget Cineribus" (It will rise from the ashes).

Detroit was founded by Antoine de Mothe Cadillac as a trading post for the French to do business with the Chippewa tribe in 1701. The Chippewa was the largest and most important Native American tribe living north of Mexico and numbered 30,000, divided equally between the United States and Canada. They called themselves Anishinabag, "original men", a phrase that would mean so much as Detroit grew and prospered. It was when Henry Ford, Ransom E. Olds, the Chevrolets and the Dodge brothers began to build their automobile empires that Detroit grew into the Motor City. Up until that point Detroit had remained as a medium sized port for over 200 years until the motor industry grew at a frightening rate in the 1920s, swallowing up the surrounding greenbelt and like the mining towns of the old West caring little about its inhabitants as greed became everything.

Elsewhere in Detroit, on Woodward Avenue, stands the Detroit Institute of Arts. Inside there are more than one hundred galleries featuring five thousand years of art treasures from around the world. There is also a mural entitled "Detroit Industry" by Diego Rivera, the renowned Mexican artist who had returned home from Europe in 1921 and embarked upon a series of outstanding murals in Government buildings throughout Mexico and the United States of America. After a successful period in New York, he travelled to Detroit in 1931 where he began sketches in the giant Ford Rouge Car Plant for a mural based on the Detroit car industry, sponsored by Edsel B. Ford and commissioned by William R. Valentiner, the Director of The Detroit Institute of Arts. Ten months later, in 1932, the work was completed on the Institute's walls; the most ambitious work Diego Rivera would ever undertake in North America. The work was indicative of the success of Detroit's motor industry. Although the bosses were happy to support the arts to the world, nearer at home they sponsored the building of segregated neighbourhoods and when production was quiet were not averse to dumping their workforce.

"Resurget Cineribus" (It will rise from the ashes)

Detroit's second most famous industry had literally been doing just that, as well as rising from basements and old houses with labels and studios like

Northern, Fortune, Thelma, Soulhawk, Golden World, Solid Hitbound, La Beat, Sid Ra, Tera Firma, Impact, Revilot, D Town, Ashford, Karen, Wheelsville to name but a few. A year after Diego Rivera had completed his mural the first of these, United Sound, had opened on Second Avenue, Number 5840 at Antoinette. It opened as Detroit's first major studio in 1933 but it wasn't until the 1960s and the rise in the popularity of local black talent that it would play an important role in the history of Soul music.

During the First World War, Detroit was a major supplier of munitions and supplies. During the Second World War the City quickly became the centre piece of the "Arsenal of Democracy", by landing 29 billion dollars in government contracts and leading the nation in war production. Factories, both large and small, from auto parts to adding machines were retrofitted to produce munitions, parts, supplies, or heavy machinery such as tanks, transport trucks, and B-24 bombers. Workers from across the country flocked to Detroit to work in the war industry, and both the population and prosperity of the city boomed. It was not only the economy of Detroit that would benefit from the war, though. Unbeknown to everyone but a few, the Germans had been developing sound recordings with the intention of confusing the Allies as to the whereabouts of Adolf Hitler. By 1943 the Nazi engineers had developed a form of magnetic tape sound recording that when broadcast had enough of the original sound quality to be able to confuse the enemy about the movements of the Fuhrer. His speeches were used on public radio broadcasts alongside music and propaganda but by 1945 the war was over.

It was then that Captain Jack Mullin of the U.S. Army Signal Corps got his hands on this new technology, immediately saw the potential of this new technology and began developing it straight after the war. His initial intention was to sell the idea to the movie studios for sound recording but it was Bing Crosby who paid for Mullin's research and development of the magnetic tape machine for his own Radio Show. The clarity of sound was going to revolutionise the way we listened to our Radio stars and it would not be long before the recording industry jumped on board. New possibilities began to emerge, as the age of Pop music threw open more and more ways of being creative and it was Brian Holland working at a small, converted house in a suburb of Detroit who would show the full potential of this breakthrough ahead of both The Beatles and Beach Boys, catapulting him into the elite group of anonymous American scientists, inventors and pioneers, those of African American descent. Alongside Garrett Morgan who invented the traffic lights and Elijah McCoy who gave us the phrase 'the Real McCoy' after he revolutionised how long-haul trains were kept lubricated Brian Holland should now be fully recognised as the first producer / engineer to realise the potential of multi-tracking sounds for the recording industry.

Some 23 years after Diego Rivera had finished "Detroit Industry", the music making machine that was Holland Dozier Holland had started to make major irreversible changes in Detroit's new commercial enterprise whilst working for the biggest of them all, Motown.

When the cover of the Four Tops first commercial Motown album was flipped over you saw the Tops striking a classical pose, mimicking the statue at whose feet they sat, Rodin's Thinker, the statue that stands, or rather sits at the front of Detroit's Institute of Arts. This was three years before the launch of their own Invictus label, with the same statue painted on the record label of Holland Dozier Holland's latest arrival. Holland Dozier Holland were obviously preparing the world for artistic excellence as well as giving the listener something to think about. Even the label's name was taken from a source far removed from any Detroit links outside of the Institute of Arts or other educational institutes and reflected the way Holland Dozier Holland liked to be perceived with their pipes and goatees. You see, Invictus was Latin for 'unconquerable'.

Detroit had not only developed into the Motor City, for the more obvious reason, but music had brought a new industry to the city. Rodin's statue has had lots to think about on Woodward over the years and had Diego Rivera lived another ten years he may well have painted this new industry as well as a city torn apart by racial tension. Since the 1950's, when Detroit was the 5th largest American city, there has been a steady exodus of people leaving. Many, no doubt driving their Fords, Chevis and Oldsmobiles whilst listening to the sound of Young America and never looking back over their shoulders. Detroit is now the 24th largest city but back in the day, no one was leaving. This was the city of dreams for so many young, gifted and black hopefuls and out of this creative cauldron of Detroit came the writing and producing team of Brian Holland, his brother Eddie and, the one in the middle, Lamont Dozier.

Brian Holland was born in Detroit on the 15th of April 1941. He learned to play piano through his going to church as a child where he would run up to the piano after the service and start jangling away. Older brother Eddie was born on the 30th of October 1939, again, in Detroit and having studied accounting and was the money-minded member of Holland Dozier Holland. The aforementioned 'one in the middle', Lamont Dozier, was born in Detroit on 16th of June 1942 and as a child he was surrounded by music, listening to his father's record collection of Nat King Cole, Frank Sinatra and Tony Bennett. He started rehearsing and singing with the local Baptist church's gospel choir along with his brother Reginald. He was also influenced by his aunt playing classical music on the family piano. By the age of 10 he had begun to collect singles by Johnny Mathis, Frankie Lymon & The Teenagers and The Spaniels as well as various Doo-Wop groups. Lamont began writing lyrics at the age of 11 and music by the age of 12. A year later he had already decided that having a recording career was what he wanted to do in life. At the age of 14 Lamont Dozier made his first recording as a member of The Romeos in 1956 on George Braxton's Fox Records also writing "Fine, Baby, Fine" for them. The Romeos also included Tyrone (Ty) Hunter who would weave in and out of Dozier's own career not only as a fellow Romeo but as a member of The Voicemasters and also as a solo artist on Chess for whom Dozier would continue to develop his song writing. Incidentally, David Ruffin was also a member of The Voicemasters before finding his way to Motown and to The Temptations. Further down the road Ty Hunter blossomed in Invictus' Glass House before returning to The Originals and being produced by Dozier in 1975 on their outstanding "California Sunset" album. It is also worth noting that Leon Ware, singer / songwriter / producer also helped swell the ranks of The Romeos.

Now, before the team of Holland Dozier Holland got together another group who would have a great impact on HDH's fortunes was already formed. The Four Tops had been together since 1954 and until the death of Laurence Payton on 20th June 1997 had held the enviable record within the recording industry of remaining unchanged for some 43 years. Previously they had been known as The Four Aims but changed this so as not to be confused with The Ames Brothers. In 1956, the same year that Lamont had made his debut, the Four Tops were still trying to find that elusive hit and tried again with "Could It Be You" for Chess with no success and so moved on to the Red Top label.

As Gordy's empire grew so too did Dozier's song writing activities, even though he was still ambitious to become a singer and as such cut "Fortune Teller Tell Me" backed by "Dearest One" on Melody, yet another label that had been added to Berry Gordy's growing roster. However, it remained his song writing for Gordy's Jobete Music, particularly when he was teamed up with Brian Holland that garnered most approval. This, in turn, only came about after one Freddie Gorman had chosen to pursue a singing career and thus ditch his writing duties to front arguably one of Detroit's most pivotal groups, The Originals.

In 1957 Brian Holland came to be the lead singer with The Satintones, a Rhythm & Blues vocal group from Detroit. The original members being Robert Bateman, Chico Laverett, James Ellis and Sonny Sanders. These singers who came together in this year were the first group to sign to one of Berry Gordy's own labels, Tamla. Across on the East Coast, The Parliaments, as they were originally known after a brand of cigarettes, had formed in Newark, New Jersey in 1955 and in 1957 released "Poor Willy" on ABC Records which did nothing. Their second release, "Lonely Island" issued on the local New Records also failed to make an impression and it would not be long before they realised that they would have to set their sights further than New Jersey and so set their compass to point towards Detroit. The same year Smokey Robinson formed a friendship with Berry Gordy at a time when Robinson led The Matadors who Gordy then re-christened The Miracles but before any recording took place Gordy helped Robinson 'unclutter' his teenage scribbles and re-structure lyrics into meaningful songs.

The following year, 1958, a small New York label, End Records, released the first record by The Miracles, "Got A Job", an answer record to The Silhouettes Doo Wop hit "Get A Job" while group members Robinson and Ron White were also recording for Chess out of Chicago as Ron & Bill. Chess would also be significant in distributing the Anna label, named after Anna Gordy, Berry's sister. The biggest hit for Anna was Barrett Strong's original version of "Money (That's What I Want)", the first release belonging to The Voice Masters with "Memories" featuring the lead vocal of Ty Hunter. At the age of 17 Brian Holland had had an early Berry Gordy release, also in '58, "(Where's The Joy?) In Nature Boy" through Kudo Records but had primarily been signed up as a recording engineer later to be developed as a writer for Gordy at the suggestion of his older brother, Eddie. Holland also met one Freddie Gorman whose earliest ventures were with the unrecorded Dynatones before moving on to The Quailtones. This group made the studio and cut "Tears of Love" and "Roxanna" for the Josie label. Eddie Holland joined The Quailtones for a brief period before bringing along his brother Brian to form part of the Fidelitones. In 1958 The Fidelitones cut one single, "Pretty Girl" for Aladdin. The patchwork quilt was still being stitched together and part of the weave included elements of the Doo-Wop groups and Rock & Roll of the late fifties being merged with the Gospel-tinged music of Sam Cooke, known to many as the father of Soul music.

In the same year of '58 Eddie Holland had had an unsuccessful solo baptism into the music business when Berry Gordy released "You (You You You You)" on Mercury by Holland. A struggling songwriter Gordy, a cousin of Jackie Wilson, chanced upon Wilson's manager who was searching for material for him. Gordy was able to get Wilson to record "Lonely Teardrops" and "Reet Petite". Gordy had met Eddie Holland at the Graystone Ballroom in Detroit when Holland, aged 16 and having a vocal range not dissimilar to Jackie Wilson vocally became the featured session singer on demos for Wilson and continued working with him until 1959 prior to his fulltime involvement in Motown.

Growing disgruntled at not receiving the financial rewards he expected, Gordy added producing to his song writing skills; Herman Griffith being Gordy's first Motown production with "I Need You" leased to the HOB (House of Beauty) label. while the first artist to benefit significantly from Gordy's growing ambition was Marv Johnson. Meanwhile, having moved to New York two years earlier, to get a 'regular job' and where he also got married, Lamont Dozier found his way back to Detroit. On his return Dozier also met up with Berry Gordy Jr. who signed him to the Anna label where he recorded as Lamont Anthony. The Anna label grew with National R&B hits for Ty Hunter, Joe Tex and the aforementioned Barrett Strong whose version of "Money" was the original that would later be adopted by, as well as be synonymous with, the 60's British Beat Generation.

Such was the buzz around Detroit that it seemed the right time for Berry Gordy to move forward and not simply remain a writer-cum-producer who was having product leased to others: Gordy was to become a manufacturer. With strong persuasion from Smokey Robinson Gordy formed the Motown Record Corporation encompassing a slew of labels, Motown itself taking its name from Motortown, the nickname for Detroit because of its then powerful car industry. Now Gordy was hiring studio time and musicians as well as developing a team of songwriters that included Lamont Dozier, grooming a sound engineer called Brian Holland and staying true to a sometime singer, Eddie Holland.

When Berry Gordy Jr created Motown back in 1959, he gave the American Dream to a portion of black America who grew and grew as Motown itself did. Some fell from the dizzy heights but, in general, many would stay at the top for a long, long time. No mean feat in itself in an industry often built on sand. Motown was destined to become the World's most successful independent record company: a black owned corporation in a white led industry. Now, although many critics condemned Gordy for selling out or 'whitening' black music with his clever mix of rhythm & blues and popular white musical trends, the fact remained that Gordy also benefited the local black community by giving opportunities, albeit as an opportunist himself, to many people who otherwise may have been destined to live a life in the Projects, inner City housing developments. Nobody was in the business to lose money and to be commercially viable it was necessary for Gordy to take up certain popular musical themes and blend them with his own ideas and traditions. An early indication of these forays into white popular culture was the initial desire to call another of his labels Tammie after the 1959 hit by Debbie Reynolds, although this was thankfully prevented because of copyright. The next two years would see significant strides that culminated in the gold "Shop Around" by The Miracles.

18

As an astute businessman Gordy had seen the marketing power of using a name freshly placed in a white record buying consciousness and white popular music had, itself, taken from black music to find its backbone and stride. Berry Gordy Jr stood as a black man who grabbed for the American Dream and made it a reality, much like Sam Cooke, opening the way for others to follow. A tradition still felt strongly today when new creators look at Motown as an organisation to emulate. Time showed though that not all the creative talent gathered by Gordy had the same eye for business. Norman Whitfield launched his own Whitfield label, George Clinton failed with his own Uncle Jam label and the Holland Dozier Holland team valiantly battled on with their Invictus Company until their own separation. Still, all of them added to the overall pattern and texture that was Detroit Soul and all of the seemingly loose threads began to intertwine as did the aforementioned Voice Masters.

The Voice Masters were formed in 1959, later joining Motown with some of them helping to form The Originals featuring Freddie Gorman. The same year the prototype of the Soul super group The Falcons scored with the R&B hit "You're So Fine" with Joe Stubbs, younger brother to Levi of the Four Tops, singing lead. Stubbs later became a solo artist for Lupine and briefly joined The Originals at Motown. Staying with the label he then joined The Contours in 1967 for whom he sang lead on "Just A Little Misunderstanding". After Stubbs left The Falcons Eddie Floyd spent a brief period as The Falcons' lead singer before pursuing a successful solo career with Stax Records and making way for yet another Soul legend, Wilson Pickett, to join the group. Back to Motown and in 1959 "Going to The Hop" was issued by The Satintones on Tamla and was followed by the very first single on the Motown brand, "Sugar Daddy". After three further singles for Motown, all continuing the Rhythm & Blues vocal group style of the late 50's, the group disbanded with Robert Bateman becoming a producer for the label. To be fair, The Satintones are best known, not so much for their recordings, but for their early association with Motown and for producing future talents in the Detroit recording scene, the most famous being unquestionably Brian Holland. Still, the group had managed to bridge the gap from the Rock and Roll and Doo Wop of the 50's to the new Soul movement of the 60's. More releases under Eddie Holland's own name followed in 1959 with "Merry-Go-Round", a Tamla production, released through United Artists and a year later he continued his allegiance to Berry Gordy with three more unsuccessful releases, also on United Artists, "Because I Love Her", "Magic Mirror" and "The Last Laugh".

Motown needed to rely on more than one artist or group and in a harsh but ultimately beneficial business move Gordy released a series of recordings between 1960 and 1964 by established R&B performers from around the Detroit area. Amongst them were Amos Milburn, 'Singin' Sammy Ward and Gino Parks but after 1964 none of these performers appeared on the label's roster. Their purpose was served: they gained Motown a local respect and boosted company sales but now had to make way for Gordy's youth policy. During 1959 and 1960 Marv Johnson gained the hits "I Love the Way You Love", "You Got What It Takes" and "Move Two Mountains", again, via United Artists but the personal differences between Gordy and Johnson prevented him from becoming Motown's first major star. By now Gordy had gained a partner and later second wife, Raynoma Liles who he had met in 1959.

During Motown's formative years Raynoma Liles found 2648 West Grand Boulevard, in Detroit, that would become recognised as the first home of Motown. It was from here that the label's earliest recordings were made. The couple were only married for 18 months but Raynoma Liles and Berry Gordy developed the Rayber Music Writing Company. Rayber, abbreviated from Raynoma and Berry, was formed to help young Detroit performers to find outlets for their songs, cutting records and demos that would be leased to larger companies. The couple gave to each other important business skills: while Gordy taught Liles a greater business sense, she gave him a smoothness that had previously been lacking in the former boxer's work. The Rayber Singers (Raynoma and Berry) were also formed to create background singing for other artists and numbered among them Brian Holland. The couple advertised on a local radio station and caught the ear of their first paying client, Louvain Demps in 1959. Louvain was born in New York on the 7th of April 1938 and raised in Detroit where she attended Pershing High, based at Seven Mile Road and Ryan Road. Elsewhere and still away from the developing Motown company, Columbia released a single on the Four Tops "Ain't That Love" but, again, it did nothing. Meanwhile Gordy was building a roster of groups and solo performers aided by writers and producers who could deliver the right sound to the right artist. Richard Wylie was one such backroom star and had landed an audition at Motown. Richard Wayne Wylie was born in Detroit on the 6th of June 1939. He grew up in a musical family and acquired the nickname "Popcorn" because he made a habit of popping quickly out of the football team's huddle at Northwestern High School. One could say that he also had a habit of popping up all over Detroit as we will later see.

It was when he was at High School that he formed his first band with his fellow school friends James Jamerson on the upright bass and Clifford Mack on the drums; the three were dedicated musicians and had a huge love of jazz. They soon became a popular band at parties, weddings, college functions and night spots around Detroit. Popcorn's band gradually evolved into Popcorn and the Mohawks. He was also a regular performer at the

Twenty Grand Club, a Detroit club where he met a fellow musician and budding songwriter Robert Bateman, then doubling up as an engineer for Gordy's fledgling Motown label. In 1960 Popcorn signed with the Northern label to record his debut single, "Pretty Girl" before signing with the Motown Label. At this stage Popcorn and The Mohawks consisted of Richard "Popcorn" Wylie on piano, James Jamerson on upright bass, Eddie Willis on guitar, Robert Finch and Lamont Dozier on drums, Andrew "Mike" Terry on the sax and future Motown producer Norman Whitfield on the tambourines.

While with Motown, Popcorn and The Mohawks released "Shimmy Gully," one of the earliest Motown releases, He allegedly played piano on "Shop Around", by The Miracles, the first Million seller for the company although Berry Gordy himself takes credit according to one source. The track was cut at 3am when all but the piano player was there, hence Gordy tickling the ivories. He also played on Barrett Strong's "Money (That's What I Want)" for Anna Records in 1960 that provided vital capital for Gordy to expand his operation. At Motown, Wylie also worked with The Contours, Marvin Gaye, Marv Johnson, The Supremes, Martha & the Vandellas and Mary Wells. He was another creative force that would blow in and out of Motown and other labels in Detroit including Holland Dozier Holland's later venture. He wanted a group of singers, The Andantes, to be his backing group. The group consisted of Emily Phillips, Jackie Hicks and Marlene Barrow. Hicks and Barrow attended Northwestern High School with Wylie. Situated further down the block at 2200 West Grand Boulevard, Northwestern was the fifth high school to open in the City and a place rife with future recording artists. Wylie brought his two classmates to Motown in 1960 along with Emily Phillips. The group acquired its name while Hicks and Barrow were singing with Emily Phillips, at Hartford Baptist Church in Detroit. It was their piano accompanist Mildred Dobey that gave the girls the name telling them it meant soft and sweet in Italian. Emily Phillips married and pressure from her husband, who didn't want her to sing, forced her into leaving. It was at this time that Louvain Demps, the Rayber Company's first paying client was invited to join The Andantes who, in turn, were invited to stay. At first, they were in the shadows of The Rayber Singers. The Andantes though would outlive The Rayber Singers and become an integral cog in the hit machine that Motown was beginning to be. In their career they remained uncredited and yet it was their unique vocalising that enhanced most of the records being created at Hitsville.

The Andantes provided flawless, but largely unaccredited studio backing on countless Motown hits and it has been written, appeared on more than 20,000 recording sessions. Early recordings that they graced were Mary Well's "Laughing Boy" and Eddie Holland's "Jamie". From within Popcorn & The Mohawks Andrew 'Mike' Terry was perhaps the least talked about but one of the most influential musicians to help formulate the Motown sound of the early 60's.

Born in 1940 in Hempstead, Texas, he moved to Detroit in 1948 and started playing baritone sax at the age thirteen. After graduating from CASS Tech in 1959, he was introduced to Berry Gordy, the founder of Motown Records. He signed an agreement with Gordy that kept him at Motown up until 1966 during which time his fluid, rolling baritone sax could be heard all over such Holland Dozier Holland compositions as Marvin Gaye's "How Sweet It Is", the Four Tops' "I Can't Help Myself" and "Something About You" The Supremes' "Baby Love," "Where Did Our Love Go" and "I Hear A Symphony" Martha & The Vandellas' "Quicksand" and "Heatwave" and complimenting Junior Walker's saxophone on "I'm A Road Runner". If James Jamerson was the genius of the bass, Mike Terry wore the same shoes in the sax department and without either of them HDH's sound would have never been the same, nor would Motown's.

The label was gradually taking shape but like any new business, cash flow problems plagued Motown. That minor issue aside, the label's first Queen of Soul, Mary Wells, was about to take her throne. Wells was signed to Motown in 1960 by Berry Gordy after the Northwestern High School girl had gone to find Gordy to try and get her composition "Bye Bye Baby" to Jackie Wilson. Fairy tale fantasy became fact when Gordy signed her to record the song herself. Guided initially by Smokey Robinson and later by the rising team of Holland Dozier Holland Wells had several hits on the fledgling label starting with "Bye Bye Baby" in that year.

In the same year Brian Holland also found himself touring as pianist with Barrett Strong while The Primettes, who had started out as sister group to The Primes, a male quartet that included Eddie Kendricks and Paul Williams who would later form part of The Temptations, were attempting to push open the door of Motown. Robert Bateman had been responsible for inviting the girls to Motown to audition for the fledgling label but after the audition with Smokey Robinson the group was turned down and so signed to another local label, Lupine. However, group leader Florence Ballard was determined to work at Motown and so day in day out the group would hang around the Motown building doing background singing or handclaps until their determination was rewarded and they signed to the label in 1960. Florence Ballard changed the name of The Primettes to The Supremes and they debuted in 1961 with "I Want A Guy" recorded on the 9th of March, written by Freddie Gorman of The Voice Masters but the song failed to make any impact and they would remain in the shadows of the label's already established girl group, The Marvelettes for quite some time.

Brian Holland was working with Robert Bateman, a singer and talent scout who had also joined the Rayber Singers and between them, as the clumsily named production unit Brianbert, had been responsible for "Please Mr. Postman" by The Marvelettes in August 1961, which also included the piano playing skills of Popcorn Wylie and was another of the Beat Generation's anthems when covered by those fab four, The Beatles. Gordy offered Robert Bateman the opportunity to manage The Supremes, he turned it down saying that "no one wanted to get involved with that skinny kid who sang through her nose". Having tasted success with The Marvelettes he seemed reluctant to take a chance with the new untried kids on the block. The Marvelettes had hailed from Dearborn, a suburb of Detroit and home of Henry Ford with the Ford Rouge Plant based there. A factory that mass-produced the Ford Model T and Mustang and at one time employed 100,000 people. The three Marvelettes attended Inkster High School, situated at 3250 Middlebelt Road. Their original version of "Please Mr Postman" became the company's first Number 1 in November 1961, although the first million seller for Motown belonged to The Miracles, led by one of the company's most significant and prolific songwriter/producers, William 'Smokey' Robinson. This was on the Tamla label, the name Gordy settled for instead of Tammie.

Another performer was beginning his career, albeit unsuccessfully across the nearby Canadian border, a white Country singer, born in Toronto, Canada in 1939 and who started his career there in 1961. He played piano and sang with various groups at the main clubs around Toronto. His first recordings were on the Audiomaster label but the inferior sound quality, of these singles, meant that they got little or no airplay. Undeterred he found his way to New York before turning his attention to Detroit where he would find fame. His name was R. Dean Taylor and he too would play a pivotal role in the careers of Holland Dozier Holland.

The Detroit music scene was made up of a mixture of local talent and talent that had migrated to Detroit to seek better opportunities within the Motor City, one exception, however, was General Norman Johnson who was drafted into Holland Dozier Holland's empire at a later date but who in 1961 was making waves outside of the city. Johnson was born in Norfolk, Virginia on the 23rd of May 1944 and took his early influence from his father who, along with a group of friends performed as The Israelites. Johnson spent six years as a boy amongst the men before moving on to The Humdingers, a group of guys Johnson hung out in the neighbourhood with and who shared the kind of bond that stays for a long time. The Humdingers recorded for the Atlantic label however no tracks were ever released. The group changed names when they signed to Minit, at the request of the label owner who thought their name was less than a humdinger. They became

23

The Showmen, a five-piece vocal group from Norfolk, Virginia. Johnson stayed with The Showmen, for 10 years and are best remembered for the Minit hit of 1961, "It Will Stand".

Back in Detroit "Shop Around" by The Miracles reached Number 1 on the R&B chart and Number 2 Nationally in America. Freddie Gorman signed to the short-lived Motown subsidiary, Miracle for one single, "The Day Will Come", 1961 but the lack of success led Gorman to drop the mike and pick up his pen. The label's motto, "If It's A Hit, It's A Miracle" was not perhaps Gordy's most inspirational moment. Gorman had started singing in his first vocal group called the Dynatones when he was about eleven. The group just rehearsed with no recordings forthcoming. William Weatherspoon who would later become an integral part of Holland Dozier Holland's work was also in the group. At this stage the Detroit scene resembled speed dating, in a constant state of flux, with names that are now familiar to us still finding their way around the groups and clubs of the city in search of that winning combination. Freddie Gorman was amongst that number before he finally settled into one of Motown's lesser known but most respected groups, The Originals. Often considered one of Motown's best kept secrets, The Originals have become an important part of this history you are reading, for without The Originals there may never have been a team called Holland Dozier Holland and not only that, the connections they formed may have remained frayed edges of Detroit's musical tapestry. Freddie4 Gorman had started to write songs with Brian Holland. He would write songs at home and then bring them into Motown where they had access to a piano so that Holland could add music. They were doing so many things at this time and that was when Brian and Freddie brought Lamont Dozier into their writing team. Gradually Gorman grew disillusioned with Motown. Despite his developing song writing he was also a frustrated singer and the company's failure to support his singing career led him to leave and to join the ranks of Motown's main rival Golden World Records owned by Ed Wingate.

The legend that was to become Golden World was born in January 1962 and was the baby of Joanne Bratton and Ed Wingate, owner of The Twenty Grand Nightclub in Detroit, a place that boasted a bowling alley as well as the main dance hall. Black acts would start their climb to the top white clubs like the Roostertail and the Elmwood from the Twenty Grand. Wingate was a larger-than-life Detroit character whose name is synonymous with Golden World and Ric-Tic, the nearest rival labels to Motown and the ones that were most likely to succeed if Gordy had not been able to make a shrewd and, to some, cruel business move later on. In its day Wingate's company made some of the most memorable Soul to come out of the Motor City.

By 1962 the Rayber Singers had disbanded to be replaced by The Temptations and The Supremes who both supplemented their early Motown careers by being backing singing to the already established acts. There was still room, however, for The Andantes. The Andantes would have welcomed a career of their own and it was up to Holland Dozier Holland to give them a rare outing with "Like A Nightmare". Even on that, though, Motown could not let the girls bathe in the glow of the spotlight and brought in Ann Bogan to sing lead on what could quite easily have been a Martha & The Vandellas track. Harvey Fuqua had discovered Ann Bogan singing in a church on Quincy Avenue in Cleveland, Ohio and from there under the tutorship of Fuqua she formed a secular group, The Messengers. Fuqua issued their first release in 1962 on Tri-Phi Records, a label he ran with his wife Gwen Gordy-Fuqua that would later be absorbed into the main Motown stable. She remained unused by Motown for several years before finally replacing Gladys Horton in The Marvelettes, the exception being her outing with The Andantes. Though the single had much potential Motown didn't promote it because the group did not make live appearances and their smooth, quality, chorale sound was so valuable that Motown never gave them a chance to record on their own in case they would no longer be available for their recording session duties. Although not allowed to record for any other company Hicks and Barrow did record on many of Jackie Wilson's hits including "Higher and Higher" which also had the moonlighting Motown musicians sneaking across to Chicago under the spying eyes of Motown.

The sound of Detroit, as we will see, may have been dominated by one company as far as the cursory listener was concerned but what lay behind the Motown sound was an existing web of musicians who had played together from the 1950's when Detroit, as well as Berry Gordy Jr, embraced the gyrating jazz sounds filtering through the City's club scene.

Still outside of the Motown organisation the last Riverside release on the Four Tops, the standard "Pennies From Heaven" released in 1962 met with no success and so Berry Gordy, having pursued the Four Tops in previous years finally signed them up to Motown's Jazz Workshop label in '62. He gave the four friends $400 with a promise of hits but their "Breakin' Through" album was shelved prior to release.

Motown may have begun to dominate the commercial Soul market but, on nearly every street corner, for every artist signed to the label there were plenty more out there trying their hardest to be heard and if Berry Gordy Jr wasn't going to listen to them then another label owner just might. Popcorn Wylie himself recorded three singles for Gordy, was Motown's first head of A&R and the bandleader on the first Motortown Special tour in 1962. However, he fell out with Berry Gordy and isn't even mentioned in his autobiography, "To Be Loved". He left the company in 1962 and signed to Epic as a solo artist and released 4 singles over 2 years including, 'Come to Me', followed a year later by the song 'Brand New Man' and 'Head Over Heels in Love'.

Motown was well-known for encouraging competition amongst its staff writers and producers, what it was not keen to do, though, was to allow the opposition to enjoy a slice of the action. Many rival label owners had a deep hatred for Gordy's empire, an unscratchable itch that would fester and even lead to their ultimate demise as in the case of Mike Hanks, owner of D-Town records. Some, though, like Ed Wingate enjoyed the challenge and came close to toppling Gordy's Motown empire, first with the Golden World label and then with the Northern Soul favourite Ric-Tic, home of, amongst others, Edwin Starr. Motown was like a reversed iceberg in Detroit. The motherload, the wide base from which life-giving fluid dripped down to smaller labels and studios; feeding them energy and allowing them the chance to try and emulate the sounds pounding out of Detroit's premier company. Some climbed the iceberg briefly enjoying wider success before sliding back down. Others would slip down the iceberg and create the same magic for the rival companies often receiving fines for committing treason but always managing to stay afloat. These were the instrumentalists.

Mickey Stevenson, the man who would eventually bring Holland Dozier Holland together as a team, was out there looking for the musicians who could hold it together and give the developing company a sound that would keep the kids dancing. They were the magic formula that Gordy had Mickey Stevenson out scouring the streets of Detroit for and he found them in the Jazz clubs of Detroit; collectively they were known as the Funk Brothers and in Earl Van Dyke he found his group captain. The sound of Detroit, as we will see, may have been dominated by one company as far as the cursory listener was concerned but what lay behind the Motown sound was an existing web of musicians who had played together from the 1950's when Detroit, as well as Berry Gordy Jr embraced the gyrating jazz sounds filtering through the City's club scene. Van Dyke, born in 1929, joined Motown in 1962 after first going on the road with Emmet Sleigh & The Sleigh Riders, a former Jazz guitarist who worked alongside Louis Armstrong in his career. Around Van Dyke he placed the drum machine known as William 'Benny' Benjamin and bass player extraordinaire James Jamerson. Names that somehow conjure up Superhero alter egos, a concept not too far from the truth. Jamerson's bass playing was the driving force of many of Holland Dozier Holland's masterpieces, Jamerson once stated that Holland Dozier Holland would supply a chord sheet but couldn't write it for him and that whenever they did, it didn't turn out right and so they would let him ad lib.

26

According to Johnny Griffiths Holland Dozier Holland's production sessions resembled more of a party atmosphere than other producers allowed. Rough notes were brought in for the musicians to get a handle on and Brian Holland would go round the individual musicians whispering and humming suggestions until the whole thing was allowed to take its natural course. These memories seem to go along with both the Holland Dozier Holland team and the musicians employed recollections. Van Dyke, Jamerson and Benjamin had moved to Detroit during the great black migration to the North with their parents and by the 1950's had all tapped into the jazz scene around the city. As musicians down in Motown's 'Snake Pit', as the studio was called, they were just what Gordy wanted, but as performers in their own right he stifled them. An album by the newly named Funk Brothers was renamed Earl Van Dyke & The Soul Brothers because Gordy didn't like the word 'funk' being associated with Motown and instead of letting their natural creativity flow into the grooves he simply had them playing by numbers, performing instrumental versions of Motown favourites. Their tightness, in more ways than one, was not the responsibility or vision of Gordy. They worked hard and played hard forming a unique bond that only broke as Jamerson and Benjamin slipped into deeper dependency and when Benny Benjamin died of a stroke brought about by a side career in drug and alcohol abuse in 1969, the year Invictus and Hot Wax took off, his technique and workload had to be replaced by two drummers, Richard 'Pistol' Allen and Uriel Jones.

The Brian Holland and Robert Bateman partnership continued into 1962 with "Twistin' Postman", a December '61 release, which reached Number 34 in the Pop Chart the following year. The Marvelettes remained in favour with Brianbert in 1962 with "Playboy" written by Holland, Bateman, William 'Mickey' Stevenson and group member Gladys Horton reaching Number 7 in the Pop Chart. Bateman left Motown soon after and set up as an independent producer in Detroit co-writing, amongst others, Wilson Pickett's original version of "If You Need Me" along with Pickett and Sonny Sanders, formerly of the Satintones. Despite his fear of public performing Eddie Holland did have relative success with "Jamie", a National hit at Number 30 after its January 1962 release. After "Jamie" he had "You Deserve What You Get" released in April and the following month "If Cleopatra Took A Chance" was released. Before Bateman left Motown, he suggested that Brian Holland and Lamont Dozier team up.

From the initial meeting they became a regular writing and producing team along with the returning Freddie Gorman. Again, it was The Marvelettes who reaped the benefits with "Someday, Someway", released as the 'b' side of "Beechwood 4-5789" in July 1962. The first tune they worked on together was "Forever", cut by both The Marvelettes and Marvin

27

Gaye. The tune saw a revival of interest in 1973 when Baby Washington recorded a version in Philadelphia with Don Gardner on the Master Five label. "Forever" entered the charts in May of '73 and reached the top 30 R&B Chart. The original tune had been started by Lamont Dozier who was busy working at the piano when Brian Holland asked him if he had got a bridge for the tune. Between them they worked out the final track and two thirds of the formidable team were there with the third and final piece, Eddie Holland, almost ready to slot smoothly into place. Holland's "If It's Love It's Alright" was released on the Motown label to a disinterested public in August, failing to emulate "Jamie".

All was not lost, though, and another Motown writer and producer Mickey Stevenson recognised the potential in the Holland Dozier partnership, so when Freddie Gorman reversed his earlier decision, dropped his pen and began performing with The Originals, Eddie Holland was persuaded to join brother Brian and Lamont Dozier. Holland himself was also partly responsible for persuading younger brother Brian, who by now was making the grade at Motown, to let him join the Holland and Dozier partnership. His argument was that three of them could turn out more tracks with Eddie Holland adding lyrics to Lamont Dozier's melodies and Brian's productions thus making more money.

In 1962, putting aside, with some relief no doubt, his own luke-warm recording career, he joined the team, thus creating the legend of Holland Dozier Holland. According to Lamond Dozier, Eddie Holland was an accountant who didn't like to be on stage, jumping around. That seemed ridiculous, he much preferred to be in the background writing lyrics. Once he was brought in things began to fall into place. As the chemistry started to work, they took on more work. The three of them working together meant that they could accomplish much more. Lamont Dozier felt that he was more of a lyricist with an ear for a melody, so he would initially work alongside Brain Holland to bring together the melody. He considered himself the ideas man of the trio estimating that he was bringing around 75% of the ideas into the team. As well as contributing ideas, Brian Holland was a recording engineer and so the two of them would work together the produce the track before hand it over to Eddie to polish up the lyrics. After that it was Eddie who then taught the song to the artist in what he called a factory within a factory. This method allowed them to produce more songs in a short space of time.

In 1962 R. Dean Taylor recorded the demo single "At the High School Dance" for Amy-Mala Records, part of the Bell company. He was now in New York but when a friend pointed him in the direction of Detroit where a new sound was exploding, he made the move. A brave 500 miles move considering that, despite Gordy's wishes to break the white market, he was primarily interested in black product. Taylor was Canadian, a Country singer and white. Still, upon arriving in the Motor City he auditioned successfully for Brian Holland who signed him to the label as an artist and as a ghost writer for their own developing writing enterprise. Holland Dozier Holland now had an apprentice. Under the guidance of Smokey Robinson, the 'no-hit Supremes', as they were cruelly nicknamed, kept up their track record with "Whose Loving You" in 1962 and Mary Wells released "Two Lovers" and "You Beat Me to The Punch". The Marvelettes "Strange I Know" written by Holland, Dozier, Gorman was released in October 1962, reaching Number 49.

Meanwhile, George Clinton was heading up the off-beat Parliaments on the East Coast and heading towards the Motor City. At one point the group was contractually tied to Motown through Raynoma Gordy at Jobete Music in New York City, in 1962 but there was some friction between that office and Headquarters in Detroit and even though they recorded, the group never had material released in their five years contract.

As 1962 rolled into 1963 Eddie Holland continued to record and January saw his version of "Darling I Hum Our Song" issued to no avail. The song would later be re-recorded by both the Four Tops and Martha & The Vandellas but as 'b' sides. "Darling I Hum Our Song" was a good enough song but not the tune the team needed to create for that elusive hit they needed to herald their arrival. The team's success began, however, the following month with the first official Holland Dozier Holland release "Come and Get These Memories" by Martha & The Vandellas which gave everybody involved their first major hit, after its February 1963 release reached Number 29 on the National Pop Chart. With "Come and Get These Memories" not only did Holland Dozier Holland begin to make noises at Motown and throughout the country but so too did Martha Reeves and her Vandellas.

Prior to this Martha Reeves was working odd jobs and singing at local nightclubs when Mickey Stevenson, Motown A&R man, happened to go along to Ed Wingate's Twenty Grand Club where Reeves was performing under the name of Martha LaVaille. Impressed by her performance Stevenson offered her an audition but when she showed up the following day, he told her that auditions only took place on certain days. Now, here is where the story of how she came to Motown as a secretary starts because Stevenson asked her to guard his office while he went off somewhere else. Martha Reeves began to earn a wage as Stevenson's secretary but continued to record as a member of the Del-Phis. The group had managed some session work for Motown but their activities were mainly restricted to live gigging around the area at weekends, due to Motown having an already established session group, The Andantes. Chicago based Chess Records signed the group to its Checkmate imprint, no hits were forthcoming though. More work began to appear for them at Motown and then in yet another true fairy tale style she was given the opportunity to record when the previous fairy tale Princess, Mary Wells, failed to turn up to a recording session for the song "I'll Have To Let Him Go". At this point Martha Reeves was not the lead singer, instead that honour went to group member Gloria Williams, but because they were tied to the Chess contract the single was released under the name of The Vells. After the group's failure to reach chart status Gloria Williams left and Martha Reeves took the spotlight. The Vells became The Vandellas, a hybrid of Van Dyke Street, home of Reeves' Grandmother and Della Reese, whom Reeves admired, with a little bit of The Del-Phis thrown in for good measure. The Vandellas signed to Motown's Gordy subsidiary on September 21st 1962 and with Holland Dozier Holland at the helm were about to hit a purple patch.

Mary Wells had "You Lost the Sweetest Boy" created by Holland Dozier Holland but The Marvelettes, sadly, were about to lose their link with HDH and as "Come And Get These Memories" hit the Top Thirty the same month's Marvelettes/Holland Dozier Holland collaboration, "Locking Up My Heart" scraped into the Number 44 position. Eddie Holland still tried his luck with an April, '63 release "Baby Shake" and again in June when he teamed up with Lamont Dozier, The Andantes and The Four Tops for the little known (or heard) "What Goes Up Must Come Down". Equally interesting was the Holland Dozier Holland 'b' side, "Come on Home" by The Darnells. The track was later issued as "Nothing but A Man" and used in the film of the same name when the soundtrack was supplied by Motown the following year. Holland Dozier Holland tunes, "Heat Wave" and "This Is When I Need You Most" by Martha & the Vandellas, "Mickey's Monkey" by The Miracles and "Come on Home" credited to Lamont Dozier and Brian Holland appeared on the soundtrack.

For the first time on record the names Holland-Dozier appeared as recording artists, a premonition of things to come and also, for the first time, Motown was linked to the movies. Another sign of things that would eventually change the game forever. It is also interesting to note the significance of the film itself, called by Malcolm X, the most important film about black America ever produced. Released at a time when the black consciousness in the south was reluctantly waking up. The central characters are ordinary people, trying to fall in love and tired of the burdens placed on them because of the colour of their skin. In Duff, the main character, a generation would see a man at the turning point of history when black America would turn around and say that it wasn't going to take anymore from the 'man'. Motown, though often criticised for its links with white Pop culture, could be proud of its association with "Nothing But A

Man". In July 1963 Martha & The Vandellas released "Heatwave" reaching Number 4 Pop-wise and Number1 on the then-named R&B Chart that preceded the Soul Chart.

1963 through to early '64 continued to be a lean period for The Supremes who could only look on with envy at the company's premiere girl group The Marvelettes who had grown from strength to strength from 1961 with their first number one "Please Mr. Postman" to become Motown's most consistent chart group. The Supremes fortunes changed because of one factor: the founder of the company seemed determined to make a star out of Diana Ross. A role Diana appeared to relish and a situation visibly evident within the structure of the group. Smokey Robinson had tried to work the same magic that he had conjured up for Mary Wells and The Miracles, this time though the spell was miscast and so another writer/production team had to be brought in, Holland Dozier Holland. "When the Love Light Starts Shining Thru His Eyes" reached Number 23 on the Pop Chart, its 'b' side, "Standing at The Crossroads Of Love" would later be re-written as "Standing In The Shadows Of Love" by the recently signed Four Tops.

Not only had the Smokey Robinson sparkle failed on a purely work basis but in personal terms a relationship with Diana Ross had also come to an end. Ross began to show interest in Brian Holland who, like Robinson, was a married man. This relationship lasted through the latter part of 1962 up to the end of 1963. Holland's wife, Sharon, would often visit the studio or, on one memorable occasion, Ed Wingate's Twenty Grand Club threatening to mess up the diminutive Diana Ross. At the Twenty Grand a fight was stopped involving Sharon Holland, The Supremes and The Velvelettes. Shortly after Ross ceased seeing Holland, probably on her doctor's advice.

The one thing that the team of Holland Dozier Holland did well was to involve other writers who would move on to greater things within the City if not within Motown. Tony Hester was one such writer. Hester's musical odyssey began on the east side of Detroit where he attended St. Catherine High school and later McComb College for two years. Sensing college wasn't what he wanted, he quit and started writing songs. Most of his writing occurred in the basement of his mother's house, first at a piano originally purchased for his sister who lost interest and later one he purchased himself. Hester never studied but was able to play by ear. However, he never played on any of his own sessions, always opting for better players. He also linked up with former Motowner Popcorn Wylie with whom he forged an outstanding creative partnership. Hester got his first song recorded at the age of 14 by The Marvelettes: "A Little Bit of Sympathy" the flip side of "You're My Remedy" written with Brian Holland

and Lamont Dozier. When Berry Gordy wanted to sign him to a seven-years contract Hester refused, not wanting to commit himself to such a length of time. Though he never signed with Motown, he spent considerable time hanging out at Hitsville U.S.A. watching HDH produce records. His own success came with Detroit group, The Dramatics at Ric-Tic Records, now, after Golden World was gone, the main rivals to Gordy's developing Empire.

"I've always felt that if you watch the creative people or listen to them you could pretty much figure out what they would need to support whatever they were attempting to do and I would try to get the people that I thought were compatible to what they were attempting to do in their creative endeavours I felt that if it could be workable then I would try to get them together."

Eddie Holland

Martha & The Vandellas were still ready, willing and able to go further and proved that the following month with a number eight position for "Quicksand" that may well have been their previous hit "Heatwave" revisited but was still able to incorporate new musical ideas.

They didn't have A&R meetings instead they were called quality control meetings and they would get people off the street to come in and listen to the new material. Eventually, through word of mouth, people got to know that on the first of the month or every couple of months there would these listening parties and so people would gather in front of the Hitsville building and then they would be brought into the studio, given Coca-Cola, potato chips and hot dogs, and play the music for them to rate. Eventually this was replaced by a nucleus of staff in the A&R department that was unmatched by any company in the world but early on they did everything to try to be on the ball and keep up with what people wanted to hear. They were trying to give people things that would touch them emotionally and they didn't think that because they were black that they would only do this for the black population. They had all mixes, all races of people in there, because Motown embodied the notion that music was a language of its own and that it could cross all barriers. The team of Holland Dozier Holland worked for a basic wage plus royalties and although Lamont Dozier usually created the song, the trio would sometimes rotate these duties and come in with a starting point for the others to pick up on and weave their magic on.

For five furious years at Motown Holland Dozier Holland proved unstoppable and because of their incredible knack for creating hits Gordy would give them even more work. Gordy was also notorious for creating competitiveness amongst his staff, promoting intense rivalry by pitching teams against each other to see who could come up with the best single on particular groups. Where Holland Dozier Holland competed many of the opposition were non-starters. Although frustrating to many of the session musicians Holland Dozier Holland would be the creative team who, more than any at Motown, were quick to embrace the new technology being brought into the contemporary field of recording. As Holland Dozier Holland grew as a team, their music could be seen to change with new ideas continually being brought forward into their productions and when Engineer Robert Dennis went to Motown in 1963 and found that one of his first jobs was to make drawings for an 8-track machine that was being built by Motown's Engineering Department, a new world of possibilities would open up to Brian Holland in particular.

James Jamerson's bass playing was the driving force on many of Holland Dozier Holland's masterpieces and he once stated that Holland Dozier Holland would supply a chord sheet but couldn't write it for him and that whenever they did, it didn't turn out right and so they would let him ad lib. According to Johnny Griffiths, another local keyboard maestro and future Motown session man, Holland Dozier Holland's production sessions resembled more of a party atmosphere than other producers allowed. Rough notes were brought in for the musicians to get a handle on and Brian Holland would go 'round the individual musicians whispering and humming suggestions until the whole thing took its natural course. Another legend of the studio, keyboard player Earl Van Dyke put a different spin on this though and claimed that Lamont Dozier always sat at the piano and came up with the same little things, then again though his criticism stretched to that other nobody, James Brown. According to Van Dyke, Dozier would take one track and clone ten songs that sounded alike but when given something back from Van Dyke would complain that this was what he gave him on the last tune. This led to conflict between the two on several occasions. According to Eddie Holland the musicians had tried to belittle his brother by playing games with him, testing his abilities as a producer but Brian Holland knew exactly what he required from the players. Holland, like brother Eddie, Lamont Dozier and their boss, Berry Gordy Jr, were all self-taught musically which wore the patience of the jazz oriented, multi-talented musicians but Brian Holland had a natural talent for picking out the sound. If James Jamerson had been left to ad lib it was only allowed to go as far as Holland let it.

The Motown session men also complained about the meanness of Holland Dozier Holland, particularly Eddie, who had taken up the mantle of team leader. Other writers and producers like Smokey Robinson and Norman Whitfield would give bonuses for players on their hit records but Eddie Holland believed that the musicians were paid a wage and that was the end of the story. They saw their own work as a nine to five, although they loved every minute of it, working on the early sessions with The Marvelettes and at this time turning out two or three songs a day. They handled it in many ways just like a person would handle a nine-to-five job. In the studio Brian led. His gift was in hearing the records before they were even recorded. His brother, Eddie saw in his younger brother a unique talent for hearing the arrangements in his head and being able to convey them to the musicians. Eddie would make suggestions like 'add two bars here, or four bars there' that Brian would add in and although the musicians were granted artistic license the singers were not. They would go through the process, knowing that they did not have that much time. They would take the basic melodies on tape, listen to them and jot down ideas on each tune as they were rehearsing. Then once they cut some tracks Eddie Holland would work through the day, through the night, wake up in the morning, just constantly chipping away at it until he was completely satisfied that they understood the song. He then directed them in the studio where they would bring the song to life.

That style of working was confirmed by a former Motown engineer in Nelson George's book, "Where Did Our Love Go": He said that they would record music tracks and that, conceptually they might have an idea of who would be right for it but often they still did not know. They had basic instruments, the rhythm section, the horns, the strings. Brian Holland and Lamont Dozier would take those tracks and fit them into the musical sequence that they thought the record should follow and Eddie would try to write lyrics to it. They would do this for four or five times until they got the perfect song and after all this was done then they would go out and try to get different artists to fit into their creation. This insight shows the foresight that Holland Dozier Holland had and how their music was more than simple composition. It was a fusion of art and technology and as such was arguably the forerunner of the 80's techno pop that led to the Hip Hop generation's skills at sampling.

The team carried on in fine dancing spirit with the same month's "Mickey's Monkey" named after the Monkey dance of the period. This time the lucky recipients of the song were The Miracles The recording of the song emphasised the then family spirit of Motown with two members of The Supremes, two Vandellas, two Temptations and Marvin Gaye all joining in to add atmosphere to the proceedings. "Mickey's Monkey" reached the Top Ten and Top Three Pop and R&B respectively. In "You Lost the Sweetest Boy" released in August going Pop # 22 and R&B #10 Mary Wells had her finest moment outside of Smokey Robinson's composition "My Guy". "My Guy" had the honour, incidentally, of being the very first Motown recording to be written and produced by a fellow artist. September gave Marvin Gaye a chance at a Holland Dozier Holland song with "Can I Get A Witness" hitting number 22 on the National Chart. "Can I Get A Witness" was a far more Gospel-tinged recording and betrayed Holland Dozier Holland's Church roots as well as continuing the family approach to much of Motown's recording with fellow performers standing in to supply the uplifting chorus.

At this stage in his career Marvin Gaye was still searching for that elusive hit that would place him firmly in the hearts and minds of the nation. Holland Dozier and Holland approached him and they said that they had a great 'thing' for him. Diana Ross as well as the other Supremes were in the studio so Holland Dozier Holland suggested using them as backing singers. The Miracles once again recorded with Holland Dozier Holland for October's "I Gotta Dance to Keep from Crying" but the track only managed to reach the Top Forty while Eddie Holland's "I'm On the Outside Looking In" bombed. It seemed strange that the team could be supplying hits for others and yet Eddie Holland remained on the starting blocks, stumbling to compete. The roll had not started to happen but when it eventually did Holland would still not be able to gain the same success as the groups that he had helped to reach the top.

The team was beginning to make those, all-important noises, at Motown and it was with their next project that they were to finally hit the jackpot. It had started in the same month of October 1963 and seen as an attempt by Berry Gordy to allow The Supremes, one of his non-hit groups, a chance at success. With the Four Tops as well as Holland Dozier Holland on background vocal duty the trio recorded "When the Love Light Starts Shining Thru His Eyes", their seventh single after Smokey Robinson had failed to secure the group as Motown's number one female outfit. This signalled a liaison that would remain until Holland Dozier Holland left Motown in 1968, giving The Supremes ten Number Ones starting with their second release by Holland Dozier Holland, "Where Did Our Love Go", also in 1964. The year ended for them with Eddie Holland once again failing to chart with "Leaving Here". In David Marsh's excellent "The Heart of Rock & Roll", 1989, he suggested that this track is what Jackie Wilson would have sounded like if Holland Dozier Holland had produced him. Mike Terry would later say that Eddie Holland was the finest male singer he had ever worked with. Still the record only reached Number 76 and Eddie Holland was almost ready to throw in the towel.

One other ingredient that was literally put in the mix was noted sound engineer, Lawrence T. Horn. Horn, Motown's Chief Recording Engineer mixed almost every Motown release between 1964 and 1968. Horn did this remarkable feat by implementing a recording "system" for Motown and by ingenious management of a staff of engineers. After innovating and improving the art of engineering at Motown he began to work closely with Berry Gordy to produce the Motown recorded "I Have A Dream" speeches of Dr. Martin Luther King. His main claim to fame came from the system he developed for 3 track recording in 1964 which opened up the way for Brian Holland to produce his own magic. As with the producers at Motown all the other engineers would compete for the mix that was chosen for release. They would be invited to mix their own production from the master reel and as with the record producers these would be submitted to the Quality Control meetings where the best mix would be chosen. Since Lawrence Horn did the transferring and mixing to make the multi-track, he did most of the mixing on the released version and since he was good at mixing, he would often be the engineer that won the mixing competition. In the days of analog recording, the engineer would clean-up and pre-master the multitrack before the mixdown process began.

For a major production, the engineer worked with the multi-track recording of a tune for around 6 sessions before mixdown could begin. During that time, that often spanned 18 to 30 hours, the engineer had to mix monitors, cues and run-offs after each session. The engineer heard the tune when it was only drums, bass and rhythm and all the way through the process of becoming a finished production. The idea was to get the tape so that it contained only the final sounds of the production. It was not uncommon to have several vocal performances on several tracks and then edit a final vocal track by editing.

If you listen to "Can't Hurry Love" by The Supremes, you can hear this, as Diana's voice overlaps from chorus to verse. It also needs noting that Motown's studio was not the only place where groups could record. The company's producers and engineers often had their own favourites. Tera Shirma was used widely by Detroit producers like Ed Wingate who recorded there after he had sold his studio on West Davison to Motown but that was only until 1964, when the Golden World Studio was officially opened, that meant that both the Golden World and Ric-Tic labels were now ready to compete against Motown. The Golden World studio was considered the best studio in Detroit for recording orchestrated pieces, witness The San Remo Strings recordings. It was later turned into Motown studio B. The Golden World label itself was a mixture of one release wonders as opposed to one-hit wonders and groups who would crop up throughout the history of Detroit Soul.

By now The Temptations reputation was growing, yet surprisingly the label's premier writing and production team were rarely matched to the label's premier male vocal group. One exception was the unreleased track "A Tear from A Woman's Eye" recorded in January 1964. The same month saw Martha & The Vandellas' "Live Wire" struggling and only being able to secure a Number 42 Chart position while February's "Run, Run, Run" by The Supremes sunk, sunk, sunk. February did see Marvin Gaye hit Number 17 on the Pop Chart with "You're A Wonderful One" though.

At Golden World Sue Perrin released a February single, "Candy Store Man" which missed but the following single was the first by Golden World's golden girls, The Adorables. During their time with the label, they would release three singles beginning with "Deep Freeze". The four Adorables were in fact two sets of sisters, Joyce and Betty Winston and Dianne and Pat Lewis. The most famous of these being Pat Lewis whose name is synonymous with quality Detroit soul and Betty Winston who took the name of Max Fleisher's sassy cartoon figure Betty Boop, dropped the 'p' and recorded with Popcorn Wylie who had left Motown in 1962 to go freelance, joining Golden World in March 1964. The Adorables single was also the first one bearing Freddie Gorman's name on a Golden World release.

In March 1964 as "In My Lonely Room" was proving a non-starter for Martha Reeves and company, despite Holland Dozier Holland's input, Freddie Gorman and Bob Hamilton produced Golden World's biggest success with "Just Like Romeo and Juliet" for The Reflections. Not all the production belonged to Detroit with vocals being cut in Chicago, the backing track though was recorded in Detroit's oldest Recording Studio, United Sound. The Reflections were the label's most successful group, releasing 8 singles along with the company's only album. By April The Reflections "Just Like Romeo And Juliet" had reached number 6 in the U.S. Billboard Charts, the same month that "Just Ain't Enough Love" proved yet another disappointment for Eddie Holland the singer.

That would prove insignificant though as a whole music form was about to be shook up and re-shaped by Eddie and his partners because from this point on the Golden Age of Motown paralleled the Golden Age of Holland Dozier Holland. For it was their creativity that would form, re-form, evolve and, eventually, dissolve the sound of Motown. However, the race was on for pole position in Detroit with creative people using the labels like revolving doors. The follow up single for The Reflections over at Golden World, "Like Columbus Did" was only "Just Like Romeo And Juliet" part 2 and while Motown's rivals were treading water all that had gone before at Motown was the calm before the storm because in the same month of June 1964 The Supremes and Holland Dozier Holland struck Gold in the form of "Where Did Our Love Go", a National Number One. The group who had been in the shadows for so long were about to become centre stage celebrities and in the full glow of the spotlights.

Within the team of Holland Dozier Holland there was a hint of conflict with Eddie Holland wanting the song to be sung by Mary Wilson as it had originally been intended for The Marvelettes. He imagined it being sung in a more sultry, deeper key than Diana Ross had so far shown herself capable of doing. Eventually he was outvoted but he still requested that Diana sing it lower than usual. Mary objected to the song as The Supremes had seen and heard more ballsy numbers being produced on other groups and felt that the teenage "Baby baby…" lyrics were too simple. Luckily for all concerned Holland Dozier Holland eventually persuaded the group to cut it and the track saw the light of day. So too did The Supremes with this, their 7th release. The backing track was cut in Gladys Horton's key, which was low but they didn't like it. So, without recutting the track they went in and got Diana Ross to do the vocal even though Eddie Holland was desperate to have Mary Wilson take the lead as Diana Ross had a high, shrill voice at the time. The Supremes were low down on the totem pole of artists needing assistance but Holland Dozier Holland decided to give the song to them. When they found out that it had been rejected by The Marvelettes they were less than impressed. Diana was already feeling unhappy about doing this song because of the key and a lot of things were said but she came off sounding very sultry as a result of that key. Lamont Dozier was trying to teach them intricate harmonies for the background and wasn't getting anywhere so he suggested that Diana sang "baby-baby" but the only way she could do it was to sing "baybeh, baybeh" in that low and sultry way. Usually, they would have put it in a higher key because that was what she was used to singing in but it wouldn't have sounded the same. Those kinds of moments in the studio were things that you couldn't explain, a magic moment that you can't explain and one that started The Supremes on an unprecedented run of hits. What had started out as an accident became a calculated risk and Diana Ross's sound had arrived. The Supremes never really acknowledged the greatness of 'Where Did Our Love Go' but happily promoted themselves on the strength of it. The Marvelettes, on the other hand, despite some outstanding tracks and a revitalised period under the guidance of Smokey Robinson, were never again to reach the same dizzy heights due partly to some bad business calls, arguably the biggest being the rejection of "Where Did Our Love Go."

Upon their return to Detroit after extensive touring duties The Supremes were a different group. Brian and Lamont picked them up at the airport and when they came off the plane, they didn't know them. They had a way of walking and talking that was almost funny, star time had arrived. They looked at each other and smiled. This success could not have come at a better time for everybody concerned and they were all riding on a mammoth crest of a wave. After "Where Did Our Love Go" came "Baby Love" a million seller and the team of Holland Dozier Holland had to take stock of just what they had started. They didn't have an album of songs, so had to get right back in the studio. Holland Dozier Holland looked at one another wondering what the hell they had started and to them feeling that they were pioneering something new felt strange.

"Candy to Me" in July was Eddie Holland's last throw of the dice as a performer before his knowledge of accounting and the fresh understanding that song writers outlived song singers led him to pour all of his creative energies into the Holland Dozier Holland team.

"After I started writing I didn't really have an interest in recording at all. Of the first few records I put out, the one that was most successful was the record Jamie but after going out on the road and performing in certain theatres, I realised that that was not my interest, not at all. I didn't like the life out there and what it gave me was a greater respect for artists and then I realised that being an artist was like any occupation or avocation, it was something that you really want to do, you had to be inspired and that really was not my forte. I wasn't interested."

Eddie Holland

Although he did find individual success with the Temptations as he continued to develop his creative skills away from the Holland Dozier Holland team and successfully collaborated with Norman Whitfield with whom he wrote "The Girl's Alright with Me", a Temptations 'B' side from 1964, "(Girl) Why You Wanna Make Me Blue", also by The Temptations in 1964 and, again the same year, "Too Many Fish In The Sea" for The Marvelettes. Apprentice R. Dean Taylor cut "Just Like In The Movies", "My Lady Bug Stay Away From That Beatle" and "Surfer's Call", all written with Brian Holland Lamont Dozier and sometimes Eddie Holland but none of them gained releases. The tracks were aimed purely and simply at the white record buying market and as such were not indicative of the label's other material. Holland Dozier Holland themselves were about to become unstoppable though and were given other acts to work with, chart success being the name of the game. So along with Martha & The Vandellas, The Supremes, Marvin Gaye, The Miracles and Mary Wells the next group to benefit most from the team's involvement were the Four Tops.

In 1964 "Baby, I Need Your Loving" was the beginning of another fruitful teaming. With the exception of 1965's "Ask the Lonely" and "Loving You Is Sweeter Than Ever" in 1966, Holland Dozier Holland were responsible for the producing and, again with two 1968 exceptions, the writing of fourteen hits including two Number Ones for their male equivalent of The Supremes, the Four Tops. The Tops had remained calm, waiting for their moment then one night, while watching The Temptations at a local club Brian Holland approached the four friends and asked them if they would go down to the Motown studios after the show because there was a tune the trio had that might just be the answer to the Four Tops' prayers. The group agreed and sure enough the magic that had worked for others was about to do the same for the patient quartet. The song had been laying around for nearly 2 years, with the instrumental track already to go.

Mickey Stevenson approached the team to see if they had anything that they could record on the newly signed foursome and "Baby I Need Your Loving" was dusted off for Levi Stubbs to work wonders with. At first though Stubbs was reluctant and was not used to the way HDH worked. He suggested that the song be given to Lawrence Payton, the Tops second lead vocalist to try out but HDH were adamant that Levi Stubbs would sing it. Finally, he agreed to work on the song and history was made. In July of 1964 "Baby, I Need Your Loving" heralded the arrival of the Four Tops and gave them a Number 11 Pop hit and by the time the first Four Tops album was rushed out to cash in on the success of the single the group was established. Frustratingly, The Fourmost covered "Baby I Need Your Loving" in England pipping the Tops to the post. Other Holland Dozier Holland tracks on the album included "Without the One You Love (Life's Not Worth While)", "Where Did You Go", "Your Love Is Amazing", "Don't Turn Away", "Left With A Broken Heart" and "Love Has Gone". When you flipped the cover over what you saw was part of Holland Dozier Holland's future as the Four Tops sat mimicking the statue at whose feet they sat, Auguste Rodin's 'Thinker', the image that HDH would use as the design for their Invictus label. The company they would set up in 1968 after they had left Motown.

September saw The Supremes second Number 1 on the Motown label, "Baby Love" while Marvin Gaye reached Number 27 with Holland Dozier Holland's "Baby, Don't You Do It" on Tamla. Two different styles that showed the breadth and depth of Holland Dozier Holland's creativity at this time. Whilst "Baby Love" was a perfect vehicle for the newly discovered soft, sexual, whispering tones of Diana Ross accompanied by the equally qualified Mary Wilson and Florence Ballard "Baby, Don't You Do It" was as hard and as raw as anything coming out of any city in America and was the perfect answer to anybody who claimed that Motown didn't have Soul.

The chart domination by The Supremes continued the next month with another Number 1, "Come See About Me". It was soon becoming apparent to all and sundry that this was the sound that other girl groups would have to live up to and live with and if stable mates The Marvelettes, The Velvelettes and The Vandellas struggled how would the competition outside of Motown cope?

The next female group to emerge from Golden World were The Debonaires; a trio that had started out including cousins Joyce Vincent and Telma Hopkins who would become backing singers for Motown and later with Holland Dozier Holland's Invictus/Hot Wax set up after The Debonaires run of singles came to a halt. They were High School students when Golden World released "Please Don't Say We're Through" backed by "A Little Too Long" in 1964. Big things were expected of the track as the same production crew who had received a Gold record for The Reflections "Just Like Romeo and Juliet", Freddie Gorman and Bob Hamilton were responsible but unfortunately it was not promoted outside of the Detroit area. The Debonaires "Please Don't Say We're Through" was released on Golden World in October 1964 and both Golden World and its sister label Ric Tic that would appear a year later would continue to be thorns in the side of Berry Gordy Jr but would also be an important feeder into the post-Motown work of Holland Dozier Holland as would be one General Norman Johnson who had yet to make his own move to the Motor City. Whilst with Minit The Showmen, Johnson's group, were only finding their feet and it was when they moved to Swan that Johnson began to diversify his talents to better effect although The Showmen's recordings of this period were criticised for being a pale imitation of what The Temptations were doing at the same time. Tracks such as "Our Love Will Grow" would prove popular on the British Northern Soul Scene. Johnson felt that the problem was in the production not the vocal preferring to have produced the sessions himself. At this time many producers were desperately attempting to emulate the successful Motown sound and Richard Barratt, the producer for The Showmen, was no exception. After the closure of Swan Records, The Showmen never recorded again with Johnson. Fortunately, "It Will Stand" was re-released on Imperial in 1964 and after four or five weeks at the top of the Detroit Music Chart his style and voice became known to Holland Dozier Holland and Brian Holland knew that one day, he would track down the General and work with him.

The year ended for Holland Dozier Holland with two more successes. Firstly, the Four Tops, "Without the One You Love" and for Marvin Gaye, "How Sweet It Is to Be Loved by You". Despite Gaye's obvious delight at gaining more success he was never completely happy with the way that Holland Dozier Holland worked. In a strange way Holland Dozier Holland were giving Gaye a new dimension in much the same way that they had done, albeit by accident, with Diana Ross but where Ross struggled to sing in a lower key Gaye was having to hit the higher notes. He tried to interpret what he thought they felt but it was very taxing on him because he was still trying to find his voice. His voice was in a very experimental stage at this point and with their kind of music. Because it needed the roughness and the softness in spots it was very difficult to control his voice like they wanted him to. He would look at Levi Stubbs of the Four Tops in the studio sometimes and could see that HDH were employing the same tactics on him.

On Golden World their most successful group, The Reflections 45's "Shabby Little Hut" was released in February 1965 but failed to do anything and with The Supremes and the Four Tops taking over as Holland Dozier Holland's premier groups at Motown Martha & The Vandellas were in danger of losing out but still, they could come through with classics that The Supremes would never have been able to cut with the same sense of purpose or energy. Inspiration for songs came from some unlikely places and during the Civil Rights unrests Lamont Dozier watched from the windows of Motown as tanks passed the Hitsville Studios. Thus, was born the next Martha & The Vandellas hit 'Nowhere to Run'.

"Nowhere to Run", released in February of 1965 reached Number 8 on the National Billboard Chart but was second best in the race to the top with the same month's Supremes outing, "Stop! In the Name of Love" climbing all the way to the top. On the strength of the growing success of the company and the interest shown by other sections of the Popular Music Industry EMI gave Gordy his own British label and at the suggestion of Dave Godin, head of the British Tamla Appreciation Society, fused the two names together to form Tamla Motown. Tammie Motown just would not have sounded right. In March, Holland Dozier Holland were also given the honour of having the first release on the British Tamla Motown label.

"Stop! In the Name of Love" by The Supremes, written by the team, appeared as Tamla Motown TMG 501. At last Gordy had a foothold in the International market and once again had done away with having to have his product leased to other labels. In the case of England previous Motown releases had appeared on the London, Oriole, Fontana, and Stateside Labels. That month Jobete Music, Motown's song publishing arm entered into a contract with Edward Holland. The contract provided, among other things, for assignment of the copyright on all musical works written or composed by Mr. Holland to Jobete in exchange for royalties and other consideration. The contract specified that accrued royalties were to be paid in March and September of each year.

The Reflections were keeping the flag flying for Golden World and their next release again hit the big time, with "Poor Man's Son", their most popular recording to the wider Pop market reaching No 55 in the Billboard Pop Chart in March 1965, although international honours would belong to a British cover by Birmingham Beat group the Rockin' Berries who secured a Top 5 position with their version. It was on an April session for The Miracles that another future behind-the-scenes star began to learn his craft.

As the 70's progressed McKinley Jackson's name began to appear on almost everything Holland Dozier Holland were releasing, beyond that he gained massive recognition throughout the wider music field for his stunning arrangements but in 1965 he was just a kid, still wet behind the ears but more than willing to learn. Jackson was another kid born and raised in Detroit's inner-city and aside from his music teacher he was seen as a non-achiever, possibly not helped by his regular truancy that saw him either hanging out at Motown or Golden World to play on sessions. These ranged from the trombone that he had started to play at school or simply hitting a tambourine, whatever it was didn't matter, the point was he was getting paid $6 a session but also gaining priceless experience. "Ooh Baby, Baby" was released in April by The Miracles on the Tamla label and was the first session that McKinley Jackson was able to sit in on. Paul Riser arranged the "Ooh Baby, Baby" session and along with Gene Page and H B Barnum would be the people who most influenced Jackson. Such was his potential and willingness to learn that by the age of 16 Jackson had worked alongside such Motor City greats as James Jameson, Norman Whitfield, Rudy Robinson and Benny Benjamin without being snapped up by Motown. Instead, he began arranging for the numerous competitors that had sprung up around the city. One of his first was The Arabians on LeMans records. He was also working his way around the clubs, sitting in with the house bands. At the Brown Bunny Club, he met his soon-to-be manager Betty Slater who introduced him to future Chairman of The Board member, Danny Woods and together they started to form The Peps, later becoming The Politicians. The early line up included Stanley Cleveland, Melvin Griffin, Chuck Boyd, Zachery Slater and Charlie Hearndon. Soon they became the house band at Ed Wingate's 20 Grand Club. This group became a formidable unit, backing all the major artists who drifted into Detroit and when Holland Dozier Holland broke away from Berry Gordy to set up Invictus records the group played on almost everything that was released on the label becoming Holland Dozier Holland's latter-day Funk Brothers. With HDH firmly in control Motown seemed to be pulling away from its rivals and April 1965 saw yet another Number 1 for the three Supremes and their powerful allies Holland Dozier Holland with "Back In My Arms Again" whilst the Four Tops were able to reach top 5 with "I Can't Help Myself (Sugar Pie Honey Bunch)".

Once the Four Tops hit the big time with "I Can't Help Myself" and the track started its descent of the charts Columbia, their former label decided to re-release one of the group's old tracks. Columbia's 'suits' had anticipated that the fledgling company would not have anything ready but what they hadn't taken into consideration was the ability of Holland Dozier Holland to come up with something new at a minute's notice, spurred on by Columbia's intentions. Lamont Dozier came up with 'It's the Same Old Song', which was similar to 'I Can't Help Myself'. He found a way of turning the bass figure around but basically the chords were all very similar He added a few chords on top of the high part just to give it some new nuances. Berry Gordy more or less brought everyone at Motown in to get this track out. At 3pm Holland Dozier Holland met chief engineer Lawrence Horn in the studio. The musicians and the Four Tops were standing by as HDH wrote "It's the Same Old Song" right then and there. Brian Holland and Lawrence Horn worked with the musicians on the tune while Eddie Holland finished the lyrics. Lamont Dozier finished the melody 30 minutes later. By 5pm Robert Gordy handed engineer Robert Dennis the mix and by 6pm Dennis was told to cut a master for a strike-off, a stamper to press out records very quickly. A strike-off generally allowed 1000 singles to be pressed. More changes were made before the track was finally on its way to Owosso, Michigan and to the American Record Pressing Plant. Bear in mind that they were still hand cutting records at this stage. Finally, almost 24 hours after the emergency was called Motown had managed to release 1500 copies to all the main Disc Jockeys throughout North America. The Columbia release peaked at Number 39.

Although other groups were given the Holland Dozier Holland treatment it seemed as though there really were only the two groups capable of doing justice to Holland Dozier Holland's material and why Berry Gordy Jr was keen to keep the trio's workload high. In July came the next two hits for The Supremes and the Four Tops. This time the roles were reversed with "Nothing but Heartaches" securing the lower position for The Supremes with the Four Tops "It's the Same Old Song" going all the way to the top. The hard work had paid off.

Elsewhere in the City Ed Wingate's operation persisted, with Motown cast-offs or disillusioned artists and writers still determined to make it as Detroit began to make more inroads into the national and international consciousness and in 1965 Wingate's company succeeded in capturing the Motown sound. by using Motown session men and offering better rates of pay than Gordy who had always worked below the existing Union rates.

The fourth release on Ric-Tic introduced us to Edwin Starr with "Agent Double-O-Soul". Born Charles Hatcher on the 21st of January 1942 in Nashville, Tennessee, Edwin was raised and educated in Cleveland, Ohio. In 1962, after completing two years of military service in the USA and Germany he moved to Detroit and by 1965 was to become part of Soul music history. In Cleveland he had met Lou Ragland and it was through his association with Ragland that Starr signed to Golden World. Here he was responsible for co-writing Starr's first two Ric Tic singles under the pseudonym B. Sharply, "Agent Double O-Soul" and "Backstreet". Just as

Charles Hatcher became Edwin Starr, the popularity of "Agent Double-O-Soul" gave Starr a stage identity that cashed in on the success of the James Bond movies. As well as this there was also a chart place for Edwin Starr's "Agent Double-O-Soul" released in July 1965 reaching Number 8 on the Soul Chart. Mickey Stevenson, the man who had brought Holland Dozier Holland together was used by Gordy to issue fines on the musicians who were caught moonlighting. Those who played on "Agent Double-O-Soul" were each fined $1,000, paid by Ric Tic boss, Ed Wingate. Golden World's subsidiary Ric Tic was gathering momentum and the first recording by the San Remo Golden Strings, "Hungry for Love" was released in August 1965 reaching Number 27 on the Pop Chart, it was also the first production for the label by Al Kent alongside his brother Bob Hamilton.

"There were many talented people in Detroit who never became what we called successful. The people at Motown were exceptionally fortunate because the type of quality competition made it easier to get better quality product and it was no accident that Motown was so successful because the competition was so fierce and you know, talent grows and thrives through competition. So a lot of people did not have that same advantage and dealing with a company that had so many writers and producers that were competing so fiercely they never developed on that level but there was a singer by the name of Albert Hamilton who I thought was one of the better singers in Detroit."

Eddie Holland

Al Kent was born Albert Prentis Hamilton in Detroit in 1937. He had made some solo recordings in New York City for Wizard, Baritone and Checker. He later had three singles released on Ric-Tic, the first being "You've Got To Pay The Price" which peaked at Number 42 on the Pop Chart and Number 22 on the R&B Chart. Robert Harston (Bob) Hamilton Jr, wrote and produced under the alias, Rob Reeco and was sadly killed in a drive by shooting in Detroit in 1969. At Golden World Al Kent met his future wife, Norma Toney. Norma was a prolific songwriter who had just co-written "Inky Dinky Wang Dang Do" for The Dramatics but would be recognised more once she began working with Holland Dozier Holland at Invictus Records. The musicians working alongside the San Remo Strings were the legendary Funk Brothers along with the same horn and string players that were on all of the records. Some of the musicians came from the Detroit Symphony Orchestra as did the Motown Strings under the guidance of Gordon Staples. The Ric-Tic label was famous for its instrumental 'b' sides but also released 'a' side instrumental material with the San Remo Golden Strings whose "Hungry for Love" was backed by "All Turned On".

45

Incidentally, the group's name was directly lifted from the Italian town of San Remo and its World-famous Music Festival (Festival Della Canzone Italiana), an annual Italian popular music festival that was the pet project of Frenchman Marcel Baison and also the inspiration for the Eurovision Song contest. Both "Agent Double-O-Soul" and "Hungry for Love" had proved highly popular singles which made the next one important if Ric-Tic was to sustain credibility. Unfortunately, Rose Batiste's "That's What He Told Me" remained in the shadows of the label's predecessors. Batiste was a native Detroiter born in 1947. Her mother persuaded her to knock on the door of Motown. Her cousin Freddie Gorman was still with the company at this point but despite encouragement she was never signed. Instead, she signed up to the Thelma label before moving on to Ric-Tic for the one release. Both sides were co-written by Bob Hamilton but somehow it failed to catch the general public the same way its predecessors had been able to do. The same did not apply to the next release though and saw the start of a Northern Soul career with the initial Ric-Tic release by the legendary J.J. Barnes, "Please Let Me In".

Another former Motowner was a jobbing writer/producer/singer Andre Williams, who released one track on Ric-Tic as he went along his own way throughout the recording industry. Born in Alabama "Mr. Rhythm", Andre Williams wrote "Shake A Tail Feather", a 1963 hit for The Five Du-Tones and worked at Motown and Fortune. He had signed to Motown in 1961 where he produced The Contours and Mary Wells and co-wrote the 'b' side of "My Guy", "Oh Little Boy" alongside Brian Holland.

If Golden World had given Berry Gordy some sleepless nights it was another Ed Wingate label, Ric-Tic that would give him nightmares. Freddie Gorman had returned to the studio as an artist cutting tracks for Ric-Tic, "In A Bad Way" and "Take Me Back". The following year Motown did just that as Gorman re-joined Gordy's empire to front The Originals with a little help from Lamont Dozier. At Motown Freddie Gorman settled into life as the recognised leader of The Originals and the first track they worked on with Holland Dozier Holland was "We've Got A Way Out Love" in 1965 but the song never appeared until four years later after Dozier had split from Motown. Although a quartet, the group started their recording career as five because Motown had Joe Stubbs on the books, brother of The Four Tops, Levi. Freddie Gorman felt that Motown hadn't known what to do with Stubbs and so put him with The Originals where he stayed for 6 months. This wasn't to suggest that Stubbs was a make weight, in fact he was the lead vocalist on the group's debut single, "Goodnight Irene", 1965 before leaving to front The Contours. After his stint with Motown, he too followed Holland Dozier Holland out of the Motown door.

One of the new breed of creators at Motown was Norman Whitfield, a native New Yorker, who had spent a big part of his formative years in the Pool Halls of Harlem before moving to Detroit where he had risen from playing tambourine for Popcorn And The Mohawks to working in the mail room of Motown, moving on to head Quality Control and co-writing with Eddie Holland. With Holland he had reached the National Top Thirty in 1964 with The Temptations and carried on not only taking The Temptations away from Smokey Robinson's control but also freeing up Robinson to concentrate on his own group The Miracles with whom he had guided to a Number 11 spot with "Going to A Go-Go" at the end of 1965.

In 1965 McKinley Jackson, who had grown up since sitting in on that Miracles session back in April, arranged the ultrarare Northern Soul classic "When You Lose the One You Love" by Buddy Smith on Brute Records. Motown had let another talent slip through the net and yet Gordy was still able to build a roster of groups and solo performers aided by writers and producers who could deliver the right sound to the right artist: but the newfound stardom was beginning to breed contempt; most significantly in the mind of Motown's first Lady of Soul, Mary Wells. Surprisingly, Mary Wells' 1964 hit "My Guy", while appearing to herald the beginning of her career in England, particularly, was in fact the final act of a successful one in her homeland. In the same year she toured England with The Beatles and achieved a first for the company by having an overseas hit. Still, Wells had dreams beyond that of a Soul singer from Detroit; she wanted to act and persuaded by then husband Herman Griffith, the former Tamla singer and Morty Craft, President of 20th Century Fox Records she was hoodwinked into believing that an acting career lay ahead if she left Motown. Instead, what lay ahead when she turned 21 and quit the company was definitely no birthday treat. After moving from 20th Century Fox and signing to Atco Mary Wells single "Use My Head" in 1965 only reached Number 34 Nationally.

This was the first time a Motown artist had tried to rock the boat and the effect on her was disastrous. Ironically, her ambition was nothing that Gordy was not going to strive for later in his own career but Wells' decision to quit was too much too soon for the company boss. From Gordy's point of view, it strengthened his grip on the other artists who saw that there could be more to Motown's management than first met the eye. Different variations on the Wells theme appeared throughout the history of Motown. As mentioned though, Mary Wells was instrumental in getting the Motown sound accepted overseas. Up to, and including, the success of "My Guy" Motown had relied on a similar set up to the one Gordy managed to break away from in his homeland; the leasing of products to other labels but all that was now in the past. By the mid-60's Motown was the largest independent record company in the world but sometimes its workings were a mystery to those nearest to the company. The label was bursting at the seams with talent and unfortunately was unable to give everyone equal treatment often overlooking the talent it was holding on to. The organisation was obligated to release one record a year on any signed recording artists and if Motown didn't release a record, then the artist could legally leave the company.

Over the years many 'one-hit' wonders would pour out of Hitsville to be picked up years later by avid collectors. Yet for all those who made it to the studio an equal amount would be left sitting on the bench in the lobby of Hitsville waiting for that call. Ronald Dunbar's butt had begun to make its own groove on that bench long before he got the chance to cut any more creative grooves. Dunbar was born in Detroit on April the 15th 1939, he was both an entity and an identity to be used when required for whatever purpose.

Now at this point that may be slightly confusing but as the story unfolds you will begin to see what I mean. Here is the start of the riddle. The first recordings of the track "Chills And Fever" was released in 1960 on Detroit's Startime label by Johnny Love and His Orchestra. Then when the larger Dot label chose to give it a National release the track was credited to Ronnie Love, Dunbar's stage name. His first credit on a Motown recording came the following year when he co-wrote "Greetings (This is Uncle Sam)" by The Valadiers. He would continue at Motown, working with Holland Dozier Holland with no credit but once they left Motown, Dunbar's name, along with an Edith Wayne, would be used as a pseudonym for Holland Dozier Holland, while he was credited under his own name at the same time. A riddle within a riddle.

At this stage in the game Dunbar was still a benchwarmer, working on the early shift at Chrysler, from there he called home and cleaned up ready to be at Motown by 4.30am. He was trying to pitch a tune for Marvin Gaye, "Your Love Controls Me." He had already spoken to Brian Holland who told him that he was preparing to take Marvin Gaye into the studio and to have the tune ready for them to listen to. The opportunity never happened. and Dunbar remained frustrated. That was until he dropped into a conversation that he was going to go to the Racetrack the next Saturday. Holland seemed keen to go and asked Dunbar to call over at his house for him. Before they left the house, Dunbar had been given a chance to hear the Four Tops single "I Can't Help Myself", to be released in April and to offer advice on which was the best mix to go with. It was, coincidentally, the same choice that Holland was going with; the day couldn't have got off to a better start. At the track Holland backed four winners and the next Monday was telling everybody how he'd been to the track with Ronald

Dunbar. The following week Eddie Holland joined his brother and Dunbar for a day at the Races where the three of them hung out in the lounge area.

From then on Dunbar worked closely with Holland Dozier Holland and although Motown continued to ignore him the trio would stay loyal to him and forge a relationship that existed up to Ronald Dunbar's passing on the 3rd of April 2018. Another one that got away was Steve Mancha but his talents would later also be grabbed by Holland Dozier Holland after their move from Motown. Mancha was born Clyde Darnell Wilson on Christmas Day, 1945 in Walhalla, South Carolina but by 1950 his family had moved Northwards towards Detroit where black migrants were finding work easier than in the South. Another ten years passed and by 1960, Wilson befriended Melvin Davis who was recording for Fortune Records. With Wilbert Jackson he recorded as Two Friends cutting the single "Just Too Much to Hope For" on Harvey Fuqua's HPC label. From there Wilson joined Motown as a staff writer and where Marvin Gaye and Tammi Terrell re-cut "Just Too Much To Hope For" as well as "Give A Little Love" the b-side of "Ain't No Mountain High Enough." The Monitors recorded his "Number One in Your Heart" and The Spinners did "Just Can't Help but Feel the Pain".

Clyde Wilson left Motown in 1965 as another disillusioned artist and began to work with Don Davis, another creator who was managing to build up a steady reputation in the shadows of Motown with his Groovesville label. Here Wilson along with Melvin Davis, for whom he had played guitar in his Jaywalkers and who would later join Invictus as lead singer of The 8th Day were signed. At the suggestion of Don Davis and with the blessing of writer/producer Don Mancha, he became Steve Mancha and as such began a singing career releasing singles on Groovesville and its subsidiaries Wheelsville and Groove City. The first Davis' production was "Did My Baby Call" backed with "Whirlpool," on Wheelsville Records in 1965. This was followed by three Groovesville releases, "You're Still In My Heart" released in October of 1965 followed by the Holidays single "I'll Love You Forever," on Golden World Records. The Holidays were a group whose line-up could constantly change depending on who was around for a recording session. This incarnation of The Holidays comprised Edwin Starr on lead vocal, Mancha and J. J. Barnes and although it became a hit in the Soul circles the group never toured.

The rest of the year was fairly quiet for Holland Dozier Holland with Kim Weston's "Take Me In Your Arms" on Gordy reaching the Pop Chart at number 50 and Earl Van Dyke & The Soul Brothers instrumental version of "I Can't Help Myself" on another subsidary, Soul, doing nothing except causing a few feet to tap. Brian Holland's young Canadian understudy, R Dean Taylor, was saying "Let's Go Somewhere", a collaboration between

James Dean and Eddie Holland which went nowhere although the track, released on yet another subsidiary, VIP, later became a favourite on the British Northern Soul. Outside of working with the full team of Holland Dozier Holland Taylor collaborated with Eddie Holland on another track "Poor Girl" also in 1965. Even the Tops only reached Number 19 in October with their fifth release for Motown, "Something About You". The next Number 1 for The Supremes was released in the same month though and "I Hear A Symphony" saw Holland Dozier Holland embark on fresh production techniques. The first evolutionary period of the Motown sound was in full swing: having continued Gordy's choice of instrumentation harking back to his late '50's productions using tambourines and flutes Holland Dozier Holland began to fill out their productions. "I Hear A Symphony" utilised classical themes for the first time in their work although classical music had always played an important role in all three of the team's musical education. Lamont Dozier had hated the '50's and the Holland brothers would play classical music to help them develop ideas.

Not only were HDH's Classical influences showing through but also Brian Holland's respect for The Dixie Cups hit of 1964, "The Chapel of Love" which became the starting point for "Symphony". The year also saw Motown open its doors to The Isley Brothers from Cincinnati, Ohio on a three years' contract and it would be the job of Holland Dozier Holland to introduce them to the world of Motown. Prior to this the Isleys had left Cincinnati for New York where they released their first single, "Angels Cried" for the Teenage label. They came to prominence in 1958 with the original version of "Shout". After this they then moved to Atlantic and Wand where their version of The Top Notes "Twist and Shout" reached Number 17 on the National Chart in 1964. Prior to their signing to Motown, they had begun to develop their own T-Neck operation. T-Neck had been named after their new hometown of Teaneck, New Jersey but the Atlantic distributed label failed to do anything for them as the opening release in 1964, "Testify" (not to be confused with The Parliaments later hit, "I Wanna Testify") saw no chart action. The track is probably more famous for including a searing guitar solo by their resident guitarist, 'Spider', known to the world as Jimi Hendrix. Likewise, the next three T-Neck productions released on the Atlantic label failed to chart. So, by the time the brothers joined Motown they were already an established act with some experience within the industry and therefore a little away from the other Motown acts who had come through the Motown groom school and, in the case of the Four Tops and The Supremes, been happy for a full make-over.

The year of 1965 ended with the latest Supremes and Holland Dozier Holland hit "My World Is Empty Without You" reaching number 5 and the underrated Elgins begging the listeners to "Put Yourself in My Place", courtesy again of Holland Dozier Holland, while sharing the stage with Detroit rockers MC5 at Wayne State University, Detroit, a bizarre mix if ever there was one. At this point in the story, I ask you to remember the name of Wayne University as it may hold the key to one of contemporary music's great mysteries. The Elgins themselves, were native Detroiters who had recorded as The Sensations on the Flip label before adopting the name of The Elgins upon joining Motown, the name being taken from a make of wristwatch. At the suggestion of Berry Gordy, the group took on a female lead vocalist, Saundra Malette, for the Holland Dozier Holland work. Work with Holland Dozier Holland came purely by chance. Group members Duke Miller and John Virgil Johnson were also barbers by trade and the three master writers and producers would frequent the shop where they worked. One day Brian Holland visited the shop on his way to catch up with the Motown Revue that was playing in Chicago. Brian Holland asked Johnson to go along with him and in turn Johnson took the opportunity to ask Holland to consider recording with The Elgins. The rest, again, became history, albeit short lived. The group proved more important to the British Northern Soul scene than their own country folk and after one album they were released by Motown in 1968.

This was a vintage period, though, for Holland Dozier Holland. Productions on The Elgins as well as the lesser successes of Marvin Gaye and Kim Weston would soon be adopted by a hungry market outside of The United States for in hindsight Motown not only created its own sound but also its own competition. The Northern Soul dancers in England performed their choreographed pyrotechnics to a backbeat of Motown sounds or sound-a-likes. Many classics of, what Dave Godin, christened Northern Soul, have a neo-Motown quality as though the producers were medieval alchemists attempting to create gold and instead coming up with the next best thing.

In January of the new year, 1966 the Isley Brothers opening release proved to be their most successful track while with Motown and, more than any, helped to establish them in the eyes of many as a Motown act through and through despite their already impressive track record. "This Old Heart Of Mine" reached Number 12 on the Billboard Chart and Holland Dozier Holland had done it again., The team were astounded. Lamont Dozier spoke to Brian Holland saying that he didn't think this was ever going to end and that they had stumbled into something that was worldwide and lasting. Brian Holland agreed, feeling that something had 'zapped' them. As the success continued, like so many, they put it down to divine intervention but it was simply being in the right place at the right time and Motown was about to happen. Holland Dozier Holland were writing pure poetry which, more than ever, was evidenced in the lyrics to "This Old Heart of Mine".

Block out the pounding rhythm and lose the image of those jam-packed dance floors and you are left with some of the saddest lyrics ever to grace 7 inches of vinyl.

> Try "With half a kiss you remind me of what I miss." or
> "You're here for a day and gone for a week."

Another Motown staff writer, Sylvia Moy, had contributed to the song but despite this ability to pull out the stops when required not all their releases were hitting the mark. Yet one only had to look at the number of singles being issued on a national level and weekly basis to realise that even top twenty success was to be commended when it was achieved with such regularity. So, although Kim Weston's February release, the rousing "Helpless" only reached Number 56 and the Four Tops struggled to find the Number 18 slot with "Shake Me, Wake Me" they should still be counted as successes.

The following month another artist was added to Holland Dozier Holland's list of achievements. This time around the vocalist was a reluctant one. His voice had always been his saxophone and yet just as "This Old Heart..." will forever belong to The Isley Brothers, "Road Runner" will remain Junior Walker & The All-Stars' masterpiece. "Road Runner" reached Number 20. With his July re-definition of Marvin Gaye's "How Sweet It is", produced by Johnny Bristol and Harvey Fuqua sounding like it had been recorded in the Motown canteen, Junior Walker & The All Stars reached Number 8 and even though it had been placed in the hands of others to produce, the Holland Dozier Holland magic shone through. Across the City another legend was in the making but it would be the next decade that would see Laura Lee explode onto the Soul scene.

Laura Lee was born in Chicago on the 9th of March 1945 before moving, after adoption, to Detroit where she was raised by the Reverend E.A. Rundless. Her musical education began as so many Soul performers did in Gospel; in Laura Lee's case with The Meditation Singers, her adopted Mother, Mrs Ernestine Rundless' group, who recorded for the HOB (House of Beauty) and Gospel labels. In an attempt to move across from Gospel into the more secular black music Laura Lee removed the Rundless part of her name and in March 1966 cut the classic "To Win Your Heart" for Ric-Tic; the vocal of The San Remo Strings "Festival Time" which, incidentally, followed Laura Lee numerically in the order of Ric-Tic releases. The San Remo Strings "Festival Time" again referred to the Italian town of San Remo while the flip "Joy Road" was a celebration of the road which ran for 40 odd miles from the heart of Detroit to the west and Ann Arbor. Despite only having the one release Laura Lee felt at home at Ric-

Tic while "To Win Your Heart" still has a big following in the UK. To her it was the kind of studio where all the singers used to hang out, people like Edwin Starr and if they knew that she was recording they would come to the studio to watch her, at other times she would help Edwin Starr with his timings. All the artists would drop by to see what was happening to chat, eat something and generally support the artist that was recording.

Brian Holland had the utmost respect for Laura. He tried to get her a contract with Motown and she went to see both Berry Gordy and Mickey Stevenson but they didn't like her singing. They liked the bubblegum type of sound and her sound was a heavier, more soulful one than what they were looking for. Brian Holland didn't have the authority to get her a contract with Motown but he always believed in her, remaining a firm fan of Laura's unique vocal style. His admiration would eventually bear dividends.

Holland Dozier Holland were often asked if they'd reach that Number One position again and there seemed little doubt in their minds that they would, despite The Supremes April 1966 single, "Love Is Like an Itching In My Heart" only scraping into the top ten. By the summer Motown and Holland Dozier Holland were ready to deliver another double whammy. Lesser hits like The Isley Brothers "I Guess I'll Always Love You", "Love's Gone Bad" by Chris Clarke, "Little Darlin'" by Marvin Gaye and The Elgins wonderful "Heaven Must Have Sent You" were all overshadowed by the return to prominence of the Four Tops and The Supremes with "Reach Out, I'll Be There", the Tops' greatest overseas success and "You Can't Hurry Love". Additional instruments such as oboes and Arabic drums combined with pounding bass lines, flutes and tambourines were most effective on The Tops "Reach Out". Holland Dozier Holland had managed to create their own Wall Of Sound not dissimilar to the fullness conceived by Phil Spector in his New York original. In hindsight there should have been no doubt that recording the track was a good move and yet Levi Stubbs, like other artists before him, was reluctant at first to sing for Holland Dozier Holland. It has even been suggested that the track was planned originally for Tom Jones who was looking to sign for Motown at this time. For HDH, the song just fell into place. Brian Holland would play half the song sometimes, he would play the intro to 'Reach Out' and then Lamont Dozier would jump in, push him out of the way and sing, "Now, if you feel that you can't go on..." They would feel it like that on the spot. Then Holland would jump back in with the bridge. They would be sliding on and off the piano stool. It was a beautiful experience and one Lamont Dozier said he would never forget.'

As well as reviving the career of the Four Tops Holland Dozier Holland, alongside Smokey Robinson, had also secured more hits for Marvin Gaye, Brenda Holloway, the newly re-named Martha Reeves and The Vandellas and Kim Weston while other writers and producers, like Kim Weston's husband Mickey Stevenson and Ivy Jo Hunter, would work in tandem with other creators to try and emulate the top dogs. As the top dogs Holland Dozier Holland were not always willing to share their honours and there was a ghost in Holland Dozier Holland's house by the name of R. Dean Taylor. Taylor, while benefiting from the team's input with "Let's Go Somewhere" in 1965 and "There's A Ghost in My House" in 1967, was also Brian Holland's understudy and as such contributed to several of the Four Tops hits as well as "Love Is Here And Now You're Gone" by The Supremes. He was paid cash by the team and left off the label.

Between 1960 and 1965 Mike Terry had worked for Motown before signing with Golden World in April 1966 at a time when the label was in its final few months. During his time at Golden World, he joined forces with George Clinton and Sidney Barnes to form Geo-Si-Mik Productions. Clinton and Barnes were well acquainted by the time they arrived in Detroit to work for Golden World. They had been introduced to each other by George Kerr in New York. Sidney moved on to Sue Records, then Red Bird Records, as a songwriter and artist. At Red Bird, he recorded some classic songs including "You'll Always Be In Style" and "I Hurt On The Other Side" a big number on the Northern Soul scene. A desire to be a part of the Motown dream had seen The Parliaments move to Detroit to work and try and get a deal. The Parliaments were all working in barbershops in Plainfield, New Jersey but after five frustrating years being signed to Motown where it was obvious that Motown were simply using them as a way of getting the Temptations to work harder, they signed to the rival Golden World company after their contract expired and released the double header "That Was My Girl" and "Heart Trouble". Joe Hunter and Bert Keyes provided the arrangements for those songs. The Geo-Si-Mik song, "I'll Bet You" by Theresa Lindsey was covered by a number of artists over the years including The Jackson Five, Billy Butler and Funkadelic. It is also credited to Theresa Lindsey as co-writer. Clinton had made the move to Detroit to be part of the Motown revolution that hadn't happened for him but that wouldn't stop him becoming one of the city's most unique, creative individuals. The first mention of the Geo-Si-Mik team on a Golden World 45 came on the flipside of "Picture Me and You", "I Love the Life I Live".

By the time the beautiful "How's Your New Love Treating You" was released by The Debonairres in June 1966, Diane Hogan was the lead vocalist on the Golden World single and by July the label was releasing many more one-off releases on acts such as Larry Knight, Dickie and the Ebbtides, Pat Lewis and Tamiko Jones, of these Pat Lewis became the most successful. After leaving The Adorables she released "Can't Shake It Loose" a superb Geo-Si-Mik production. The final San Remo Strings release came in August 1966. "Quanto Sei Bella" c/w "International Love Theme" continuing the unusual link with Italy whilst The Adorables final Golden World release was "C.O.D. (Collect on Delivery)". Golden World's time was nearly up.

Golden World was gaining a reputation as being the best studio in town and Berry Gordy was showing increased interest in the label. It was The Holidays who would steer the label into mythology with the final release "No Greater Love" and in September 1966 Gordy bought out Golden World. Future Golden World material was now released exclusively on the Ric-Tic label and all other subsidiary labels became extinct. A record that many believed to be a Motown recording was released at this time, "S.O.S (Stop Her on Sight)", recorded by Edwin Starr. Edwin Starr's original was issued in England on the Polydor label before finding its way onto Motown Chartbusters 3 and adopted from that point on as belonging to Motown to the dancing masses but the initiated knew different.

As well as owning the studio, Motown now owned the Publishing Company and contracts that numbered Edwin Starr and JJ Barnes. J.J. Barnes was born in Detroit, Michigan on the 30th of November 1943 and after an up and down career that included a period away from the industry Barnes learned of the Ric-Tic label where "Real Humdinger" would put him on the map. The track gave him his first entry into the R&B Top Twenty in early 1966. The next disc, a George Clinton produced cover of the Beatles' "Day Tripper" introduced J.J. to Britain when it was issued by Polydor, beginning his Transatlantic love affair with the UK. Ed Wingate's Headquarters were now based in his home on Edison Avenue and the legend of Golden World didn't transfer to Motown but instead it went to the smaller Ric-Tic label. Time was to tell another tale and Gordy's eye now turned to Ric-Tic records and the remaining foundations of Golden World.

After the less-successful J.J. Barnes single "Say It", a thunderbolt would hit the Ric-Tic label. Berry Gordy was no lover of healthy competition and decided that Ric-Tic was stealing too much of Motown's limelight. Ric-Tic's days were numbered. The Parliaments couldn't believe their misfortune, having released themselves from their Motown contract the label they had escaped from were about to buy the company they'd moved to and so they fled to LeBaron Taylor's Revilot label where they finally succeeded with "I Wanna Testify" the following year.

Criticised by musicians and reluctant to share credit with other writers Holland Dozier Holland were still proving themselves to be the best creative force at Motown and as such had little time to worry about treading on others' feelings. Their feelings came out in the songs they crafted. If proof was needed to show their remarkable variety and, equally, if proof was needed to show Motown's versatility, then October's threesome was just that. "I'm Ready for Love" by Martha Reeves & The Vandellas, "You Keep Me Hanging On" by The Supremes and "Come 'Round Here" by Smokey Robinson & The Miracles.

The Number One unsurprisingly belonged to The Supremes and yet any one of the three deserved top billing. "Come 'Round Here" continued Holland Dozier Holland's love affair with classical themes with its elaborate orchestration, cut in September 1966 and released a month later with Smokey Robinson doing his best to input the lyrics in a mock-Levi Stubbs manner that would have remained better suited to The Tops. Both "I'm Ready for Love" and "You Keep Me Hanging On" relied heavily on the beat. However, the two differed in their musical construction. "You Keep Me Hangin' On" relied on chattering guitars and an almost stop start arrangement for its hook whereas "I'm Ready for Love" was bass driven and relentless from beginning to end. The most obvious but least gutsy won out in the end and gave The Supremes their seventh Number One.

Not to be left behind the Four Tops ended the year with a Number 6 hit "Standing in The Shadows of Love". Levi Stubbs once stated that, for a group to be identified with one particular song was an achievement but they were lucky to have recorded so many that were easily identifiable as belonging to the Four Tops. What would also be recognised soon was that at this point in their career the Four Tops not only belonged to Motown but deeper still and with more devastating effect to Holland Dozier Holland. Still, there was much for Berry Gordy to feel proud about. As well as having a built-in record making machine The Miracles also benefited from having the Midas touch of Holland Dozier Holland pointed in their direction. Critics of Motown have often condemned the almost factory production line quality of the label arguing that everything sounded very similar. I would swap the word similar for identifiable plus, the more you hear the more differences, or rather, the more the progression becomes clearer.

As David Morse pointed out in his in-depth analysis of Holland Dozier Holland in his 1971 book "Motown" the team's assembly line quality was their hit-formula repetitiveness, not only in song structure but in lyrics that recalled earlier efforts. A familiarity that kept the buyers buying. For example, you could compare "Baby I Need Your Loving" to "Without The One You Love" where both are tales of love that isn't necessarily lost but love that is on the back burner, waiting to heat up again into passion, equal to the pleading voice of Levi Stubbs. "Standing in The Shadows of Love" visualises in poetic form mythical shadows where love bears down dark and foreboding upon the singer as in "Seven Rooms Of Gloom"; another dream-like vision of a house not built of bricks and mortar but broken hearts and misery.

Flutes and tambourines had always been a part of Gordy's productions way back to 1959 but now the use of harpsichords, full orchestras and the aforementioned developments of Holland Dozier Holland and the rising genius of Stevie Wonder added much more to the basic ingredients. Lamont Dozier acknowledged the greatness of the artists they worked with and how they were quick to get a handle on the team's working pattern. In the case of Levi Stubbs, it was usually in one take. The Four Tops would be given the song, told what to do, they'd learn it in a day or two, come in, record and be out of there. If they weren't like that, they would never have been signed to Motown in the first place. The talent was there and that made the work much easier. Dozier said that if the talent had been of a poorer quality, then they wouldn't have been able to get the songs out as fast as they had. Elsewhere at Motown experimentation was taking place as the pull of the 60's stopped Motown from becoming an anachronism. Still, in general terms the mainstream of Motown remained relatively safe.

At Atco Mary Wells had more success with "Dear Lover", a Number 8 R&B hit that didn't manage to show on the main Pop chart. After even less success with Jubilee and Reprise Wells seemed destined to forever walk up a dead-end street that only offered brief spells of success and a final U-turn some 30 years after her sparkling debut when Wells' career was somewhat revived by Ian Levine's retro Motor City set-up.

The Temptations album track "Just One Last Look" from the 1966 album 'With A Lotta Soul' was another rare matching of The Tempts with Holland Dozier Holland but the team of Holland and Whitfield came up trumps with "He Was Really Sayin' Something" for The Velvelettes later re-cut by British group Bananarama in 1982. In 1966 Florence Ballard of The Supremes began to struggle within the group and started to miss performances, so Marlene Barrow of The Andantes was used as a substitute.

Before the end of 1966 other moves were afoot within the engine room at Motown. William 'Mickey' Stevenson who had been one of Berry Gordy's most loyal subjects was made an offer by MGM to head a new West Coast label. When he left, he took his wife, Kim Weston, along with him. In two moves that Gordy would later regret he gave more power to the Holland brothers. To plug the gap, left by Stevenson's departure, he made Eddie Holland head of A&R and at the same time, Billie Jean Brown took 18 months off to go to Spain with her husband, thus leaving another gap unplugged; this time as head of the Quality Control department, to which he appointed Brian Holland. By year end Holland Dozier Holland had gained 24 Citations of Achievement from BMI as well as bringing into the Motown fold two new creators Nicholas Ashford and Valerie Simpson. Ashford and Simpson met in the choir of Harlem's White Rock Baptist Church and after having unsuccessfully recorded as a duo, they joined forces with Jo "Joshie" Armstead, at the Scepter/Wand label where their compositions began to gain notice. The three of them hit paydirt with "Let's Go Get Stoned" by Ray Charles, reaching number 1 US R&B hit in 1966.

Towards the end of the year The Fantastic Four's first recording for Ric Tic hit the streets in December 1966, this was Gene Redd's "Girl Have Pity" which, although an excellent song, did poorly in the charts. Formed in 1965 The Fantastic Four eventually became Ric Tic's most successful act even out-selling Edwin Starr and J.J. Barnes. More changes, not all positive, began to take place as 1967 started. Perhaps the title of The Underdogs January V.I.P. release summed it up, "Love's Gone Bad", also reflected in The Supremes latest Number 1, "Love Is Here and Now You're Gone". The Four Tops continued their run of success with February's "Bernadette" reaching the top four while out of the past came "Jimmy Mack" by Martha Reeves and her neglected Vandellas; lifted off the shelf for a Number 4 National chart place and a Number 1 R&B hit. It would prove to be their last link with Holland Dozier Holland.

Because the situation at Ric-Tic was becoming increasingly rocky, Chess, the Chicago based label, took up Laura Lee's contract in the same year. A string of rocking dance and ballad tracks overseen by Rick Hall at his famous Fame studios in Muscle Shoals, Alabama followed. However, her first release, written by Laura and James Cleveland was "Stop Giving Your Man Away" produced by Leonard Caston who himself would wander in and out of the Chicago and Detroit Soul scenes. In 1967 "Dirty Man" established her firmly in the non-Gospel arena and although it didn't score high on the national chart it did reach Number 68 Soul wise and begin to establish Laura Lee as a singer not to be overlooked.

The aforementioned "Bernadette" was another difficult one for Levi Stubbs in so much as he could not 'connect' with the tune. That was until an Italian gentleman was brought into Motown to teach the group some Italian lyrics and their meaning. This ignited a spark in Stubbs that made the song more accessible. The influence of the song came from Holland Dozier Holland's separate romantic histories, the girls who got away, the composite Bernadette. One night, Eddie Holland was working past midnight to complete the song when his girlfriend called him. Desperate to see Holland she blurted out the words, "Some people search their whole life through to find the love I found in you." Another hit was born.

In February 1967 across at Ric-Tic, the label released the latest single on The Fantastic Four, "Can't Stop Looking for my Baby" backed by the beautiful "Just the Lonely". The single, "The Whole World Is a Stage," was their major hit reaching Number 6 on the R&B charts in 1967. Their next release, "You Gave Me Something (And Everything's Alright)," reached Number 12 in the same year. Their final recording for Ric-Tic was the fabulous "I Love You Madly", cut at Magic City Studios and later re-issued by Motown on the Soul subsidiary. The Debonairres re-surfaced on Solid Hit with the ultra-rare "Loving You Takes All of My Time" and "I'm In Love Again". Both were backed by "Headache in My Heart" which saw George Clinton re-cutting it with Funkadelic four years later and included it on their second album "Free Your Mind and Your Ass Will Follow ".

The girls later found International fame as the backing duo for singer Tony Orlando with his group Dawn. Dawn was among the biggest pop acts of the '70s and it was also Hopkins who delivered the line "shut your mouth" on Isaac Hayes' "Theme from Shaft". Back at Motown "There's A Ghost in My House" by R. Dean Taylor disappeared although Taylor re-emerged with a British hit and a Northern Soul following in 1974.

In Detroit, a rumour had started that The Supremes were about to undergo an internal change. The rumour was that Diana Ross was going to embark on a solo career, still, in March, the group took care of business as usual with "The Happening" happening for them as they took the theme from the movie of the same name right to the top. This latest release was seen by the public as yet another winner from Holland Dozier Holland although in front of their names was another, DeVol. Frank DeVol came from Canton, Ohio, where he followed his father into a musical career which would eventually lead him to work as a musical director for some of the biggest names in 50's show business including Rudi Vallee, Dinah Shore and Jack Carson. By the early 60s he was becoming more focussed on writing music for both television and the movies, winning five Oscar nominations for his scores and five Emmys for his television themes and scores. He continued arranging for the likes of Tony Bennett, Doris Day, Vic Damone and Peggy Lee and in 1967 he worked on the comedy crime caper, "The Happening". Although it was not Motown's first foray into films it was another step on the path that Berry Gordy would later choose to walk.

It was equally important for Motown to keep the names of Holland Dozier Holland on the label and in an unkind but legal move, the label enlisted the services of a young eager songwriter from New York called Ron Miller. Eddie Holland had Miller write the lyrics for the tune but was convinced that the label would say "Holland Dozier Holland and Ron Miller". A meeting was held with Berry Gordy Jr and Holland Dozier Holland to sign the contracts. Instead of having his name on the label Miller was given $5000 and told to "sign here". Unfortunately, copyright laws state that when someone pays for something to be written they become the writer under "Work for Hire" provisions and if Miller wanted to carry on working for Motown, he was left with no other option but to sign. Miller had been too desperate and overkeen to bring Berry Gordy a song he had composed, "For Once In My Life", a song that had originally been written for an off-Broadway play and been released locally in the New York area. Despite such a rocky start to his Motown career "For Once In My Life" became a 1968 hit for Stevie Wonder and an evergreen standard since then. Meanwhile "The Happening" was later used as a promotional item released on The City of Detroit Presents label by Detroit Tiger's Baseball star Willie Horton backed by Supremes Mary Wilson and Florence Ballard. The intention was for the record to help support the Mayor's Youth project with Horton calling out phone numbers to call up about the project while the two Supremes sang the song behind his talk over.

This was shortly before Hell broke out in the City.

The Supremes were elected as the new spokespersons for the United Foundation's Annual Fundraising Torch Drive. Then the rumour became the truth. On the 30th of April 1967, the trio known as The Supremes separated though, not as expected with Diana Ross. Instead, Florence Ballard, The Supremes acknowledged founder, left the group. Her departure was not under the happiest of circumstances and Diana Ross's name was added to the front of The Supremes while Ballard was replaced by Cindy Birdsong, formerly of Patti Labelle & The Bluebelles. Florence Ballard continued as a solo artist with Robert Bateman, the man responsible for inviting The Supremes to Motown producing her solo recordings for the ABC label. May saw the release of the Four Tops "Seven Rooms Of Gloom" a Pop Number 14 while June gave Marvin Gaye a Number 33 with "Your Unchanging Love".

Freshly signed to Motown were Gladys Knight & The Pips when Norman Whitfield became their designated producer. Again, the team of Holland and Whitfield were successful with the single "Everybody Needs Love" in June 1967. R Dean Taylor had two further collaborations with Eddie Holland "Don't Fool Around" 1967 and "Gotta See Jane", written by the team of Eddie Holland, Ronald Miller and R. Dean Taylor.

On the Gordy label Eddie Holland, Norman Whitfield's protégé Frank Wilson and R. Dean Taylor cut "All I Need" by The Temptations. Within the HDH creative team Brian Holland would once again show his progressive production techniques this time with the use of electronic gimmickry on the immediately recognisable 'beep beep beep' introduction to "Reflections" by the newly named Diana Ross & The Supremes released in July and reaching number 2. The song featured one of the earliest uses of an oscillator on a major recording while the lyrics continued Holland Dozier Holland's earlier themes pioneered by the Four Tops, those of a world where emotions and memories took on solid forms to haunt the living.

Eddie Holland and Norman Whitfield had four more hits on The Temptations, the gut-wrenching David Ruffin vehicle "Ain't Too Proud to Beg", "Beauty's Only Skin Deep" and "(I Know) I'm Losing You" before a final success with "(Loneliness Made Me Realise) It's You That I Need". It would be another ten years before the Holland Brothers got their chance to work with the tempting Temptations when both teams had seen better times.

Berry Gordy Jr was losing track of what was going on 'back home' as he began to spend more time trying to develop links away from Detroit in the film industry of California. During 1967 Gordy was spending more of his days looking away from the General Motors sign in Detroit and focusing on the Hollywood sign, California dreamin' his time away in Los Angeles. There he was planning the move that would break up the established Motown empire and fail to emulate his rise in the music industry, for lightning rarely strikes twice. As a writer and producer Gordy possessed a natural flair; now that he had made enough money through his natural abilities, reality gave way to fantasy; money being the one commodity that allows the rich to act out their fantasies often with less than fantastic results. Something else was also about to hit the City, something so devastating that it would never truly heal. A city like Detroit could offer maybe two or three routes out of the Projects, the Car Plants, music or crime and the three were often interchangeable either through opportunity, missed opportunity or sheer bad luck coupled with misunderstandings and racial intolerance. In Detroit, Motown was changing as was the city itself and Gordy was so totally out of touch that he failed to even notice.

In July, the city came to the boil and in three days a riot split Detroit wide open. The riot began early in the morning of Sunday, July 23rd when the police, led by Sergeant Vic De LaValla, raided a Blind Pig, an illegal bar located at Twelfth Street and Clairmount Avenue. They were expecting to arrest a few customers but instead found 82 people inside celebrating the return of two Vietnam veterans. The Vietnam war had created a visible division throughout the country. The growing tremors carried on and threatened to overturn the growing belief that America had relegated black people to second-class citizenship for far too long. That included fighting and very often dying for a country that didn't appear to want them. Martin Luther King Jr's march to Washington in 1963 and his historic "I Have A Dream" speech was in danger of becoming a voice from a bygone era as white America began to rethink its newfound acceptance of its black brother and sisterhood. Even liberal Americans questioned the actions of the Detroit rioters feeling that it was nothing more than radical protest. Through all of this, Detroit tried to get along with its business. Meanwhile, a crowd gathered in protest and within a short time mobs of young men were engaged in burning, looting and acts of random violence. Earlier riots had been blamed on police "overreaction" to minor incidents, so authorities did not at first dispatch large numbers of officers to the area. They further tried to keep things low key by persuading the media to impose a news blackout. Neither tactic worked and things were soon totally out of control. The rioting spread to take in fourteen square miles of black neighbourhoods and unlike some earlier outbreaks, it was quite indiscriminate: mobs torched and plundered black businesses as freely as white ones and burned down a number of black homes as well. In the latter stages of the riot, blacks from outside the inner city entered the riot zone to participate in the looting.

Vast clouds of smoke were seen rising from black neighbourhoods as Detroit Tigers' star player Willie Horton stood on a car in the middle of the crowd, still fresh from a baseball game and still wearing his baseball uniform, tried desperately to calm the increasingly angry mob. "The Happening" had found a new definition. Maybe not something to confess to but Ken Knox, saxophone player for Chairmen Of The Board said that his first horn came out of the Detroit riots. Everyone was running down the street with televisions and couches and a guy with a saxophone ran past. His brother bought it for him right there in the street for $50.

In three days, a riot split Detroit wide open. Soon afterward the media lifted the news blackout and people began to get the details. By Monday morning news reports indicated that the police and National Guard had matters under control but that night the rioting resumed and intensified. After midnight, the rumblings of troop vehicles moved along the expressway. For the first time in the decade, a riot had got so out of hand that the authorities had to call in federal troops. It took five days to restore order and afterwards there were 43 dead, 7,000 arrests made, 1,300 buildings had been destroyed and 2,700 businesses looted. The riots in Detroit and elsewhere had a devastating effect not just on the communities themselves but on the entire nation.

When they were in tenth grade at Pershing High School, Roderic Davis and Larry Reed formed, along with four other school friends a group to play at local talent shows. As they honed their craft, they would still play free to any appreciative audience. These were the legendary Dramatics. The Dramatics were able to escape the muddle of Detroit, sign a contract with Stax Records in Memphis and continue through the 70's and 80's to be one of Soul's most consistent acts with the guidance of producer Don Davis and writer Tony Hester, whose creativity had grown enormously since being that 14 years old kid whose first song was that Marvelettes flip side "A Little Bit of Sympathy" written with Brian Holland and Lamont Dozier back in June of '64. Like many others The Dramatics joined Motown but never had anything released and were then signed to Ed Wingate's Golden World company where they found success on the Wingate imprint with "Inky Dinky Whang Dang Do" co-written by Norma Toney. She also co-wrote three songs by the Fantastic Four plus the Flaming Embers "Bless you". Her finest moment, however, came with Holland Dozier Holland when she co-wrote the BMI award winning song "Deeper and Deeper" for Freda Payne.

On Wednesday July 26th 1967 the lives of two of the group members came close to a dramatic end, at the hands of the Detroit Police Department at The Algiers Motel. Every year The Fox Theatre, on Woodward Avenue held the weeklong Swinging Time Revue. The Dramatics lined up alongside The Parliaments and J.J. Barnes for the 1967 Revue. Their repertoire included a version of The Young Rascals "Groovin'", a Temptations number "I Want A Love I Can See" plus their most popular song to date, "Inky Dinky Whang Dang Do". Earlier on that Sunday Larry Reed called one Fred Temple to ask him to help out as a valet for the group, sorting out the clothes, making sure towels were on hand to wipe the sweating brows of the dynamic Dramatics.

On that Sunday afternoon in July a man ran on the stage telling everyone that a riot had started and that everybody should go home or to the nearest hotel to find safety. It was mid-afternoon, the temperature was somewhere in the mid-eighties and as the group left The Fox Theatre the smoke was already blowing its way across the troubled skies of Detroit. The six young men hopped on the Woodward Avenue bus but was stopped a few blocks past Grand Boulevard. A policeman stepped on and told the passengers to leave and find cover because there was likely to be shooting around the area. They walked a block north and came upon the neon palm tree that advertised The Algiers Motel. There they paid for a room from the show's takings and once inside Fred Temple phoned his mother to tell her of his whereabouts. This was the first day of the three days riot.

By the third day, Tuesday July 25th the stores had re-opened and some of the group strolled across to The Lucky Strike Market on the corner of Woodward and Euclid. Three of the group prepared to go home, Ron Banks' parents picked him up and later Larry Demps and Michael Calhoun left. Roderick Davis and Larry Reed chose to hang around, along with Fred Temple. One of them would not live to see the day out. Shots had been heard earlier from upstairs. These, it later transpired, were from a starter pistol that could only fire blanks. At about eleven o'clock they were lying around watching tv in room A3 when the door burst open and in swarmed the police.

By now the remaining Dramatics were being herded into the corridor by the police. Lined up and afraid, Roderick Davis had twenty or thirty dollars lifted out of his pocket. What followed was humiliation and abuse of authority as the innocent were told they were going to die. Threats that were only made more real by the dead bodies glanced through open doors. "Pray out good and loud" shouted one of the officers. Larry Reed recited The Lord's Prayer followed by Roderick Davis. The police found this fun and broke into laughter. Davis witnessed the police attempts to bring about more deaths by dropping a knife in front of one of the men lined up and telling him to pick it up. When the man refused, he was beaten. This continued with the police picking out different men to abuse. Davis was hit in the head and told to keep his face to the wall. The humiliation didn't stop at the men. Two white girls present, who only added to the growing officers' anger and frustration, were stripped down to their underwear. The girls were returned to the wall then Roderick Davis was pulled from the line and taken into a room. Systematically the police officers were pulling men from the line-up and taking them into separate rooms where they fired shots into the corners for the others to hear and left to imagine what was happening.

Meanwhile television viewers sat horrified as American tanks moved through an American city hunting American citizens while helicopters scrutinised the city below. That night Tonia Blanding, aged four, was killed by a tank's .50 calibre machine gun when someone in the same room she was in lit a match and the flare was taken as a sniper's gun fire. At the other end of the spectrum Helen Hall, a fifty years' old white woman from Oakdale, Connecticut, died as she opened the curtains of the Harlan House Motel to get a better look at the tanks on the street below. At the Algiers Motel Fred Temple lay dead. Patrolman Robert Paille was charged with Temple's murder and was eventually acquitted due to the lack of evidence. In 2017, Kathryn Bigelow Directed the movie, "Detroit" based on the Algiers Motel events.

The city was torn apart and for many it was the beginning of the end. The city's economy took a dive as property values dropped, signalling a drop in tax revenues. Motown valiantly attempted to mend the broken body with an Elastoplast by releasing "I Care About Detroit" by Smokey Robinson & The Miracles, on Tamla, to the local radio stations. After the riots, Motown founder, Berry Gordy Jr., was honoured at a United Foundation dinner where Motown's participation in the pre-riot Torch Drive's record-breaking campaign was recognised but post-riot, Detroit seemed destined never to recover from this violent period in its history and Berry Gordy Jr was about to escape from it.

In 1967 Holland Dozier Holland hatched their own plot to move away from Motown and would later follow their former boss to California but the departure from Detroit had begun long before 1967. The riots of that year only added to the exodus for when one thing happens in isolation there is no effect but when that occurrence reacts with something else, then you have cause and effect.

"I went to Detroit in '68-'69 and people were still talking about the riots. People in Canada could hear the gunshots from over the border... I found Detroit completely hostile, I'd never seen so many bloody guns before! You know, you walk into a store and there's a guy with a gun on his hip. Well, I'm sorry but that shocked me, you know. You get into a cab and there's a plate glass window between you and the cab driver .... I just couldn't believe the rudeness. I just couldn't get over that shock."

Harrison Kennedy

Artists, writers and producers were becoming increasingly critical of the Motown organisation. Again, as if to give Gordy subtle hints the Four Tops next release of August was the aptly titled "You Keep Running Away" reaping a Number 19 position while October saw "In and Out of Love" by Diana Ross & The Supremes. The main issue amongst the Motown employees was that of money. Gordy had signed up many people at an impressionable age but now it seemed time to renew and review the contracts. People were being overlooked or simply not receiving what they felt was their rights. The company was about to hit a crisis that would ultimately destroy the Motown sound as it was right then. As a producer Brian Holland was considered a genius and as a full team Holland Dozier Holland were proving to have enough ability to run their own show: but that would only come about after Motown had grown unrecognisable even to its founder Berry Gordy Jr. If the importance of Holland Dozier Holland at Motown needed spelling out it was done so in the title of the album, 'The Supremes sing Holland Dozier Holland'. Sure, there had been Stevie Wonder's tribute album to Ray Charles and The Supremes had paid tribute to The Beatles, Rodgers & Hart and Sam Cooke. Here, though was a rare opportunity for the backroom staff to be given top billing. Aside from "The Temptations Sing Smokey", no other Motown songwriters would be given this star treatment. Despite being given this high profile and adulation the team of Holland Dozier Holland were not happy with the financial rewards the company was prepared to offer the writers and producers of what they saw as more than 50% of all the hits Motown had had until now. While they were at Motown, they claimed that they had been responsible for writing and producing about 90 million sales of records but had never gained the kind of money they felt they had the right to expect.

When Motown exploded onto the music scene in 1964 it had been largely due to the work of Holland Dozier Holland. In that year Motown had been able to gain 10% of the Pop market and within this figure 75% of the releases that were hits were written and/or produced by Holland Dozier Holland team members. It began to feel as though, by themselves, they could have potentially been the biggest hit record company in the world. Added to this they had to keep coming up with the goods and were not in the best of shape health-wise. Everything began to take its toll. The problems of not getting enough rest meant that they were getting over tired and anxiety was beginning to set in followed by mental exhaustion. For Lamont Dozier and Brian Holland, it began to get rough at Motown.

Not being given special acknowledgement wore on Holland Dozier Holland and when Berry Gordy began to consider offering the next Supremes release to someone else despite the impressive track record of the team, the damage became irreparable. By now money had become the root of all the evil that Holland Dozier Holland saw in Gordy. As a team they were now feeling that they had been excluded from sharing in the billions of dollars that Motown was making and became disenchanted. Gordy had, at one time, told Brian Holland that he would be getting a block of stock in the company but never did. Eddie Holland could tell that Brian had been deeply hurt by this decision and in turn became angered by Gordy's reluctance to share.

They tried to talk about it and come to some agreement, but any time they brought it up it fell upon deaf ears. They were making this well-oiled machine stronger and richer but were reaping less of the benefits. Surely, it was only fair that their successes were reflected in their rewards. Eddie Holland began to let Gordy know how the team felt and suggested a subsidiary label deal with Motown. They wanted Berry Gordy to agree to them developing new artists exclusive to themselves and this label, while producing other Motown artists in the spirit of the Quality Control method where they remained in competition with the other staff writers / producers.

"That was the breakdown in communication, when he thought that that wasn't to Motown's advantage."

Eddie Holland

If Gordy had of agreed to this would it have kept a stronghold in Detroit while he pursued his West Coast ambitions?

"Absolutely, especially with being head of A&R but let me say this, I can understand why Berry didn't want to do it. Berry Gordy, knowing my personality, he felt that I would spend more time on the label that Brian, Lamont and myself were at and that although I told him that I did not believe that that would happen, that Brian and Lamont would forego what they had with The Supremes and the Four Tops to do that but he thought that I would be persuasive enough to cause them not to do it so I understood his apprehension."

Eddie Holland

Gordy's refusal moved the team to begin digging their escape tunnel out of Motown. Eddie had made the decision to quit without consulting either his brother or Lamont Dozier. Brian found Eddie contemplating on the porch of the house next door to Motown. He shared the rumour that had been circulating Motown that Eddie Holland was getting ready to quit. If that was true, then he was ready to go too. Without even discussing a move away from Motown Lamont Dozier had made up his mind to move on. He had other aspirations and wanted to move out to California to venture into the motion-picture business himself. To make matters even worse Berry Gordy Jr was about to make another move that did little to endear him to his artists.

In 1968 Ed Wingate decided to sell Ric-Tic and Golden World and the labels were about to be buried by a business deal with Gordy. Wingate's decision was possibly brought about by increasing difficulty in getting distributors to deal with the smaller independent label when Berry Gordy was offering more lucrative returns. Gordy, 'sensing' this problem, chose to buy the product but not the labels and in so doing crushed any opposition to the Motown stranglehold. For years Berry Gordy Jr was lambasted for what he did to Ric-Tic Records, a small, seemingly inconsequential label based in Detroit. A collection of Ric-Tic recordings issued in England on Tamla Motown as "Ric-Tic Relics" was even condemned because British Motown had dared to put out the tracks under their imprint. The British always shout for the underdog and in many Northern Soul fans eyes Ric-Tic was the underdog to top dog Gordy. Four acts went to Motown, Edwin Starr, the Fantastic Four, Al Kent and J.J Barnes. Laura Lee and The Flaming Embers reached much greater heights during the 1970's with Holland Dozier Holland at the Hot Wax label and the same was true of The Detroit Emeralds at Westbound. The Emeralds final Ric-Tic release came in July with "Take Me the Way I Am" and then in 1969 they moved to Westbound by which time Berry Gordy had snuffed out the opposition and begun his West Coast interests. Westbound was nowhere near the threat that Golden World and Ric-Tic had been.

Two months after the Emeralds final release, the curtain came down on Ric-Tic when Berry bought out the remaining assets. Edwin Starr was groomed to stardom by the Motown machine, George Clinton and Al Kent were made staff writers/producers for Jobete Music while all the other writers, producers and artists steered clear of Motown. J.J. Barnes remembered that the Motown take-over had been announced to the key artists and producers before Ed Wingate handed over control. He gave them the choice to go to Motown, Gordy, though, was primarily interested in the studio and the catalogue, not the artists. To J.J Barnes a move to Motown sounded good and so he was one who agreed to go there. At Motown Barnes was constantly kept busy in the studio cutting tracks with a variety of producers but none were ever released during a frustrating year that finally saw Barnes quit the company. It took Eddie Holland to make Barnes realise that he was never going to fit in at Motown. The reason being, he sounded too much like their number one solo star Marvin Gaye and the label didn't need two. It was rumoured that Marvin Gaye was unhappy about the similarity of J.J.'s voice to his own. Never the most self-confident of artists, it was also suggested that Marvin may have leaned on Berry Gordy to suppress J.J.'s recordings. Whether this is true, speculation or merely sour grapes will probably never be known for certain. However, there's no doubt that J.J.'s time as a Motown artist was an unhappy experience. He summed it up very simply, saying that he got the hell out of there as soon as he could.

The Fantastic Four moved to Motown's Soul label but felt that it was a wasted spell. They had only gone after Wingate convinced them that it was the right choice to make to ensure them national prominence and in fact, they had another Top 20 R&B hit with "I Love You Madly," which came out in 1968 and re-issued on Soul. They lasted for two years with Motown before semi-retiring in 1970. Several years later Armen Boladian persuaded them to sign with his Eastbound label, although most of their product appeared on the sister label, Westbound produced by Al Kent. Kent himself had had just one hit for the company, "You've Got to Pay the Price", which went to number 22 in 1967. In 1969 a vocal version of the song by Gloria Taylor was an even bigger success on Silver Fox.

As mentioned, Holland Dozier Holland took charge of other strays including The Flaming Embers, as they were originally named. They had taken their name from a famous downtown Detroit eating establishment of the early sixties and consisted of Jerry Plunk, lead vocals and drums, Joe Sladich, Lead Guitar, Jim Bugnel, Bass (Mike Jackson later replaced Bugnel) and Bill Ellis, Keyboards. The group had formed in 1964 but it wasn't until the move in 1968 to Hot Wax that they took that giant step from local bar favourites to national prominence and for a brief moment burned as bright as any Detroit star before returning to the bar circuit. Prior to all of this The Flaming Embers recorded one single on the Fortune label, "You Can Count on Me" backed by "Gone, Gone, Gone". As well as this single they also backed Paul London on "Don't Believe Anybody". On the strength of these tracks, they were signed by Ed Wingate for a short period to the Ric-Tic label. They started their Ric-Tic career in 1967 with "Let's Have A Love-In" backed by the instrumental version by Wingate's Love-In Strings reflecting the nation's mood whilst expressing lyrics usually avoided in the usual Soul recordings, something the group would return to once established at Hot Wax. So popular, seemingly, was the instrumental 'B' side that it was re-released as the 'A' side two records later with "She's A Real Livewire" by The Flaming Embers being relegated to the 'b' side, again in 1967.

The next Ric-Tic release in 1967 was a re-issue of "Let's Have A Love-In" backed by the George Clinton song, "Hey Mama, What'cha Got for Daddy". A year later and "Bless You", a most pleasant mid-tempo item full of pathos and the unique vocal delivery of group leader Jerry Plunk with the equally lilting instrumental 'B' side supported the release more than adequately. "Children" followed in 1968 and their final Ric-Tic release was "Just Like Children" backed by "Tell It Like It Is", the Aaron Neville standard was their parting shot in September 1968. Flaming Ember never saw themselves as anything other than a Detroit band, and were proud of this: they were first and foremost Soul performers who just happened to be white. The group was made up of players living within the Detroit City limits, even players from the suburbs weren't even included. Many record buyers were convinced that Flaming Ember were a black group. It wasn't a black thing or a white thing though, it was a Detroit thing! When they were at Ric Tic Records, they got a lot of recognition from the black recording industry. George Clinton was a friend of theirs and he wrote "Hey Mama Whatcha Got Good for Daddy." They were also doing the music tracks for other artists, so had a reputation for being a funky group. Black audiences were well aware of them by reputation, so when they played the 20 Grand Club for the first time, the place was packed with superstar artists and record people. They were well received and got a standing ovation. They met boxer Joe Louis and a few of The Temptations were there, along with other Motown and Ric Tic artists. One night, after doing their show, group member Jim Bugnel was walking down the centre isle and a lady sitting at the bar stopped him and said that they were really great. He thanked her and went to sit at the end of the bar. The owner asked if he knew who that was that stopped him, he shook his head. It was Dionne Warwick. Kenny Gamble and Leon Huff had The Soul Survivors with "Expressway To Your Heart" on Crimson in 1967 flying the flag for Philly and Impact had released The Shades Of Blue in Detroit a year earlier with their original version of Edwin Starr's composition "Oh How Happy"; but these were isolated acts who lasted one or two singles. On Holland Dozier Holland's new labels, they would without doubt be what was then tagged 'the great white hope'.

In that fateful year of 1968, The Flaming Embers were given another unique opportunity. They were at Ed Wingate's house rehearsing when he showed them an invitation he had received for them to play at The Apollo Theatre on Thanksgiving night. He said that we were the first white group ever to be asked to play the Apollo, but he wouldn't let them go because they had other commitments at that time. Wingate called Bugnel one morning at 6:00 a.m. and told him to get the group together telling him that they were going to Las Vegas to appear with Solomon Burke, Tamiko Jones and Louie Prima at the Sands Hotel. The Apollo honour would go to another Detroit group, Rare Earth. Rare Earth had made a single appearance on Golden World towards the latter part of 1965 under the name of The Sunliners with "The Swingin' Kind". A second single, "Heart Of The City', was recorded but never released. After leaving the Sunliners, the group's Russ Terrana wanted to join the company's staff and Ed Wingate offered him a job on the engineering team. It wasn't long after this that Berry Gordy bought Golden World and Russ became an employee of Motown. Terrana was responsible for engineering over 80 Number One hits during his Motown career whilst The Sunliners eventually renamed themselves Rare Earth and joined Motown. Rare Earth, though, held on to its black indulgences becoming that first white band to play the legendary Apollo Theatre in Harlem as well as benefiting from the production wizardry of Norman Whitfield. Meanwhile, The Flaming Embers headed for Nevada. Upon their return from Las Vegas, they heard that Ed Wingate had decided to sell the record company. He sold most of the artist contracts to various other labels including Motown Records. Wingate gave the Flaming Embers an outright release from their contract to sign with any company they wanted. He told them that he received numerous calls from major labels like Atlantic, Stax, Columbia and Capitol. All were interested in the group but when Eddie Holland told him that they were leaving Motown to form their own labels, Hot Wax and Invictus in Detroit The Flaming Embers decision was made.

By now Holland Dozier Holland had created their last work for Berry Gordy even if he didn't know it yet and the most recent hits by Diana Ross & The Supremes, "Forever Came Today" and the Four Tops, "Walk Away Renee: plus "I'm In A Different World" were all in 'the can', the term for being recorded and stored away. The foundations at Motown were crumbling. Even the structure within groups was changing. "Forever Came Today" was cut by Holland Dozier Holland without The Supremes backing

Diana Ross. The track had been cut the previous year when the other two members were out of Detroit but by 1967 the Andantes were used on all the Supremes songs, replacing Mary Wilson and Cindy Birdsong. For other artists they had been used to smooth The Marvelettes' infectious, but sometimes shaky harmony and were also used on the Four Tops records for high end as well as backing Martha Reeves on every Martha & the Vandellas' recording after Annette Beard left.

"So Long" by Marvin Gaye was written by the team of Norman Whitfield, R. Dean Taylor and Eddie Holland whilst Ronald Dunbar wrote "Sing What You Wanna" with Shorty Long on Motown's Soul subsidiary. As noted earlier, Dunbar had already worked with Holland Dozier Holland while at Motown and when they left several creative and technical people left with them including Dunbar who would later prove a major force for Holland Dozier Holland, eventually receiving a Grammy and four Gold record awards and choosing to stay with the Holland's after Lamont Dozier had made his decision to leave the team. He later moved on to George Clinton's P-Funk Empire before returning to Holland Dozier Holland and becoming A&R director.

Outside of the rumours that Holland Dozier Holland were setting up their own shop there was the story circulating that they were going to reunite with another disillusioned ex-Motowner, Mickey Stevenson in L.A. with his Venture label. Holland Dozier Holland's earliest post-Motown material was cut at the Tera Shirma studio and there were other more bizarre rumours that private investigators, or worse, were seen hanging around studios or on rooftops filming Holland Dozier Holland entering and leaving recording studios other than Motown's. Bass player Bob Babbitt recalled that Holland Dozier Holland had just left Motown but he didn't think that they were legally out of their contract so they had other producers and writers doing the sessions for them. As a studio musician he was doing two sessions one day at Terra Shirma and in between the sessions he went out back of the studio were there was a parking lot. For whatever strange reason he chose to take a broom with him out the back door. At that time the Detroit studios and musicians were getting unknown phone calls threatening the musicians not to work for Holland Dozier Holland. Outside in the car park he spotted a strange looking guy standing by a car. Babbit put the broom on his shoulder and started to creep towards the car. He thought that he saw a gun and a hand grenade on the front seat of the car and so took the broom and started sweeping the parking lot back peddling to the studio back door.

Out of Holland Dozier Holland's moonlighting sessions came the early production, "She's Not Just Another Woman", by the 8th Day, eventually released in May 1971 by which time the group was fronted by Melvin Davis. However, in 1968 the group was simply a piece of a jigsaw and as such its elements resembled the same being put together by former Motown bass player Tony Newton although Newton himself had yet to be slotted into place. The song was written by Ronald Dunbar, along with Clyde Wilson who would prove inseparable from the session's vocalist Steve Mancha; Wilson and Mancha being one and the same! The song had been written by Clyde Wilson and Ronald Dunbar and it was Wilson in his Mancha manifestation that appeared on the initial single. The "She's Not Just Another Woman" session took place at Tera Shirma Studios at 15341 Livernois, Detroit and the musicians brought in for the track included Chuck Boyd on bass, Willie 'Preacher' Hampton on guitar and Melvin Griffin on keyboard. The 'B' side, the beautiful "I Can't Fool Myself" was handled magnificently by Eddie Anderson, formerly of The Holidays, who was also to become another member of 100 Proof Aged In Soul. "I Can't Fool Myself" was also cut by Steve Mancha but Anderson's version got the nod.

As all the rumours and cloak and dagger shenanigans were going on a call came from Jeffrey Bowen for General Norman Johnson to join HDH in Detroit. Bowen, another Motown staff producer had been working for Berry Gordy's empire since the mid-sixties.

"Jeffrey Bowen was extremely responsible and involved in helping me put those groups together. I could not have moved that fast without a person like Jeffrey Bowen who would go out and find the talent and help me put them together. Years ago, I'd heard General Johnson's voice I did not know who he was but I remember telling Jeffrey Bowen that I thought this guy had a very unique sounding voice and had him track him down to find out where he was and have him make arrangements for him to come to Detroit because I would like to talk about signing him."

Eddie Holland

Edna Wright, who would eventually lead The Honey Cone into pole position ahead of the '70's version of The Supremes, felt that as early as 1967 Holland Dozier Holland were planning their move away from Motown because after a chance meeting with the Holland brothers, they kept calling her explaining that they were trying to form their own label. Whatever the truth was eventually going to be Holland Dozier Holland were most definitely on the move having remained active for themselves by laying down the foundations that would become Invictus Records while still in the employment of Berry Gordy Jr.

Gordy was genuinely surprised when he was informed that the trio were no longer producing anything for him and that they were rumoured to be in negotiation with Capitol regarding their own concern. After the Holland Dozier Holland team had approached Gordy about money without satisfaction they had gone on a 'go-slow'. Gordy would call Brian Holland's office then Eddie Holland's to find neither of them around. After checking up he discovered a two months' period of inactivity.

Gordy had been blind to Eddie Holland's constant request for a fair share in the profits. Motown was in turmoil with Gordy's heads of A&R and Quality Control on strike. Holland himself felt confident that, despite other Motown creators having fallen into relative obscurity after leaving the corporation, that he could run an operation like Motown himself. Smokey Robinson felt that Eddie Holland alone instigated the breakup and that Brian Holland remained faithful to him because he was his brother while Lamont Dozier was simply swept along by the proceedings. Robinson was also of the opinion that Eddie Holland had shown less ability than his partners and had often used others to assist him in his song writing without crediting them: this was something that R. Dean Taylor had passed comment on at an earlier date. In a spectacular flurry of lawsuits Eddie Holland, Lamont Dozier and Brian Holland quit Motown and in 1968 Invictus Records was about to be launched and it would soon fall to people like Nicholas Ashford and Valerie Simpson to plaster over the gap left by Holland Dozier Holland.

Their first song, which was already in the can, was given to another secretary who wanted to have her five minutes of fame, Rita Wright. "I Can't Give Back The Love I Feel For You" failed commercially despite a sterling production by the now departed Brian Holland and it would take a name change to Syreeta and a new liaison with future husband Stevie Wonder to make her the star she had always dreamt of becoming.

In April 1968 Laura Lee's "As Long As I Got You" was followed by her reading of Curtis Mayfield's "Need To Belong" and "Hang It Up". Sadly, despite the quality of these recordings no hit ensued. Her Chess career ended with the double-header, "Love More Than Pride" and "Mama's Got A Good Thing" but despite these commercial failures and the loss of a recording contract the best was yet to come for Laura Lee.

The war was about to start, Motown firing the first shot in the Wayne County Circuit court on the 29th of August 1968, asking Holland Dozier Holland to pay damages of $4 million and further asking the court to restrain them from doing work for any other record company. Holland Dozier Holland had, according to Gordy, violated their song writing agreements with Jobete publishing by not producing anything since the latter part of 1967. When asked what he had been doing during 1967 Lamont Dozier claimed that he had been mowing the lawn or playing tunes on the piano that he forgot afterwards. The lawsuit emphasised just how

73

much in royalties the team had earned from 1965 to 1967, $2,235,155. Holland Dozier Holland retaliated, counter-suing Motown.

Holland Dozier Holland had a 40-page suit prepared by three Detroit law firms and one from New York. At the time the suit was for the highest amount ever requested in a lawsuit of this type. They claimed that they "never read their contracts, and if they had read them, they could not have understood their legal wording." The song writing team's suit claimed that Motown's three attorneys had told them that they had nothing to worry about and that the company had their best financial interests in mind. Furthermore, they were told that the contracts were only written documents, even referring to them as 'a matter of fun'. Holland Dozier Holland also claimed that their contracts violated both state and federal anti-trust laws by forbidding the recorded use of their material by any company other than Motown. This had given Motown a monopoly position in the industry. Holland Dozier Holland claimed conspiracy, fraud, deceit, over-reaching and breach of fiduciary relationships to the amount of $22 million through exploitation. They also asked the court to put Motown, its accounts and copyrights into the hands of the receiver.

The charges further claimed that since Brian Holland and Lamont Dozier's joining of the label way back at the company's conception no contracts had been seen and when their contracts ran out in 1967 that verbal promises were made instead of written agreements. As High School students, they had signed with the company for $2 a week plus royalties. After "Please Mr. Postman" and "Playboy." had hit the big time then, Holland said, Berry Gordy increased his royalties to 1/2 cent per record and bought him a new Cadillac. According to the suit, Gordy offered Brian Holland stock in the company instead of an increase in royalties in 1964. Despite the ongoing legal battle, the three had cause to celebrate elsewhere when they received the NATRA award for R& B producers of the year, an honour they shared with Jerry Wexler for his Atlantic label outings.

By now though the three were older and wiser to the music industry and yet Eddie Holland, upon reflection, felt that more was going from beyond their control the deeper they got into the lawsuit. He didn't feel that it was so much over money but more about dealing with a wider creative outlet and that the company was not structured for that at that moment in time. He described the problem as a failure to communicate with Berry Gordy because of their closeness and that everything had escalated to the point where suddenly the next person he spoke to would be an attorney. To Holland it was like standing on one end of a bridge with Gordy on the other with somebody setting fire to the middle. Still before long they would get what they wanted; to develop new artists exclusive to themselves and their label, the one difference being that they were going it alone under the nose of Berry Gordy Jr, their former boss.

Gordy had shown a willingness to let go of creative talent who had been Motown's backbone to be replaced by a new wave of writers and producers who, in general, were Los Angeles based. The original Motown sound was being phased out but one survivor who would lead the new wave was the rising Norman Whitfield, who as it has already been noted, would himself become despondent and try his luck at being a label owner. Unfortunately, success breeds success but very often a biproduct is failure. Berry Gordy's battle with Holland Dozier Holland continued well into the 70's, the period when they were striving to emulate the Motown boss.

The war raged with Holland Dozier Holland accusing Gordy of intimidation and blacklisting musicians who worked with them whist Gordy would still complain about the trio's timing, accusing them of setting up shop while still under contract to Motown. When they were riding this crest of success they had to keep coming up with the goods and they weren't in the best of shape health-wise. Eventually everything took its toll. The problems of not getting enough rest meant that they were getting tired and anxiety was setting in. They were physically and mentally exhausted; for Brian Holland and Lamont Dozier, it got to be rough at Motown. Also, given the emphasis that was placed on Motown as this all-powerful force, they didn't really feel that they got the credit that they thought they should have and eventually left because of some of that but mostly because of the money part. Finally, the cases were settled out of court with no publicity.

The three team members of Holland Dozier Holland were still under exclusive writing contracts with Motown, but nothing prevented them from being music publishers which brought in just as much money. They used their vast talent to develop new writers for their new publishing company, keeping a flow of hit songs coming. Lamont Dozier and Brian Holland were under exclusive production contracts with Motown but Eddie Holland was not. Eddie had been helping with production for years, so there was nothing preventing him from being the producer. It looked like they could keep the team operating much like it did before but without Motown. Almost instantly the new Holland Dozier Holland labels started getting hit records. They had the Hot Wax Records label distributed by Buddha Records and the Invictus label distributed by the giant Capitol Records.

During this time Holland Dozier Holland were prevented from recording for two years and so had to rely on other creators or 'ghost write' for themselves which is when we will reunite with Ronald Dunbar and the mysterious Edith Wayne.

Featuring

- **If Cleopatra Took A Chance**
  - **LAST NIGHT**
  - **WHAT ABOUT ME**
- **JAMIE**

Eddie Holland had the voice, the looks and the stage fright.

Mickey Stephenson (left) put Brian Holland and Lamont Dozier together and later Eddie suggested that he join their team.

Ric Tic and Golden World would later supply acts to HDH's post-Motown company.

The Marvelettes (top left) were some of the first artists to work with Brian Holland and Lamont Dozier Holland. Holland had already scored bit-time as co-writer of "Please Mr Postman". The Elgins' (top right) most memorable recordings were created by the team of Holland Dozier Holland, including "Heaven Must Have Sent You". Mary Wells (left) was dubbed the first Queen of Motown and also benefitted from the team of HDH but it was Martha and The Vandellas (bottom left) who scored the first hit with 1963's "Come And Get These Memories". Marvin Gaye (below right) started out as a session drummer for Motown but was gathering momentum when Holland Dozier Holland weaved their magic with their unique songwriting and production skills.

Freshly signed to Motown, the Isley Brothers (bottom left) also found success with the trio. More hits for The Supremes and the Four Tops continued with Holland Dozier Holland.

Berry Gordy Jr, founder of Motown, refused to give HDH a new deal and so the team chose to move on and create their own labels, Hot Wax and Invictus. An early Four Tops back cover was a premonition of things to come whilst the Four Tops were left to ponder their future.

Holland Dozier Holland had started to develop material before they cut their ties with Berry Gordy Jr and because of legal obligations they were initially unable to sign their names to new songs. Even though Gordy had shown little interest in the team towards the end of their tenure with Motown, he was not going to make their lives easy and throughout their post-Motown career they were dogged by lawsuits making it difficult for Eddie Holland, particularly to maintain the level of creativity that he had been used to.

The Detroit music scene had always been blessed with great musicians and throughout their career HDH were able to utilise the best. Members of the legendary Funk Brothers and newer instrumentalists, including members of Funkadelic and Brainstorm joined forces with The Politicians, their 'house band'. Alongside them were talented individuals like a 15 years' old Ray Parker Jr and Dennis Coffey.

Much of Holland Dozier Holland's post-Motown success was due to their ability to develop other creators. Four of their most successful protegees were Greg Perry (top left) who Motown had wanted to sign at the age of seventeen, General Johnson (top right) who, as well as writing and producing with Perry ,was also leader of the group Chairmen Of The Board. Lyricist Angelo Bond (bottom left) was an integral part of their team and Ronald Dunbar (bottom right) was there at the labels' birth

Melvin Davis (right) was already well established in Detroit as a singer and songwriter. At Motown he was a session drummer, mst famously playing on "Tears Of A Clown" but his talents were wasted there.

He had collaborated with Steve Mancha (bottom right) before they both joined HDH. Mancha, along with Eddie Anderson (top right) and Joe Stubbs (bottom left) formed 100 Proof (Aged In Soul) on Hot Wax.
Both Stubbs and Anderson were well known on the local scene, making the name 100 Proof more than appropriate.

With the success of Hot Wax and Invictus, it looked like Holland Dozier Holland were set to continue their assault on the charts. Honey Cone were their answer to the Supremes with just a hint of the Jackson Five thrown in for good measure and in the Chairmen Of The Board they had found their new Four Tops.

Alongside Greg Perry, General Johnson's creativity with Honey Cone surpassed anything The Supremes were doing at this time.

Diana Ross (right) was looking over her shoulder at HDH'S new leading lady, Freda Payne (left).

Holland Dozier Holland had struck Gold with her single "Band Of Gold" and were now pushing towards capturing the album market..

The team's feminine side was even more successful though with Laura Lee (below). William Weatherspoon whose credits at Motown included Jimmy Ruffin's "What Becomes Of The Brokenhearted was responsible for much of her success at Hot Wax.

The Invictus Years

1968-1977

Invictus

Out of the night that covers me,
Black as the Pit from pole to pole,
I thank whatever gods may be
For my unconquerable soul.
In the fell clutch of circumstance
I have not winced nor cried aloud.
Under the bludgeoning of chance
My head is bloody, but unbowed.
Beyond this place of wrath and tears
Looms but the Horror of the shade,
And yet the menace of the years
Finds, and shall find, me unafraid.
It matters not how strait the gate,
How charged with punishments the scroll,
I am the master of my fate:
I am the captain of my soul.

William Ernest Henley

The Invictus sound was tight, percussive and funky, supplied by the finest of the more established Detroit session men such as Earl Van Dyke, Johnny Griffith and Rudy Robinson on keyboards. Eddie Willis, Dennis Coffey, Willie 'Preacher' Hampton and Ray Monette on guitars, with the likes of Bob Babbitt and Tony Newton on bass, Uriel Jones, Andrew Smith and Richard "Pistol" Allen on drums with Jack Ashford on tambourine and vibes.

Bob Babbit recalled that when Hot Wax issued the debut album on Flaming Ember they gave credits to the band members when in fact the only member of the group on the recording was Jerry Plunk the lead singer. "Little" Charlie Hearndon, guitarist, moved on from The Fabulous Peps to join McKinley Jackson & The Politicians, from there he enjoyed a stint with The Night-Liters co-writing the funk anthem "K-Jee" with that Detroit stalwart of old Harvey Fuqua. Don Hatcher began his career on bass and vocals in the band known as The Fun Company which he formed alongside

87

Zachary (Zack) Slater (or Frasier), a future 'Politician', on drums. Don became part of the 100 Proof Aged In Soul unit alongside guitarist Ron Bykowski, who would later join the ranks of Funkadelic. Tiki Fulwood, Bernie Worrell and Billy Nelson also from Funkadelic and Larry Sims, Renell Gonsales of the group Brainstorm and individuals such as guitarist Rodney Anderson added to this mesmerising collective. All of this was supplemented by fine orchestration produced and arranged with far more passion than anything Motown was issuing at the time.

Holland Dozier Holland's studio was a converted movie theatre, The Town Theatre on Grand River Avenue whilst the musical force harnessed behind the scenes was the responsibility of many masters. Dennis Coffey had performed his guitar tricks on most of the Ric-Tic material, featuring heavily on the instrumentals, notably Al Kent's Northern stomper "You Gotta Pay The Price" as well as The Parliaments breakthrough "I Wanna Testify". Coffey was, to his knowledge, the first guitarist to bring the wah-wah pedal to Motown on "Cloud Nine" by The Temptations. He branched out to become a recording artist in his own right with accompaniment in his Detroit Guitar Band by Jack Ashford and Bob Babbit, hence a sound not dissimilar to the work on Invictus. Coffey would head over to Tower Studios for Holland Dozier Holland's sessions around at 9:30pm or 10:00pm after he'd finished recording at Motown during the daylight hours.

Babbit, a young white bass player had been the house player for the old Golden World company alongside Coffey on guitar. Ray Monette, another Caucasian player had been raised in Detroit's R&B scene and after working for Holland Dozier Holland progressed to Motown's premier Rock band, Rare Earth. Earl Van Dyke, keyboard-god of Detroit who had been critical of Holland Dozier Holland's handling of musicians at Motown was still prepared to work for them in their new kingdom. His approach to the work was, however, less than personal and once claimed that when the music was brought into the studio, he saw it and when he left, he forgot it. Being a studio musician kept your mind focussed on the job at hand that sadly meant that none of the players responsible for the sound ever really sat back to reflect on a good day's work.

The rhythm was a direct descendant of the Motown sound that, after all, was the dominant paternal voice of Detroit. It was comparable with the sound of post- Holland Dozier Holland Motown, a sound the trio had directed in their later years with Gordy and epitomised by new artists The Jackson Five who arrived a year after Holland Dozier Holland departed. Greg Perry said that as producers, they just mouthed things, telling the musicians what they wanted and then leave them to get on with it. A far cry from the rigidity suggested by musicians during the halcyon says of Motown, the exception being Holland Dozier Holland. Despite the input from several quarters one group was acknowledged as the House Band for the company. These were The Politicians led by McKinley Jackson, a Chicago arranger who had "Love Machine" issued as a single on Hot Wax. The 'a' side being a vocal handled by Ronald Dunbar whilst the instrumental 'b' side became the British 'a' with another instrumental, Holland Dozier Holland's "Free Your Mind" becoming the 'b'. Incidentally, this track had previously appeared as the flip side to The 8th Day's second release, "You've Got To Crawl" under the title "It's Instrumental To Be Free". This was confusing to the British public. Despite the fact that Funkadelic members, Tony Newton on bass, Detroit session guitar aces Eddie Willis and the new axeman Ray Parker Jr were on guitar and pianists Sylvester Rivers, Johnny Griffiths and Earl Van Dyke and Eddie 'Bongo' Brown and Jack Ashford on percussion on numerous Invictus tracks, The Politicians remained named the resident house band in much the same way that The Funk Brothers were at Motown, MFSB were in Philadelphia or Booker T & The MGs and/or The Bar Kays were down in Memphis.

All these labels would also have other musicians on the periphery. The Politicians had been together since 1968 and comprised of Melvin Griffith, Roderick 'Peanut' Chandler, Clarence 'Clay' Robinson, the aforementioned Zachery Slater and McKinley Jackson, Jackson was rapidly becoming the most in demand arranger alongside the more established Paul Riser, arranger for much of The Temptations psychedelic period under producer Norman Whitfield as well as a respected horn player, H.B. Barnum who, as an artist in his own right, had cut the Northern soul classic "Thumb A Ride " fame as well as having a solid background of playing with '50's group, The Robins, The Du-tones, The Penguins and B. Bumble & The Stingers and Tony Camillo who arranged much of the orchestrated parts of Freda Payne's first Invictus set, "Band Of Gold". Camillo, a college professor in New York moved into the music business in 1969 after realising that there had to be more to life than academia.

After some early stabs at recording, he was invited to start a Motown career with Holland Dozier Holland who in turn persuaded him to join them in the new Invictus company. Here he arranged all of the early successes for the company. Eventually the relationship with Holland Dozier Holland cooled off when he refused to sign a seven years' binding contract with the label and they in turn stopped including his name on the albums. These musicians, who had gone for so long without the full recognition they deserved were the backbone of not only the labels but the sound of that City. The reason why Golden World and Ric-Tic had the same sound as Motown wasn't because the company painstakingly researched every chord and rhythm pattern laid down by the musicians at Motown. Much simpler, they were the same musicians; and as new pretenders to the Detroit throne Holland Dozier Holland employed a blend of established Detroit session men alongside a new breed who were given the opportunity to learn from their heroes, throwing in their own innovations along the way. A perfect example of this was fifteen years' old Ray Parker Jr. At the age of thirteen Parker had been employed by The Detroit Spinners as their guitarist before being signed up by Holland Dozier Holland in 1970 where his unique chattering wah wah sound was in evidence throughout their productions. Later in his career he was responsible for writing the Number One Soul hit for Rufus "You've Got The Love" in 1974 before establishing himself further with his own group Raydio. As with Motown the Detroit Symphony Orchestra performed the string and horn chords for Holland Dozier Holland's company.

One other ingredient that was literally put in the mix was noted sound engineer, Lawrence T. Horn. In 1969 Barney Perkins started out as an apprentice with L.T. Horn at Holland-Dozier-Holland Sound Studios in Detroit and after working his way up to being a full-time recording engineer, he gave an idea for a song called "Put It In The Want Ads" to producer Greg Perry. The record went platinum and Barney doubled his money that year off the song writing royalties. Other Engineers included Robert Dennis. Dennis went to Motown in 1963 and found that one of his first jobs was to make drawings for an 8-track machine that was being built by Motown's Engineering Department. Like so many others Dennis grew disillusioned with Motown and had started taking 'sick days' off to go to job interviews in Chicago. He was about to sign a contract with Chess Records when one of Motown's technical engineers who was planning to leave to join Holland Dozier Holland told him in confidence of the trio's plans to leave the label. Dennis took up an offer from Holland Dozier Holland and remained in Detroit. He gave his notice at 5:00 pm Friday evening and the following Monday was on a plane to New York along with two other engineers all with 'secret' identities.

Over the next 6 weeks they worked on designing and constructing a custom recording console as well as 'sourcing' all the other recording and engineering equipment required to build HDH's own recording studio. Last, but not least Greg Reilly, best known for his engineering of George Clinton's late 70's and early 80's recordings, started as an apprenticed guitar player with Holland Dozier Holland. He had also become Robert Dennis's business partner after quitting Motown and opened their own Recording Studio, Superdisc. Still, L.T. Horn remained kingpin in the studio and yet, for all his astounding and innovative feats at Motown and later at Invictus, Lawrence T. Horn's place in America's history books will sadly be for infamy as we will see later.

After a modest start The Creative Corporation, as Holland Dozier Holland tagged their company, would prove everyone right and by 1969 the Hot Wax label along with its sister label, Invictus was beginning to turn heads and melt the turntables of America. The company's administrative offices were situated in Cadillac Tower a 40-story office occupying the corner of Cadillac Square and Bates, one block east of Woodward and two blocks north of the Coleman A. Young Municipal Centre. It was designed by Architects Bonnah & Chaffee and built in 1927. The original Detroit Historical Museum opened on November the 19th 1928 on the 23rd floor of the Cadillac Tower (then known as the Barlum Tower) and was referred to as the "highest Museum in the world". An impressive place to house what was hoped to be an equally impressive addition to Detroit's music history with Invictus being Latin for unconquerable and Eddie, or Edward Holland, as company President, taking the role of master of his fate and captain of his soul, ably supported by a cast made up of Detroit's finest and equally outstanding 'incomers'.

The first release on Hot Wax belonged to a newly formed trio, Honey Cone, with "While You're Out Looking For Sugar" making the Top Thirty Soul Chart. In Honey Cone Holland Dozier Holland found their female equivalent of The Jackson Five who epitomised the new pop age of Motown whilst on more feminine issues the group would reign supreme for the time that The Supremes floundered. As with other groups in their roster the trio had been pieced together by Holland Dozier Holland in a shrewd move that meant that they would retain ownership of the name and thus if, as happened, the group members split then a totally different Honey Cone could still appear.

Honey Cone were Edna Wright, Carolyn Willis and Shellie Clarke. Wright, the lead vocalist, was born in 1946 and began her showbusiness career when she was 15 joining a travelling Gospel group, The COGIC Singers (Church Of God In Christ). Through her sister Darlene Love she then met Phil Spector. Spector's associate Jack Nitzsache produced her first recording, "Yes Sir, That's My Baby" by Hale & The Hushabyes; a group made up from Sonny & Cher, Jackie DeShannon and Brian Wilson from The Beach Boys. Edna sang lead vocal on this mish mash of Popular cultural figures, interestingly, the roles would reverse as Cher became the 90's re-tuned superstar and Edna Wright returned to background singing for her. Four years on, under the name of Sandy Wynns, she had a hit on VeeJay with "A Touch of Venus" and two years later she began concentrating on background singing in her native California for Johnny Rivers, Bill Medley, The Righteous Brothers and Ray Charles. Ray later invited her to join The Raelets, his own backing singers and recording artists. She remained as a member for 6 months between 1967 and 1968.

Honey Cone were indirectly formed by Darlene Love who had had her own solo success at the hands of Phil Spector both as a solo performer and as a member of Bob B. Soxx & The Blue Jeans and who just happened to be Edna Wright's older sister. She was asked to form a trio to work on an Andy Williams Television Series but because of prior arrangements wasn't able to commit herself. At this point she was committed to her work as a member of The Blossoms.

Edna Wright contacted Shellie Clarke, born Mashelle Clark in Brooklyn, New York in 1947. The family moved from Brooklyn to Los Angeles, California in 1957 and later won a scholarship to The University of Southern California and then Darlene Love recommended Carolyn Willis who had also worked with Bob B. Soxx as well as being part of the one hit wonder group The Girlfriends who had "My One and Only Jimmy Boy" in 1964. Edna Wright came to the attention of Holland Dozier Holland by default. The Supremes were doing the TAMI Show with Marvin [Gaye] and a load of others and Frank Wilson asked her to go into the studio and stand in for one of the girls as they were having Union problems. At that time, the Union insisted that the artist had to be in California and Motown wanted her to stand in and to just act like she was singing but because she could read music, she started humming the song and unbeknown to her, Lamont Dozier and Eddie Holland were in the booth. As previously stated, Edna Wright had already sensed back in '67 that Holland Dozier Holland were ready to move from Motown but it took her sister to push her onto a plane heading for Detroit, where she met up with Holland Dozier Holland who outlined their intention to make her a solo star. As the aforementioned Sandy Wynns she had made a relatively good living on the West Coast but had grown tired of the gigging and so refused their initial approach.

Honey Cone's first unofficial outing came on the previously mentioned Andy Williams show in 1969. Edna rang Eddie Holland up that night and told him to watch. That night Eddie Holland saw Edna on TV with Carolyn Willis and Shellie Clark. What he liked was that Edna's voice had a mellow quality and an intensity at the same time. They put the group together and named them after an ice cream that Holland loved as a child. Honey Cone were not a new Supremes, though. Each artist was a new personality to them and so they wrote songs that would fit Edna's voice. The way she sang was sensitive and vulnerable and a little tough too. It was Holland Dozier Holland who were responsible for guiding the initial successes for the girls. Eddie Holland had in his mind that he had always enjoyed working with female artists at Motown and as a lyricist had noticed that women were more interesting to write for. To him women had a broader sensitivity to emotions than men who he felt were taught, growing up, that you didn't cry, you took it on the chin. Men couldn't say that they hurt if they were but that Holland Dozier Holland could deal with those subjects through writing for women. That was why they liked writing for girl groups so much. It wasn't because they were easier to direct, in fact the women got away with more in the studio than the men. Groups like The Four Tops and Chairmen Of The Board always took much better direction. Remember back to the Supremes and The Marvelettes studio traumas but they were sure that they wanted to go on working with women artists in their new company and just as important, they also knew there was a market there for this music. Demographics showed that it was women who bought most of their records. Not just the Supremes records but the ones by male groups like the Four Tops as well, because they had shown a sensitive side and Holland felt that women liked to see that side of men. He knew that he was able to write in a way that appealed to women and said that he spent a lot of time listening to women talking about their views, their problems and so on, something that he found interesting even if most men didn't.

Songs were written to fit Edna Wright's voice, to capture that sensitivity and vulnerability as well as the toughness that was there. Shortly after that they were signed to Hot Wax by Holland who, as mentioned earlier, had taken up the position of company President. Holland Dozier Holland knew that they wanted to go on working with female artists in their new company and were well aware of the potential market out there. Because in the world of Holland Dozier Holland for every girl who was asking the question, "where did our love go?" There was a man, standing in the shadows of love, reaching out to be there and if love was like an itching in your heart, then Levi Stubbs was equally in need of your loving.

Success didn't prevent the three girls from continuing their background singing chores in Los Angeles and instead they chose to commute to and from Detroit whenever they were needed to overdub their voices onto tracks. Early on this job had fallen to Ronald Dunbar and later Greg Perry, Holland Dozier Holland being tied up in a lawsuit with Motown which prevented them from writing and producing their own acts, or at least under their names. Greg Perry was the nephew of Motown writer and producer Robert Bateman, he of "Please Mr Postman" fame and the other half of the Brianbert partnership. He had worked under the guidance of Billy Davis, A&R Director over at Chess Records in Chicago where he cut "Love Control". Greg Perry was the second of five talented brothers, the eldest, Leonard had written songs with Dennis and Zachery whilst the middle brother, Jeff, later formed a trio with Dennis and Zachery recording as Three of A Kind for Sussex records. It was Greg, though, who would have the most influence on Detroit's music scene of the '70's. Perry turned down a Motown publishing deal because of its dubious contract terms and instead chose to sign up with Holland Dozier Holland. He was just 17 when he came on board, signing up to do album projects. They didn't think there were going to be any singles but then they started competing. Perry got together with General Johnson and they started to crank material out. Like Lamont Dozier before him, he would come up with an idea and maybe the chorus line. He felt that Johnson was better lyrically than he was in the early days. They welcomed Angelo Bond to the team, who was phenomenal with lyrics.

"You know, a lot of it came from Greg Perry, General Johnson and Angelo Bond. Because I felt that they were creative people within their own right and I was instrumental in putting them together. I thought that General Johnson was unique and I thought Greg Perry was unique and so I thought that if they worked together that they could have a pretty successful mergence of all those talents. Angelo was such a great lyricist that he was very supportive in the lyrics structure of their songs."

Eddie Holland

They were deliberately trying to resemble the Holland Dozier Holland team, where Brian and Lamont would come up with the chorus lines and melody, then they'd turn the lyrics over to Eddie. Laura Lee worked closely with both Angelo Bond and William Weatherspoon. She thought of Bond as a sweet, happy-go-lucky character who she never had a disagreement with. Weatherspoon also contributed lyrics but it was Angelo Bond who was viewed as the better when it came to putting word to paper and if Holland Dozier Holland had housed a number of their songs in that dream world where love took on either a physical or ethereal presence and walked this dream world haunting and taunting those poor souls who were so desperate to be loved, their protegees were writing adult fairy tales where all the king's horses and all the king's been couldn't put a broken heart back together again or somebody was sleeping in my bed and it sure wasn't Goldilocks.

Invictus opened its innings with Glass House's "Crumbs Off the Table" and New Play's "Music Box". Whilst Glass House would prove an ever-present group of players throughout the Invictus story New Play would only last for the one release. However, the woman behind New Play, Ruth Copeland from Durham in England was an interesting addition to the Invictus catalogue.

Ruth Copeland had a normal family life in Consett, County Durham in the North of England and like most people in the town her father was employed by the steel works. She loved to cycle in the green Durham countryside and became an art student, but when she was just 16 her world was turned upside down when her mother died suddenly from a rare medical condition. Before the death of her mother, she had felt quite satisfied and secure within herself and her life and was confident that had her mother not died that Ruth Copeland would have stayed in Consett and become an art teacher. Ruth didn't become a teacher. She moved south to London and started singing backing vocals with a group called Ed and The Intruders. It wasn't long before she was offered recording deals by two new record companies. The first being The Beatles Apple label in London and Invictus in Detroit. She chose Invictus because her sister was already living in the States. Her debut single, 'The Music Box', was released in 1969 and credited to the New Play starring Ruth Copeland. It was co-written with Ronald Dunbar and Edith Wayne. Soon after arriving in Detroit, she met and married Jeffrey Bowen, a Motown staff producer who had been working for Berry Gordy's empire since the mid-sixties, producing the Temptations and Marvin Gaye along the way. The Invictus marketing machine promoted Ruth as a feisty sex symbol, describing her music as 'female chauvinism' and proclaiming, that on the eighth day, God created Ruth Copeland.

If 1969 had heralded the arrival back on the scene of Holland Dozier Holland, then 1970 was the year that Invictus and Hot Wax exploded for real. Once again, it was in the hands of one of Eddie Holland's favourite protégés, the female of the species, to deliver the goods and in Freda Payne they hoped to have the start to compete with Motown's own Diva, who owed so much to HDH, Diana Ross. Freda Charcilia Payne, born on 19th September 1945 was another native Detroiter. She had graduated musically from Jazz into Pop and had previously recorded for MGM, Impulse and ABC before joining the Invictus roster. Even further back than that Freda and her sister Scherrie at the age of three and four respectively had recorded an acetate, "Hey-Bop-A-Be Bop" recorded when their uncle took them to a local store where for a dollar you could cut your own acetate. She had first met Eddie Holland when she was thirteen; Holland was seventeen and just beginning to work for Motown. Freda herself had also worked for Gordy as his protégé coaching her as a singer and dancer as well as cutting the unreleased "Father Dear" and "Save Me A Star" under the name of Little Freda Payne but parental advice had kept her in school. Swings turned to roundabouts for Freda Payne who, had she remained with Motown, may well have found her career bulldozed onto the side lines by Gordy's fascination with his rising solo star Diana Ross. Two years after her first encounter with Eddie Holland she met brother Brian. She was still in school, years that had also seen Lamont Dozier as a fellow student. Some time passed and Freda had moved to California where she shared an apartment close to Tamiko Jones who had also made her name in Detroit for the Golden World label. Here she met Brian Holland again, this time at a party.

On learning that Freda had got no management or recording contract he discussed the trio's intention to form its own recording complex and after a year of formalities Freda's first record was released, "The Unhooked Generation" The lyrics were similar to the equally bitter Gladys Knight Motown outing "Didn't You Know (You'd Have To Cry Sometime)" although the rhythm made for a more upbeat performance. After this initial American release failed to open the charts up Payne's second release, and her first for Invictus in England, proved to be one of the years' biggest successes, "Band Of Gold"; which, unfortunately, gave Payne little pleasure in trying to emulate.

To the uninitiated Freda Payne will always remain a one hit wonder, if that be the case one can only listen in admiration at that one hit, the perfect marriage between Soul and Pop that only Holland Dozier Holland could conjure up. Recorded at the Tera Shirma studio "Band Of Gold" remains one of those unmistakable tracks from the second it begins. With Dennis Coffey supplying the sitar riff and Bob Babbitt pounding out the bass line, the track had Detroit pedigree all over it and yet within its grooves there lay a mystery.

The label credited Ronald Dunbar and Edith Wayne with writing chores. Holland Dozier Holland were all under exclusive writing contracts with Motown's publishing company Holland Dozier Holland had to therefore develop other song writers. Under the terms and conditions of the contract they still had to adhere to with their previous employer Berry Gordy Jr. they were allowed to suggest, coach, as well as analyse and reject sections of songs as part of their rights as music publishers with their own Gold Forever music company. According to Lamont Dozier, he and Brian Holland came up with "Band of Gold" and "Give Me Just a Little More Time" but they didn't put their names on them because they were in a lawsuit and couldn't use their names. So, they used Ronald Dunbar, who was an employee of theirs and Edith Wayne, who was a friend of the Holland family. After that they brought in Greg Perry and General Johnson as well as Ronnie Dunbar. Credited as lead writer on "Band of Gold" Dunbar told a different tale to that of Lamont Dozier. Dunbar told of how they helped to develop, by coaching and by directing the writers and producers that they were "mentoring," and that he was one of those people helped in development. He said that he was given certain projects to write. "Band of Gold" was one of those projects and that he came up with the title "Band of Gold" first. His partner, Edith Wayne wrote the lyrics with him according to how the track was and used the melody structure that they got by listening to the track. He stated that he was part of the "in-house" team that was being developed at the time and that it was a great opportunity for newer writers, like himself and to some other people in getting their careers developed.

After completing the song, Holland Dozier Holland's own version of Motown's Quality Control department considered the track too long and at the advice of Brian Holland removed a whole section of the track. Although initially unhappy at the cuts Dunbar was allegedly left acknowledging the mastery with which Holland had lent his unique production skills to the tune. If he needed any more convincing, he just had to look at the initial 5 Million sales. The edit was credited with the reason for the air play but the lyrical content also provided an unexpected following from the Gay community. The reason being that lyrics explaining that Freda Payne had actually rejected her husband lay dead on the cutting room floor and what was left was more than a Band Of Gold it was a mixed message about the man's sexuality.

In England EMI launched the Invictus and Hot Wax labels and whether intentionally or not gave Invictus the same cataloguing numbers beginning with 501, "Give Me Just A Little More Time" by Chairmen Of The Board, as it had done for Tamla Motown in 1965. Perhaps the powers that be were expecting a carbon copy success story. Could Holland Dozier Holland's Midas touch work for them again? Only time would tell. "Band Of Gold" stood at Number One Nationally whilst the Number Two position belonged to Chairmen Of The Board with the original version of "Give Me Just A Little More Time". Both compositions were again credited to Ronald Dunbar along with Edith Wayne, whose names would be matched to much of the company's early success although it was later learned that Holland Dozier Holland had used their names because of contractual problems hanging on from Motown.

Here, there are variations on the truth. One story implied that at the time Holland Dozier Holland were trying to come up with a pseudonym they looked out onto Woodward and saw the sign Wayne State University, Edith was Lamont Dozier's mother's name. Coincidentally as soon as Holland Dozier Holland started using their own names Edith Wayne disappeared totally. Others claimed that Eddie Holland wrote most of those songs credited to Dunbar/Wayne with Ronald Dunbar. Wayne was the pseudonym for Eddie Holland. Whilst Wayne was sometimes credited as the co-writer on many songs with Lamont Dozier and Brian Holland, the name never appeared with Eddie Holland. So, for Dunbar and Wayne you may wish to read Ronald Dunbar and Eddie Holland although to this day Holland Dozier Holland remain adamant that Edith Wayne was a real person and responsible for these tracks. Then again, what is favourite now is that, for Dunbar and Wayne, read Holland Dozier Holland.

General Johnson said that they were playing games. He and Greg Perry worked as a team both writing and producing but when it came to putting producer credits on, they would only pay for one producer. He also said about the tracks with Edith Wayne as writer that Edith Wayne <u>was</u> Holland Dozier Holland but they weren't allowed to have their name on the records.

"There was still some legal thing with Berry that stopped them from using their own names. Edith Wayne was in fact Eddie Holland's girlfriend ... every time you see the name Edith Wayne on a record it's Eddie Holland".

Steve Mancha

Whatever the real truth was, the fact remained that Holland Dozier Holland were now away from Motown, if not free from the clutches of Berry Gordy Jr and their new productions were about to begin where their Motown career had left off. If Motown had had the Four Tops Invictus had the Chairmen of The Board. The Chairmen Of The Board were, on one hand, an attempt to fill the gap left by The Four Tops for Holland Dozier Holland upon the Golden trio's departure from Motown, while on the other it was a brand-new attempt at revolutionising the tradition of Soul vocal groups. The lead vocalist on this track, General Norman Johnson, was far less aggressive in style than The Tops' Levi Stubbs and I, with untrained ears back in 1970 could not equate the two singers. Strangely enough it was only upon purchasing The Four Tops 1972 album "Nature Planned It" in 1997 and listening to the track, "You Got to Forget Him Darling" that I heard the similarity. That said, this was a time when The Four Tops were still suffering from post- Holland Dozier Holland blues and were obviously trying their best to find a winning formula. Hence Levi Stubbs even resorting to the, by now, legendary telephone ringing effect of Johnson, "Brrrrrrrrr", on "Give Me Just A Littler More Time". As well as fronting the Chairmen Johnson was soon to become one of Invictus' most prolific writers and producers working alongside Greg Perry.

"He was the heartbeat of the company."

Danny Woods

Between times nearly two and a half years had passed during which time Johnson had been locked away living in Lamont Dozier's Detroit home concentrating on writing material for the group. The people at Invictus kept saying that the Chairmen Of The Board were on the way and that it would be worth waiting for. The group was originally to be named The Gentlemen and was to break away from the traditional R&B groups where one vocalist would stand out front while the other members would stand behind performing intricate dance routines and perfect backing vocals. The Chairmen were, however, condemned on their first British tour for this break away from tradition. As one member left the stage another came on, so rather than a group performance there were four individual performances. Again, though, right from the very beginning they were publicised as four individuals and even with the departure of Eddie Custis, after the second album, "In Session", because he didn't like the direction the group was going in, the group had no reason for becoming a more formalised unit.

Invictus hit England like a hurricane. Holland Dozier Holland were back and yet for the successes that would eventually prove minimal its sister label would have none at all. Still, America accepted the product readily and Honey Cone were riding high with their second Hot Wax release "While You're Out Looking for Sugar" in July 1969, which seemed something of a companion record to their stable mates, 100 Proof (Aged In Soul), who had found their initial success in June of 1970 with "Somebody's Been Sleeping In My Bed". 100 Proof Aged In Soul were just that. Made up from Steve Mancha, Joe Stubbs, Don Hatcher and later Eddie Anderson. Eddie Anderson had worked in and around Detroit as a member of The Holidays, again part of the Golden World organisation. Carlis Sonny Monroe from the re-incarnated Falcons was also tipped to join 100 Proof but it was Joe Stubbs from the earlier Falcons incarnation who joined. His stay with 100 Proof Aged In Soul would turn out to be a short one; in July 1970 Stubbs left the group to be replace by Herschel Hunter formerly of the Motown group The Monitors.

Another refugee from the Ric-Tic label also found her way to the doors of The Creative Corporation and the Hot Wax label in 1970. To most casual listeners mention Invictus and Hot Wax and their roster of artists and you can bet that the top female artist in their eyes was Freda Payne. Look closer and ask them to name another Freda Payne track outside of "Band Of Gold" and they'd probably be stuck despite the award-winning follow up, "Deeper And Deeper", a success despite a heavy-handed edit that saw the heavily orchestrated intro being dropped awkwardly into the mix as the instrumental break. Ask them to name **ANY** track by Laura Lee and they'd be lost up the proverbial creek without a paddle. Yet looking closer, and deeper, and you'll see that the most consistent act that Holland Dozier Holland signed up was Laura Lee.

99

Her Hot Wax career was launched with "Wedlock Is A Padlock" in January 1971 but it was the follow-up, the similarly slanted "Women's Love Rights" that really heralded her arrival back on the scene. From the start Laura Lee felt that it was a hit song because at that time women were so pent up and afraid to do this and do that with their man. When those lyrics were sung it was like the song liberated women. She received letters and phone calls and women in person used to say to her that she had really opened their eyes because the men had got them so scared. It still felt like it was the man dominating the woman all the time. Lee denied that this was a Women's Liberation song and was adamant that it wasn't based on her own personal circumstances: still she was finding her own niche that the company would exploit for as long as it could. The album was recorded at the HDH Studios on Grand River Street and completed in about 6 weeks. They would cut the tracks and then arrange for her to come in. It was all very laid back and she went into the studio when she felt like it. William Weatherspoon and Angelo Bond would sit her down and go through the song with her and also give her a cassette to listen to and to live with for a while so that she could get the best out of it.

Even more refugees appeared with Ric-Tic's white Soul band The Flaming Embers dropping 'The' and 's' and signing to Hot Wax. Sadly, when one talks about blue-eyed soul the name Flaming Ember rarely springs to mind and yet name a more consistent exponent of this genre and I'll eat my record collection! Over at Motown both Chris Clarke and R. Dean Taylor were creating great music but once established on Hot Wax Flaming Ember would last for two albums before finally dying down. I would go as far as to say that the fact that they were white allowed Holland Dozier Holland to explore other dimensions of Soul and within the lyrics of the group's songs wet dreams, lesbian love and, dare I suggest, even erections are mentioned. Flaming Ember had launched into a relatively comfortable groove with their initial Hot Wax release, the easy-going ballad "Mind Body & Soul" in November 1969. The follow up Hot Wax single, though, was the one with which the group would gain immortality; "Westbound Number 9" This saw them into May 1970 and was followed by their second strongest release, "I'm Not By Brother's Keeper" in October. The 'B' side of "Keeper" was a non-album gem, "Deserted Village" written by former Motown and Fortune staff writer/producer William Weatherspoon.

"Westbound Number 9" by Flaming Ember became the first single to be released on the British Hot Wax label and by the end of 1970 Holland Dozier Holland had made a firm stand in Detroit against their former boss. Most of the company's major acts were well on their way to success with three more waiting in the wings and some older established names ready to have perhaps their finest hour. 1971 saw the British release of Honey Cone's debut album along with the first single by The Glass House fronted by Freda Payne's sister Scherrie, "Stealing Moments from Another Woman's Life". Glass House were an ever-present group of players whose line-up appeared throughout the Invictus story either on group outings or solo performances, despite never reaching the heights of others on the label. Somehow, they never seemed destined for stardom, which is strange, considering that the quality of their music was the match for any of their contemporaries: but their story was riddled with legal disputes and plain bad luck. Glass House was a fourpiece group made up of Scherrie Payne, Ty Hunter, Pearl Jones and Larry Mitchell. Mitchell was relatively unknown outside of the Glass House having worked within two local groups, The Classics and The Sierras whilst Scherrie Payne had not pursued a singing career, unlike her older sister. Instead, she had studied medical technology before choosing a career in teaching. However, she had started dating Lamont Dozier and followed Freda to the doors of Cadillac Tower in 1969. Freda was on the phone discussing her contract with Eddie and in the background younger sister, Scherrie was playing the piano and singing. Holland heard her and asked she would like to come along to audition.

As Scherrie Lavette she wrote material recorded by sister Freda, "The Easiest Way to Fall" and "Now Is the Time To Say Goodbye" both from the "Band Of Gold" set. Mitchell too had moved away from music to become a copywriter with Detroit's Campbell-Ewald Advertising Agency. Ty Hunter, as already mentioned, had been a long-time acquaintance of Lamont Dozier while Pearl Jones who hailed from Port Huron, Michigan had made an early career out of local television appearances as well as vocally supporting Marvin Gaye, Patti Labelle, Billy Stewart and Martha Reeves and being part of The Embracables and Aretha Franklin's Sweethearts of Soul. As Glass House their first single had been "Crumbs Off the Table" a September '69 Soul hit and Scherrie Payne co-composition with guest harmonica support by the Chairmen's own Harrison Kennedy, backed by Clyde Wilson's composition "Bad Bill of Goods". As with Edna Wright of Honey Cone Scherrie Payne shared the same vocal style delivery as her sister. The driving, pulsating rhythm created by the funky harmonica blowing of Kennedy and chopping guitars makes this one of the most infectious tracks the company ever produced. Gritty and unglamorous when compared to the later plusher productions coming out of the label and yet hypnotically compelling on every listen.

Flaming Ember's "Westbound Number 9" Album was issued in the UK along with their second single, not off the album, the aforementioned "I'm Not My Brother's Keeper" but without the haunting 'B' side. At the same time America received their newest single "Stop the World And Let Me

Off" with its risky lyrics of lesbian love between the singer's girlfriend and her girlfriend! Holland Dozier Holland's new babies were both doing fine, the company's sales were healthy and the quality of the product was fine. Freda Payne had a new release in "Cherish What Is Dear to You" the first tune away from her debut album for the company and a Holland Dozier composition: then the first signs of rot started to show, as far as British buyers were concerned.

At the time it seemed little more than a delayed release but in March 1971, The Barrino Brothers led from the front by the rip-roaring voice of Perry Barrino, only British release, "I Shall Not Be Moved" written by Holland Dozier was cancelled. This was in fact their second Invictus outing. Their singing credentials were endorsed by Motown legend Ivy Jo Hunter who sent them to David Hamilton's TCB label to start their Detroit career. Apart from one release in 1968, "I'll Take My Flowers Right Now" with the wonderful "Just A Mistake" on the 'b' side, little was known about the group. The Barrino Brothers consisted of one friend, Bobby Roseboro plus the three brothers, Julius, Nathaniel and Perry, incidentally uncle to Fantasia Barrino, 2004's American Idol winner whose debut album "Free Yourself" was a commercial success earning four Grammy nominations during 2005. Two other of Perry Barrino's nephews, KC and JoJo Hailey, were also part of the 1990s group Jodeci. Perry Barrino said that the performing genes stemmed from his father, Curtis Barrino. One of his father's favorite performance venues was at local baseball games, where he stole the show as umpire, incorporating dance moves when striking players out or sneaking up on the batter as he prepared to hit the pitches and snatch their caps. A lot of people would go to a game just to see his dad, the clown umpire.

They moved onto Invictus where their debut single, "Trapped In A Love" was issued in January 1971. In lead singer Perry Barrino Holland Dozier Holland stayed true to the same formula that they had tried and tested at Motown with Levi Stubbs and Marvin Gaye. The voice echoed those two greats down to the high key that tested Perry's powerful voice on this Greg Perry, General Johnson, Ronald Dunbar and Zachary Perry composition.

Despite the problems with shipping new material April, did bring the overseas buyers one of Hot Wax's finest albums, "Somebody's Been Sleeping" by 100 Proof Aged In Soul. It was a showcase primarily for the vocal talents of Steve Mancha and Joe Stubbs and got off to a flying start with the extended version of the title track giving the tight rhythm section the chance to break out. Personal favourites of Steve Mancha's appeared in the form of the initial single's 'B' side, "I've Come To Save You" and "Love Is Sweeter (The Second Time Around). Duke Browner's classic

"Ain't That Loving You" was given a unique treatment with Joe Stubbs rapping to a young woman who he is trying to woo back. The female part was performed by a secretary on the front desk at the company. Her and her husband were both friends of Mancha and despite her shyness she was able to add another dimension to the tune.

Also released was the second Chairmen album, "In Session" showing more variety than their first but also showing why Eddie Custis was leaving. His handling of Simon & Garfunkel's "Bridge Over Troubled Water" and Johnny Mathis's "Twelfth Of Never" were perfect vocalisations and no doubt would see Custis served well on the Vegas circuit but this was Detroit and the Chairmen were a far more progressive outfit than Custis could cope with. Also, in April 1971 the three members of Honey Cone hit Gold with the much imitated "Want Ads", a record that gained a following in the UK if not a chart place. General Johnson and Greg Perry had written a song called "Stick Up" which was rejected. They changed the chord progression and then added new lyrics. It was first recorded by Glass House but this version didn't seem to work out. Likewise, an attempt by Freda Payne was also shelved. As if the saying third time lucky rang true the newly named "Want Ads" did the job for Honey Cone. The song had come to Johnson and Perry through the studio sound engineer Barney Perkins. Perkins also used to work at another small studio. Greg Perry went over there and they got talking. He said that somebody should write a song about the want ads. About a week later Perry was sitting at the piano and the song came out. He wrote the chorus line but it was a little different. The lyrics said, "Going to put it in the want ads, I need some love for sale." When he told this to General Johnson, he said that he was making the girl sound like a prostitute so, they changed it and went from there. It was cut a couple of times and the second time they came up with "Wanted, young man single and free."

Edna Wright recalled that moment when a judgement call made one group reach the top and another, Glass House, remain as also rans despite solid material. In a story reminiscent of the Marvelettes/Supremes story, Edna Wright walked into the studio to do something and Scherrie Payne was working on "Want Ads" but it was different. The lyrics were different and so was the chorus line. Scherrie came out and told her that she could do it and that she didn't care for it. Edna asked if she was serious, which she most definitely was. Greg Perry and General Johnson went back in the studio and did it again. Johnson changed a few lyrics on it and Perry upped the track, made the bass lines and everything tighter and better.

The story had a slightly different telling from Scherrie Payne who recalled that "Want Ads" was the first track recorded with the Glass House as a whole unit but they we were irate when they found out that Honey Cone had recorded the song. Payne said that she walked into the studio one day to discover that she was listening to it. She hadn't heard the song for several months and thought that it was her singing. She didn't know the difference to the very end. Edna Wright did a little lick that was a little different than herself. Then she realised that it wasn't her voice, because Eddie Holland had this thing where he would coach each singer the way to sing a song and they all sounded a bit like female Eddie Holland's.

So, Freda, Edna and Sherrie Payne sounded quite a lot alike because of the way he would phrase a song and he wanted them to sing it exactly the way he phrased it. Later the same applied to The Jones Girls and yet interestingly, when they left to join Philadelphia International, their vocal sound changed too. So, when Scherrie heard Edna Wright's version it didn't bother her until they put it out and it became a million seller. Then she was really upset. The single climbed to a National Chart position of Number 2.

On the strength of the Gold single Honey Cone were given the complete treatment by Holland Dozier Holland who, taking a leaf out of their old boss's book, sent them to Charm School. Hollie Atkins, choreographer supreme to the entire Motown family, was brought in as well as vocal coaches. The group also hit the road despite making a good living from their continued background singing. They never felt that they needed to go on the road but did until the end of 1972. They took with them their own people, including Dick Griffey who would later head Solar Records (The Sound Of Los Angeles Records) to handle their financial affairs.

Critics started to suggest that the formula Holland Dozier Holland had adopted was making the music impersonal with Honey Cone resembling Glass House or Freda Payne and their male counterparts sharing the same delivery as the 8th Day / Barrino Brothers and 100 Proof. The Holland Dozier Holland method of working lent itself to this style of production, a trick they had pioneered at Motown where backing tracks were laid down and handed out to whoever it was considered would come up with the goods. Martha Reeves once told of how she could tell that the Vandellas were out of favour when she came across a tape can with her group's name crossed out and The Supremes marked on it. MGM, in an attempt to cash in on the newly found fame of Freda Payne, also re-released an album of hers. The Barrino Brothers "I Shall Not Be Moved" album was released in The States as was the first single by the 8th Day, "She's Not Just Another Woman" in May. The Track had previously appeared on the 100 Proof album and the vocal was identical, leading many people to question the identity of the 8th Day and adding to the criticism of the label's sounds. Was it in fact the same group as 100 Proof but placed on another label just as Funkadelic and Parliament who we will look at later were? The simple answer was 'no'. This was another perfect example of the way Holland Dozier Holland worked at Motown, laying down rhythm tracks and handing

104

them out to whoever they felt would benefit most from them. So, you would find Eddie Anderson singing a track that became credited to the 8th Day, Steve Mancha doing likewise and Darlene Love trying out for a track released by Glass House.

This does seem to contradict Eddie Holland's comment about treating every artist as an individual. The 8th Day was another group pieced together by Holland Dozier Holland and the track had actually been recorded back in 1968 when the pieces that would eventually become Invictus were still being shaped. As we would see time and time again Holland Dozier Holland had moved on from their Motown days of putting the track first and then fitting the song to the singer. Now they were fitting the singer to a group. Tracks cut by Steve Mancha and Eddie Anderson were therefore put out as the 8th Day, as were solo recording by the next lead vocalist for the group, Melvin Davis. After "She's Not Just Another Woman" the next single was sung by Davis and released again as the 8th Day. Now there are tracks, and there are records. Then there are track records. Melvin Davis, it was once said, never cut a bad track and as far as I'm concerned you won't find any finer recordings to come out of Detroit. So, therefore, his track record speaks for itself.

Melvin Davis was born on August the 29th 1942. As a child, he would share time in both Detroit with Milledgeville down in Georgia, where his grandparents owned a farm. He was developing his interest in music and was inspired by seeing Little Richard perform in Georgia as well as Sam Cooke & The Soul Stirrers. At the age of 17 he left to join the Navy but kept up his passion for music, teaching himself how to play the piano as well as guitar and writing songs. In 1961 Melvin Davis released his first single, on a local label, Jack Pot. This was "I Don't Want You". His next release saw him step up a gear as Fortune Records, a more famous Detroit company issued "Playboy". The multi-talent Davis was already establishing himself as a vocalist, who could also write and play two instruments. He continued developing those skills by taking up the drums which helped him secure a regular gig at the Ebony Club in nearby Muskegon with his group The Jaywalkers. As well as the live reputation he continued recording, this time on a third label Ke Ke, a short-lived label but one that was another step forward in his career, this time he moved on to Mike Hanks' D-Town label where he recorded "Find a Quiet Place (And Be Lonely)" in 1965, a British Northern Soul favourite. This was on Hanks' Wheel City imprint. By this time, his writing skills were beginning to get noticed and his work was being recorded by other established Detroit acts such as J.J. Barnes who recorded Davis' "Chains of Love" with the producer Don Davis, who would often call on his namesake for new songs.

Next Melvin Davis formed a trio along with noted guitarist Dennis Coffey and keyboard player, Lyman Woodard. The trio had a successful residence playing at Detroit's Frolic Show Bar and then at Maury Baker's Showplace Lounge. Dennis Coffey began producing some sessions for Melvin Davis that were picked up by Mala Records and which included "This Love Is Meant to Be", a regional hit for the guys. As the 60's Soul scene began to evolve so too did Coffey's guitar style. His first solo album, "Hair and Thangs" was augmented by Melvin's drumming. Coffey's style wasn't the only music to go through changes and Woodard's keyboard work was morphing into something different which, again, was backed by Davis' drumming skills. Lyman Woodard formed his trio in 1965 with Melvin Davis on drums/vocals and Dennis Coffey on guitar and before joining Holland Dozier Holland Melvin Davis was also drumming at Motown both in the studio and on tour where he became Smokey Robinson & the Miracles drummer. In the studio he had most famously been the drummer on "Tears of a Clown."

Ronald Dunbar had been responsible for many of the company's early successes and had previously recorded under the name Ronnie Love also for Mike Hanks D-Town label, situated in another house-cum-studio within spitting distance of Gordy's growing empire. There he opened the label's account with "Judy" and released a further two singles "Deed I Do" and "Come Dance with Me" before finishing his tenure with a re-issue of "Judy" backed by "Detroit Michigan". Mike Hanks was another of those unique and tragic figures so often associated with Soul music. He owned his own labels, was a musician, songwriter and performer and met an untimely end being shot dead outside Ed Wingate's Twenty Grand Club. Hanks had hovered around Detroit's underworld courting danger. As Melvin Davis put it, something you can get away with when dealing with musicians but when you try it with real gangsters, it ain't the wisest move. With Holland Dozier Holland, Detroit's creators were pulled together under one roof. Many had seen Berry Gordy's dominance of Detroit music as a negative and yet it was Motown that had put the City on the International music map. If these artists wanted to reach a global audience outside of Berry Gordy's empire, then the obvious path seemed to be the one leading to the door of Holland Dozier Holland.

When they got there, though, some of the lessons Holland Dozier Holland had learnt under the guidance of Gordy seemed lost. Performers such as Melvin Davis were also recognised as gifted songwriters but they rarely got the chance to show what they could do. Both he and Steve Mancha had weaved in and out of each other's careers in Detroit but with Holland Dozier Holland they very rarely met during this period. One group would be booked into the studio for a certain time and then leave before the next group came in and cross-pollination of group ideas was never encouraged. Weekly meetings took place but as Melvin Davis put it,

"They would listen but they weren't about to give up that control…. They really kinda kept everyone separate and that was one of my complaints at one of the meetings. I said that you've got all these different facilities, people should be able to meet one another and exchange ideas because, from my experience, that is the way you develop a healthy competition that really allows you to rise to the level of greatness. I mean, if I write a good song and then I go and I hear someone who writes a better song then that's gonna inspire me to go and write an even better song tomorrow night but when you keep everyone separate and you try and critique everyone's material then what you are doing is stifling the company's progression".

Melvin Davis

The 8th Day, as the name implied, was an eight-piece band. The group was formed around Tony Newton, saxophone player for Melvin Davis' Jaywalkers and former bass player for Smokey Robinson and The Miracles, who had replaced his idol James Jamerson in Robinson's road band. Along with Melvin Davis and the legendary David Ruffin, Newton had also worked in a band called the Mount Royal Clefs. Shortly after Newton's stint with Robinson, Holland Dozier Holland started to experiment with two bass players and so Newton found himself working alongside James Jamerson on such Motown evergreens as "Nowhere to Run" by Martha And the Vandellas, "Baby Love", "Where Did Our Love Go" and "Stop! In the Name Of Love" by The Supremes. When Holland Dozier Holland left Motown Newton followed, becoming the in-house bass man on the majority of recordings. Newton gradually pieced together the band using multi-racial musicians from Los Angeles and Detroit including the aforementioned Lyman Woodard on keyboards. Woodard was born on March the 3rd 1942 in Owosso, Michigan and started his musical training at age four on the piano. In 1962, he attended the Oscar Peterson School of Contemporary Music in Toronto but having watched the great Jimmy Smith in concert he made the decision to change from piano to Hammond organ. From 1970 to 1973 he became the musical director for Martha and the Vandellas.

More album tracks appeared as singles in America with Flaming Ember's "Shades of Green" being the latest in a long line. Clearly Invictus and Hot Wax were following in the great tradition of Detroit Soul, still for every rule there were exceptions and besides tapping the commercial vein

Holland Dozier Holland were still prepared to go 'left field'. The final bunch of refugees, or rather renegades, arrived from Solid Hitbound, George Clinton's Parliament. Parliament released "Red Hot Mama", a far cry from their earlier recordings for Golden World and Revilot, the label formed out of the ashes of Ric-Tic by LeBaron Taylor and in May 1971 Dave Godin, former head of the British Tamla Appreciation Society stated that the single was 'as funky and as real as they come' but did concede that it probably wasn't a chart contender. He said that the track was what funky soul was about, a rough quality polished up to be a little gem. It was never given a UK release and after the initial "Red Hot Mama" single Parliament would experiment with Heavy Metal, Folk, Gospel and Country & Western before leaving the label and taking off to the stars on board The Mothership. At the same time the group behind the group were untitled but when misfortune struck once more and the Revilot label went out of business in 1969 selling all its masters to Atco the group had to wait another year until the Atco contract on them expired. Although Atco bought the masters, due to complications they could not take up individual artists contracts which meant that as The Parliaments the group would have become inactive. Returning from a gig one night, bass player Billy Nelson suggested the name Funkadelic and, signing to another new Detroit label, Westbound the dual personality of the band began. When The Parliaments finally escaped from the chains of Atco, they dropped ''The' and 's', taking a leaf out of Flaming Ember's book, they became plain Parliament. Although plain is perhaps the wrong word.

Also important to Parliament during their Invictus days was Ruth Copeland, the English folk singer who had had that early Invictus outing under the group name New Play with "Music Box". Copeland contributed to the first Parliament album "Osmium" as a writer and co-producer although the chores may have fallen to her husband Jefffrey Bowen who, because of his contract with Motown, was, just like Holland Dozier Holland before him, unable to put his name to the project. Perhaps so but the influence of Copeland was strong enough to cast doubt on this. She felt at the time that, if you were a woman, nobody saw you as a producer and further felt that musicians who were generally men would not take guidance from a you. Ruth Copeland's "I Am What I Am" album, as well as her "Self Portrait" set were ideal companions to "Osmium" with Funkadelic supplying the instrumentation. Invictus released "Hare Krishna" as a single by Copeland, artistically interesting but, commercially, a non-starter.

The change in the Chairmen's personnel meant a delay to their May tour of Europe but Freda Payne had made the crossing. Unfortunately, the new American product, not culled from an album, wasn't ready for the tie-in and so instead of "Bring the Boys Home" the UK received the Ronald

Dunbar/General Johnson/Greg Perry composition "Rock Me in The Cradle" taken from her debut album. Also, in the UK Flaming Ember's "Stop the World And Let Me Off" was demoted to the 'B' side making way for the ballad "Shades Of Green". Two weeks later a reverse was made and "Stop the World and Let Me Off" was promoted but to no avail. Over Stateside the group had a new single in the form of "Sunshine", a schmaltzy ballad that contained lyrics that implied that the love of Jerry Plunk's life would watch football with him but would rather watch Tom Jones. The melody, if not the lyrics, was quite beautiful with similarities to the work of Jimmy Ruffin but with Flaming Ember Weatherspoon had been able to spread his creative wings a little, ranging from ballads to pop to downright dirty. "Where's All the Joy" painted a bleak picture of lost chances and lost love in a way far removed from the fantasy land of "What Becomes Of The Brokenhearted". Here was a man coming home from the factory every day, dragging his tired ass back and forth in a dreary existence that repeated itself on a daily routine. "The Empty Crowded Room" was a boppy, sing a long number that seemed to contradict the sadness of the lyrics. "Heart on Lovin' You" on the other hand would never had made it on air had it been issued as a single. Not only did the lyrics talk about wet dreams, explosions in the night and waking up with puffed swollen eyes but the chorus played on the words "heart on" or could it be "hard on"? Jerry Plunk certainly pronounced his 't's' like a 'd' and delayed saying "loving you" so that the emphasis remained on the two lead words. "Sunshine", their second album, was released in America but never seen by British collectors. Like other albums from the company, it unfortunately also contained tracks from the previous set. Here two tracks re-surfaced but amongst the newer tracks "One Step Beyond" written by the ever-reliable team of Johnson/Bond/Perry and "1200 Miles from Heaven" with its anti-war sentiments stood out as the most intriguing.

By May of 1971 Blues & Soul Magazine in England announced its Poll Results. "Band Of Gold" was voted top single whilst "Give Me Just A Little More Time" was second. Freda Payne and the Chairmen Of The Board both figured again further down with numbers 54 and 32 respectively while Honey Cone appeared at 25 with "While You're Out Looking For Sugar", 100 Proof Aged In Soul's "Somebody's Been Sleeping In My Bed" at 26 and Flaming Ember at 33 with "Westbound Number 9".

The organisation's first five major releases had all made the grade with the British record buying public, despite the fact that only Freda Payne and the Chairmen charted. The most promising act for 1971 placed the Chairmen Of The Board in Gold position with Freda Payne collecting the Silver. Further down Glass House gained a healthy 29th position but it was Payne and Johnson's crew that received most of the accolades. Freda Payne was voted third top female vocalist, Chairmen 9th top group and General Johnson 29th top male vocalist. As stated earlier when looking at the number releases weekly, one has to remember the deluge of new acts appearing continuously in the American Soul genre alone and Johnson was not 29th in a field of 30.

The awards were also being handed out in America. The 1971 NATRA Awards voted Honey Cone best female group while Holland Dozier Holland were voted producers of the year, something that rubbed General Johnson up the wrong way for it had been him and his partner Greg Perry who had virtually been the creative force behind the prolonged success of Holland Dozier Holland. Johnson did win BMI's "R&B Songwriter of the Year Award and on the strength of this asked Holland Dozier Holland to renegotiate his contract to reflect his accomplishment. They refused and history seemed to be repeating itself with the 'abused' becoming 'the abuser'. Sales again were healthy with "Want Ads" by Honey Cone when June brought the American release of the much anticipated second album by Freda Payne, "Contact". This was the first time that Holland Dozier Holland attempted 'the concept album'. The first album had been a pleasant collection of tunes, some mediocre and others instant classics.

With Motown doing everything they could to create their own superstar in Holland Dozier Holland's previous diva, Diana Ross this second outing had to work for Gordy's apprentices. One revue suggested that commercially there wasn't another "Band of Gold" in sight but by the same token gave credit to Invictus for building not only an artist who was capable of selling singles by the lorry load but more important an artist who was able to sell in vast quantities as an album seller. The musical arrangements and the production showed a newfound confidence and assurance in their product. From the opening brass laden, string-swirling mood setter to the superb orchestral highs and lows and solo piano breaks that introduced themes that re-occurred within the album, the album had winner written all over it. "I'm Not Getting Any Better" and "Suddenly It's Yesterday" started the proceedings and complimented each other by contrasting one another. "I'm Not Getting Any Better" showed the gentler side of Holland Dozier Holland as the wistful ballad moved closer to the bridge where the trio would create a dangerous journey back in time. "Suddenly It's Yesterday" sang Freda as she entered Holland Dozier Holland's very own Twilight Zone, where memories became the real deal with danger stalking her every step. She is lulled into a false sense of happiness before being hurled back to a bumpy reality courtesy of an outstanding string ensemble. This montage remains the albums creative masterpiece. The next track is a solid enough dancer, "You Brought the Joy" again strings dominate the pounding rhythm complimented by a horn section. The sound was recognisably

Detroit and Holland Dozier Holland but the whole production standard seemed to have matured. The uplifting feel of this track was then offset by "He's in My Life", a tale of deception where the man Freda loves failed to disclose to her one minor detail, he was a married man. The newfound maturity continued with the production qualities in, "You've Got to Love Somebody", a most beautiful beat ballad with an infectious hook. At the beginning of the second side, we are once again reminded of the opening stages of the album as the side started with the 'Prelude'. Soon we were drifting back through time again as Holland Dozier took us down "The Road We Didn't Take". If this had been ten years earlier the chances were that this would have been another rousing dance track given to The Supremes for in "The Road We Didn't Take" we were treated to those Motown melodies but wrapped up in the most delicate of ballads. Another ballad followed and although not penned by Holland Dozier the melody suggested their own past composition "Reflections" as we once more found ourselves in the past with "Odds and Ends". As the tempo was upped Holland Dozier returned for the next track, the single "Cherish What Is Dear to You (While It's Near to You)". However, we remained in reflective mood until the next up-tempo track, Freda's handling of the Barrino Brothers "I Shall Not Be Moved". Before we knew it the record was coming to an end and Freda was in the present but taking that one last look at the past as General Johnson supplied her with a female counterpart to his greatest success, the song "Patches". This time it was the family coming together to remember the maternal head in "Mama's Gone".

Considering that there wasn't another "Band of Gold" in sight, before Invictus finished with, it every single track had either been made into a 45's top or flipside. Still, for all the tricks the company pulled to milk the product the album stood up as a successful project and "Contact" was nominated for a Grammy Award. It seemed obvious that Holland Dozier Holland although appearing far sighted in terms of production capabilities where still locked into the singles market mentality. After all, they had helped to pioneer those three minutes plus masterpieces and extending to thirty plus minutes was like comparing the difference between a sprinter and a marathon runner. The preparation and pacing had to be perfect.

The Chairmen Of The Board had arrived in Europe for a British tour and in America their new single was "Hanging On To A Memory", taken from their "In Session "set and sung by Harrison Kennedy. After a lack of response, the record was flipped making "Tricked and Trapped" sung by Danny Woods and lifted from their debut set. In some ways "Tricked and Trapped" reprised an earlier solo effort by Woods "90 Days In The County Jail" on the Smash label. In this, 3 minutes, tale of woe our leading man tells of his problems brought about by a relationship with an underage

111

girlfriend. As he is led towards the Jail, he cried that he wished he had a hacksaw or that a blowtorch would be all right. In "Tricked and Trapped", however, the sentence appears to be carried out by the girl's brothers despite Woods' pleading that he didn't know that she was sweet sixteen and that he was in the worse mess you've ever seen. 90 days in the County Jail would probably have been less painful.

This latest single had been issued against the group's wishes as they felt that they had a potential Number One record just around the corner in "Elmore James". Nothing to do with the legendary Bluesman, "Elmore James" trod similar territory to another of Johnson's greatest and most prized compositions, "Patches". "Patches" had first made an appearance on the first Chairmen set and then again "In Session"; as well as this, the song had given an international hit to Clarence Carter on Rick Hall's Fame label distributed through Atlantic Records in 1970. At first the inclusion of the track on both Chairmen long players looked like yet another example of Invictus padding out albums but after Johnson's departure from Invictus to Arista the track re-surfaced on his one and only album for the label, the self-titled "General Johnson". Certainly, it was a creation to be proud of, having earned Johnson and Ronald Dunbar a Grammy Award and one that he had begged Holland Dozier Holland to release as the follow up to "Give Me Just A Little More Time".

Johnson never got over the disappointment of "Patches", the first song he had written for Holland Dozier Holland. He had worked on the melody and chord progression of the song for weeks and it was featured on their first album, "Give Me Just A Little More Time". Everybody was begging them to release "Patches" as their follow-up single but instead Holland Dozier Holland released "Dangling On A String", a song that was written after "Patches" was completed. Johnson also felt that Holland Dozier Holland had taken his melody and sped it up which, if you listen to the hook in "Patches" and then, in your mind, try to speed up the melody to "You've Got Me Dangling On A String" the two are close to being identical. Incidentally, Dunbar's Grammy Award was the subject of a 2011 episode of the television show "Pawn Stars" after someone tried to sell it.

"Want Ads" was Number 2 in America with "She's Not Just Another Woman" at Number 3. Further down at Number 70 came "Touch Me Jesus" by Glass House. On the album front the Glass House, along with award winning cover, released "Inside the Glass House" The album opened with the Ty Hunter led "Look What We've Done to Love", a perfect example of the ballad side of the label. A song capable of making you want to turn back the hands of time if you have ever let love slip away and one to win an argument if people ever question if violins have soul. Track 2 carried on in a downbeat way with Hunter once again delivering the song before Scherrie

Payne took over the lead with a rousing stomper, "I Surrendered". If the opening track had emphasised the strength of the ballads, then this one offered the listener everything you could desire in a dance track. After this the pace slackened again as Ty Hunter once more resumed lead with a cover of Eddie Holman's "Hey There Lonely Girl" and the melancholy "I Don't See You in My Eyes Anymore" (later cut by Brotherly Love on Music Merchant). Sparks started to fly on the next track as Hunter and Payne exchanged lead for the infectious, "If It Ain't Love, It Don't Matter". The rest of the album was taken up with up-tempo material all of which should have been enough to secure a chart placing. Then, arguably, the most polished, complete and irresistible album Holland Dozier Holland would ever release, Honey Cone's "Sweet Replies" arrived.

The UK received a totally unexpected assault from left field in the form of the Ruth Copeland composed and Parliament performed "Silent Boatman". This track and the subsequent album were instrumental in making me an obsessive collector of George Clinton's creations. The single was a complete departure from anything else either Invictus or other black groups in general were doing at this time. This takes into account the funk of Sly Stone and James Brown, the progressive soul of The Temptations or the chants of The Last Poets. Opening with an acoustic guitar the strings made way for bagpipes playing "The Skye Boat Song" before the organ came in, followed by a disembodied voice floating through lyrics about Aaron the ferryman sent to guide us across the river Styx to the next world.

Back in the real world, General Johnson had a solo outing away from his fellow Board members, "I'm In Love Darling", then the financial troubles began. The Blossoms, Darlene Love's group on MGM's Lion label sued Invictus for $300,000 claiming that they had been the group performing on the Glass House single "Touch Me Jesus". Darlene Love had figured earlier in the conception of the company, remember that it was her sister, Edna Wright, who was leading Honey Cone's chart assault and it was feasible that The Blossoms had cut the track under another name to get around their own contractual problems. Still, despite the problems Invictus was still doing the business in the charts with "She's Not Just Another Woman" destined to turn Gold for the 8th Day; the group that had started the ball rolling way back in '68 and who were an example of how messy contracts and moonlighting could be with the confusion surrounding themselves and 100 Proof Aged In Soul. The single saw a British release as did Parliament's "Osmium" set.

After fifteen years in the business Parliament got their first long playing release, although rumours were doing the rounds of a lost album, a soul version of "Sergeant Pepper's Lonely Hearts Club Band" being left in the can at Revilot. People in the Soul press didn't know what to make of it.

Funkadelic albums were too ear piercing, mind bending and rock oriented for the discerning Soul man or woman and those poor and confused people who were looking for an extension of the Golden World / Revilot material from Parliament. The album was seen as a softer, soulful version of Funkadelic, although the fact that every track was a complete contrast from its predecessor was to be commended. "Osmium" was the most successful blend of Rock and Soul that Holland Dozier Holland would dabble with. Their interest in other musical forms outside of the mainstream Soul had always played a significant role in their musical development but their choice of influence could be questioned in these more progressive post-Hendrix times.

Lucifer was a more rock-oriented outfit that made no impact as did, or rather didn't, the later signing Warlock. Lucifer was a Canadian rock group that formed in Hamilton where members of the line-up included lead singer and guitarist Eugene "Jay" Smith, bassist Bobby Washington, and guitarist Christiaan Kooij. Collectively they were nicknamed, Snap, Crackle, and Pop. Eugene first stepped onto a stage at the age of 14 doing his best to emulate the Rock and Roll and Doo Wop that he heard coming from across the border between Canada and America. The professional career of Eugene 'Jay' Smith started when he became a member of Ronnie Hawkins' backing band The Hawks. Hawkins is credited with being the man who brought Rock & Roll to Canada, having moved there in 1958. For four years, from 1959 through 1963, Ronnie Hawkins & the Hawks were one of the hottest Rock & Roll bands working, which was very special, in a time when Rock & Roll had supposedly died. The group had played R&B-based Rock & Roll, heavily influenced by the sound of Chess Records in Chicago and Sun Records in Memphis whilst Hawkins himself was practically Toronto's answer to Elvis Presley and he remained true to the music even as Presley himself softened and broadened his sound and waistline. Finally, the Hawks parted company with Ronnie Hawkins during the summer of 1963. The singer's, at times overbearing personality and ego getting the better of the relationship. The Hawks decided to stay together with their oldest member, Levon Helm, out in front, variously renaming themselves Levon & the Hawks and the Canadian Squires and cutting records under both names. A hook-up with a young John Hammond Jr. for a series of recording sessions in New York led to the group's being introduced to Bob Dylan, who was then preparing to pump up his sound in concert. In 1968, the group changed its name to The Band and joined the ranks of other Rock legends with their ultimate split and farewell concert being the Martin Scorcese directed "The Last Waltz. Away from The Hawks, Eugene Smith began to build his own reputation starting out in 1965 as Jay Smith and The Majestics cutting "Howlin' For My Baby" backed by "Driven From Home" on Clip Records but the name changed to Shawne and Jay Jackson and The Majestics when Shawne's brother and ex-Pharaohs member, Jay Jackson joined the group. Two more singles were released in 1966, "Respect" and "No Good to Cry". A year later their debut album " Instrument R&B " was issued with 1968 seeing three albums issued, "Funky Broadway", "Tribute To Otis Redding" and what is acknowledged as their finest, "Here Come Da Judge". Tracks include the often-sampled "Here Come Da Judge", "Soul Serenade", "Mr Pitiful", "The Horse", "Do Your Own Thing", "Tell Mama", "Dock of The Bay", "Tighten Up", plus "It Should Have Been Me" and "I Got You Babe" featuring guest vocalist Jackie Gabriel.

After leaving ARC they issued one single "Hey Joe" on Goodgroove before splitting in 1969. Shawne Jackson would also play with The Stone Soul Children who included soon to be Chairman of The Board member, Harrison Kennedy alongside future Funkadelic member Prakash John before embarking on a successful solo career in the 1970's. By the late-1960s Smith had formed the band Lucifer with Kooij and Washington. Following a stint in military service, drummer/singer Eddie 'Duke' Edwards studied at Berklee in Boston between 1958-1961. Joining the north-eastern US chitlin circuit, he later travelled up to Montreal where he met jazz musician Sun Ra. During his 3-year stint working with Sun Ra, he appeared on the soundtrack album 'Grain of Salt'. In 1964, he was introduced to Canadian booking agent Ron Scribner and together they formed a company to promote local talent in Toronto. They formed the music agency, 'Music Canada' but in mid-1967 Edwards returned to Montreal to work as the musical director for the World Fair. Scribner continued to promote local talent as well as branching out to become Parliament's first manager in 1969.

Scribner was approached by Holland Dozier Holland, who had wanted Smith to do work in the style of Ray Charles. He refused and they went with the Lucifer proposal instead. Scribner was also responsible for hooking up Harrison Kennedy with Holland Dozier Holland. 1971's self-titled "Lucifer" album is simply unlike anything else released by Invictus. Propelled by Smith's instantly recognizable voice, the album featured a strange combination of blues, the bizarre 'For Kids Only' and Blood, Sweat and Tears-styled jazz-rock. Smith himself was responsible for most of the ten tracks and they would often add a horn-section to augment their sound. Throughout his remarkable musical career tenor guitarist, harmonica player, percussionist Eugene Smith performed with or been the opening act for such legends as Ronnie Hawkins, B.B. King, Gordon Lightfoot, James Cotton, The Beach Boys, Peter Tosh and Canned Heat. The reason why Parliament's "Osmium" was more successful was because it belonged to George Clinton's genius, plus, the fact that he was surrounded by a group of multi-talented individuals that also showed on the two Ruth Copeland albums but was totally missing on material by the aforementioned Lucifer and Warlock.

"Bring The Boys Home" was Number 5 in the Soul Chart for Freda Payne with vocal interplay from an uncredited Steve Mancha.

"I really didn't know that much about it. I remember one day when they were writing the tune I had no idea, I don't think they had any idea, at the time about using me. You know, the track was just laying around. They cut it and suddenly one night they got excited about it and they called me up and I did my part."

Steve Mancha

Entering the chart at Number 70 were Mancha's own 100 Proof, having dropped the "Aged in Soul" tag with "Driveway" complete with car horns and innuendoes. As co-writer of "She's Not Just Another Woman" Mancha may have innocently created the line 'She's got electrifying lovin', as warm as my Mother's oven' but "Driveway" was a lyrical throwback to an earlier time when Big Joe Turner shook, rattled and rolled his lyrics to an unsuspecting 50's audience. When Mancha sang about not wanting anybody parking their car in his baby's driveway the implication was obvious. The prolific General Johnson had contributed to both songs and yet still had time to oversee the Chairmen of The Board,

"I really admired General. I liked his work ethic, that's what impressed me the most about him. Not so much the success he was having but what he did to get that success. He worked 18 hours a day to write those tunes......... he did it basically right under our noses next thing you know you're looking at the charts and saying "General, you know, the Honey Cone "Want Ads", "Bring The Boys Home" this is great, but at the same time we're out on the road, everybody's looking, we're together, we're going to studios; General was there in everything. It never, ever interfered with the group."

Harrison Kennedy

Failing to chart anywhere was Lucifer with "Old Mother Nature". In England United Artists released "Deeper into The Vaults" which featured The Showmen's classic "It Will Stand". Away from the "Sweet Replies" album Honey Cone's follow up single chose to carry over the same successful formula as "Want Ads" with "Stick Up". It surpassed its predecessor gaining a second Gold award and reaching the top Soul spot.

"Stick Up" was written the same day the team wrote "Want Ads" which was about a year before it came out. They wrote six or seven tunes which were started at the same time and about five became hits. They got together one night and it was instant. Everything they did was like magic."

Despite its success the track was relegated to the 'b' side upon its eventual British release. Staying with Hot Wax Laura Lee followed up her debut single with "Women's Love Rights" Lee denied any Women's Liberation involvement and would also suffer internationally through a lack of distribution. Another single that failed to see the White Cliffs of Dover was "Breakdown", the latest dance craze from America as performed by Rufus Thomas, The Clown Prince of Dance on Stax and here on Invictus by Parliament. The Parliament single was written by Ruth Copeland and Clyde Wilson and it was Wilson, as Steve Mancha, who supplied the main vocal. Mancha would work again, later, with Clinton's crew and again it would be with Ruth Copeland. Copeland herself had "Gimme Shelter" The Rolling Stones number backed by her own mournful ballad "No Commitment" out as a single but again there was to be no chart place for her.

"She was fantastic, a lot of fun. She kept me laughing. She came up with the idea (for "Breakdown"). *We sat down in the studio one night and just wrote it you know, and she said, 'Why don't you try singing it' and I tried it and blew it away".*

Steve Mancha

"Contact" was released in England while the 8th Day's debut set was overlooked despite rising to critical acclaim in America. If certain areas of the industry chose to ignore the product coming out of Invictus and Hot Wax others were quick to acknowledge this new vibrant sound spreading out of Detroit and the sound of Honey Cone began to bring forth imitators in the form of Krystal Generation's "Wanted Dead Or Alive", First Choice's "Armed And Extremely Dangerous" and Bobo Mr Soul's "Answer To The Want Ads" finding US releases. None could attain the quality that the trio was able to and "Sweet Replies" arrived to emphasise that fact to an eager British following. Honey Cone's Edna Wright felt tha they were good teachers who knew what they wanted. What she loved about working with Eddie Holland and especially Greg Perry and Norman Johnson was that they were perfectionists. She said that they would not let a song go until it was right. They would re-cut and re-cut, and she would re-sing and re-sing until she dropped.

The 8th Day had settled down, seemingly free from the mystery that had surrounded their birth and the eagerly awaited follow up came forth, this time delivered up front by Melvin Davis. Written by four of the company's finest, General Norman Johnson, Greg Perry, Angelo Bond and Ronald Dunbar, "You've Got to Crawl" epitomised the Invictus sound and sounded miles away from the slower but infectious sound of its Golden predecessor. "You've Got to Crawl" had a hook and a beat yet could not be classed as a dance track. Maybe the fault lay in the fact that here was a song with lyrics to be listened to and a group of people, taking up the dance floor, just are not there to stand and ponder. Nobody complained, though, at least not in America where the single gave the group and the label another Gold Disc. Britain got nothing. The 'B' side also received attention, "It's Instrumental to Be Free" written by Holland Dozier Holland as the title implies was a non-vocal track that highlighted the Invictus sound but not necessarily the group's versatility. Unless of course you count the fact that the same track with additional wah wah guitar was released in February 1972 as The Politicians' "Free Your Mind" on Hot Wax. Considering the pedigree of the 8th Day's members, the question once more was, who are the musicians on the track? Yet another unsolved mystery.

September saw the re-issue on Action in England of "You're My Everything" by The Showmen from their Swan recording days, while in America "Bring the Boys Home" had done the golden thing and along the way had also become the label's most controversial release outside of songs like "The Medal" by Ruth Copeland and "1200 Miles from Heaven" by Flaming Ember. The difference here being that both Copeland and Flaming Ember were not the high-profile artist that Freda Payne was. She was the flag bearer for the company and as such had been groomed as an ambassador of it. The American involvement in the Vietnam war was still strong and anti-American material was obviously going to touch a few raw nerves. That had been the reason why Edwin Starr released "War" over at Motown instead of The Temptations who had cut it originally as an album track. "Bring the Boys Home" was banned from the Far East Network radio stations that served the American Servicemen in Asia. There was a lot more depth to "Bring the Boys Home" than was immediately heard. Perhaps this was due to the commercial sounding nature of the song itself. For such a polished star as Payne to suddenly turn from a singer of love songs to one of protest was also running the risk of taking more time than necessary to acclimatise to in the record sales war that was not Vietnam. The song was originally intended for Laura Lee whose output, although commercial, was raw but the company needed a hit for Payne and so she got the nod. The lyrics evoked a ghostly image of fallen soldiers walking across the sky as she sang, bring the boys home, bring them back alive. "He's In My Life" was replaced by "Bring The Boys Home" on the British release of "Contact".

EMI seemed to have it in mind that the track could help to push the album sales but if it hadn't sold on its own merit then putting it onto an album was hardly going to increase its popularity. Instead, the British collector lost out again and also, although the power and sentiment of "Bring the Boys Home" should never be ignored, the track lay uneasily amongst the love songs surrounding it. The chance to give the company the nearest thing to a concept album was blown on the British release.

The distributors seemed to have a knack for turning album tracks into singles and vice versa and completely ignoring the tracks that were charting in America, all in all giving less value for money. By this time EMI's handling of the labels was being questioned: American releases like the 8th Day's second Gold single "You've Got to Crawl" were being ignored while others were either being replaced by album tracks or demoted to 'b' sides. There was even the suggestion that EMI had bought the company's catalogue as a tax scapegoat. One had to accept, though, that Invictus itself was not guiltless. Still, "Stick Up" had reached the top spot in the Soul chart and "You've Got to Crawl" was at Number 7. Both fell victim to EMI's handling.

Back home Holland Dozier Holland were guilty of other crimes. Aside from Freda Payne's second album, "Contact", the company seemed to struggle when putting albums together relying heavily on previously released material. New albums by Honey Cone, Glass House, Chairmen Of The Board and Flaming Ember had tracks carried over from their debut sets. Again, conflict struck: this time Holland Dozier Holland were doing the suing. Freda Payne and her management were being sued for breach of contract and in November it was rumoured that Flaming Ember were burnt out. Even so, Hot Wax issued "If It's Good to You", a Holland Dozier Holland composition. England got the instrumental 'B' side only while the 'a' side belonged to an old track from their debut set, "The Empty Crowded Room". Despite the group's releases on both side of the Atlantic the rumour was true.

By the end of 1971, the company began to falter with only Honey Cone and Laura Lee able to keep Hot Wax from cooling down. The Chairmen Of The Board had an American release in "Try on My Love For Size" which was condemned by critics and there were fears that the group was deteriorating with a publicised album "Men Are Getting Scarce" failing to appear. In England Hot Wax surprised everybody with a single by Silent Majority, "Frightened Girl". The surprise didn't last long when it was discovered that Silent Majority were in fact The Formations whose re-release of the Northern Soul classic "At the Top Of The Stairs" from the Philadelphia Bank Records had become a National Pop hit. The strategy employed by EMI, though applauded did no good. The time difference was too great and the sounds of the groups so different that the Silent Majority as far as the general punter was concerned was a completely different group to The Formations. The group members themselves were, however, doing bigger and better things in their native Philadelphia as songwriters where they had just come off with a Number One Soul hit for Wilson Pickett "Don't Let the Green Grass Fool You".

The final release for 1971 was "90 Day Freeze" by 100 Proof, a title reflective of the current world energy crisis. The track was considered good of its kind, although some critics were beginning to feel that the company's output was beginning to sound a little samey. Mancha himself disliked the track. The release had arrived after an out of sorts 100 Proof (Aged In Soul) had disbanded for three months. When they re-formed, they had become a more self-contained outfit but with personnel changes. Steve Mancha and Hatcher remained with the rest of the new line-up consisting of future Funkadelic member Ron Bykowski on guitar, Dave Case on percussion Darnell Hagen on drums and a fugitive from Funkadelic, Billy Nelson on Bass. Nelson was in dispute with George Clinton and left the Parliament/Funkadelic outfit choosing to go on the road with 100 Proof. Honey Cone's next success came via the infectious "One Monkey Don't Stop No Show" written by General Johnson and Greg Perry. When it received a British release "Stick Up" backed it. Their third album, "Soulful Tapestry" played on Carole King's original "Tapestry" and was acclaimed as being superior to anything Motown was putting out at that time.

At the beginning of December there were no records from either label on the UK charts. One single, "You've Got Love Somebody" from Freda Payne's "Contact" set was lost in the Christmas chart rush but whether it would have fared better at any other time is doubtful. In America Payne had a pre-Invictus set on the USA label released "In Stockholm". The record may have been better staying there as it did nothing in The States. Lost at years' end were the self-titled set by Lucifer and Ruth Copeland's "I Am What I Am". Copeland's record was a well-balanced mix of commercial Rock, Soul and Blues that relied heavily on input from George Clinton and his band of outlandish followers as well as two Jagger/Richards compositions, "Gimme Shelter" and "Play with Fire". "The Medal" opened the set with Bernie Worrell's classical piano solo that led into a hard-hitting power pack of a track augmented by searing guitar courtesy of Eddie Hazel. In "The Medal" Copeland screamed with anguish at the arrival of the medal and letter from the Government telling of her man's demise in Vietnam. During their Motown days Holland Dozier Holland had steered clear of controversy and stayed inside clearly defined perimeters of love songs sung simply and effectively but here it was, another time and America was another place. Copeland spat out the venomous lyrics at the US

Government asking if this medal was capable of giving her love in the morning or even replacing her dreams and plans. Furthermore, could it kiss her on cold evenings. The answer was a cold, no. This piece of gold could not replace her man. "I Am What I Am" was recorded using many of the same musicians as before except now they were acting as her own band with Eddie Hazel, Bernie Worrell, Tiki Fulwood and Billy 'Bass' Nelson leaving Parliament/Funkadelic.

The Funkadelic members stayed together to support Copeland on a successful tour but supporting Sly Stone led to problems, however. When she introduced her band as Funkadelic and even allowed them to take one of her encores. Stone insisted she either leave the tour or lose the band. The band went but not for long. The album failed to sell despite the success of her live shows and in fact the only album to make it over into 1972 was Laura Lee's "Women's Love Rights" long player, which also helped to re-invent the career of William Weatherspoon who Laura Lee felt was a little hard on her. He wanted her to say something his way and they argued a lot because she wanted to do the thing her way. Sometimes she would even leave the studio. They would fall out many times but there was definitely a love there for each other. He would argue that this was the way he wanted it and she would counter the argument by saying that he had given her the song, she wanted to make it hers and this is how she wanted to sing it. She did admit that they always had fun but that she never had any problems with his writing partner, Angelo Bond.

So, 1971 was over with two lawsuits, one for and one against and one loss. Flaming Ember died down never to rise again although after a brief rest, Plunk and Ellis bounced back with a reformed group, Mind Body and Soul, in the spirit of Flaming Ember and named after their very first Hot Wax release. An album was recorded but never released and the group continued playing throughout the Metro Detroit area up to the late seventies. As 1972 opened the ongoing lawsuit between Holland Dozier Holland and Berry Gordy Jr was settled on January the 3rd.

"Personally, I believe that dealing with lawsuits connected with Motown sort of took me away from creating as much as I normally would have."

Eddie Holland

Elsewhere in the company the Chairmen Of The Board were beginning to show signs of strain but instead of looking to solve problems in their existing ranks, Holland Dozier Holland went ahead with what would prove a disastrous decision. The launching of a third label, Music Merchant, distributed, as was Hot Wax, by Buddha. Music Merchant was seen by some parties as the successor to Invictus that seemed to be steering up a dead-end street under Capitol's distribution. Keener eyed observers noted that the label was the same shade of blue as its sister but there the similarities ended. Sadly, the new label would prove a financial disaster that eventually collapsed without one major success although both Eloise Laws "Love Factory" and Just Brothers "Sliced Tomatoes" would become rarities on the British Northern Soul scene. Just Brothers were Frank and Jimmy Bryant and had previously recorded for the Empire and Lupine labels. The guitar on Sliced Tomatoes belonged to Funk Brother Eddie Willis whilst the rest of the instruments were amply played by the legendary Benny Benjamin on drums, Joe Hunter on keyboard and Frank Bryant on bass. Bryant also co-wrote "Deeper In Love" with Don Davis recorded by J.J. Barnes in August 1966 for Ric Tic and produced by Don Davis. He later toured with Junior Walker & The All Stars. Ironically, for all the wealth of material Holland Dozier Holland created during this period "Sliced Tomatoes", an outside production would bring in more royalties than any other when "The Rockafella Skank" by British musician Fatboy Slim was released as a single from the 1998 album "You've Come A Long Way Baby".

The Jones Girls could also be found on the label prior to their amazing success at Philadelphia International under the guidance of Philadelphia's own Holland Dozier Holland, Kenny Gamble and Leon Huff. What happened to make Music Merchant such a disaster then? The product was equal to the other two labels. Holland Dozier Holland themselves contributed several songs as well as General Johnson and Greg Perry. Warlock's "You've Been My Rock" written by Holland Dozier, powered along in the best Chairmen Of The Board / 8th Day vein, although the ensuing album seemed to suggest that outside of the single an entirely different band had been responsible for the lightweight Rock on show. The Jones Girls came across as the company's Honey Cone with their catchy performances whilst Eloise Laws sat somewhere between Freda Payne and Laura Lee. Brotherly Love, a family group called Jackson believe it or not, sounded remarkably like their namesakes and gave Holland Dozier Holland the chance to put together what might have been, had they stuck around for an extra year at Motown. The Smith Connection hung in like The Stylistics under the writing skills of Ronald Dunbar and group leader Michael Smith. Smith would later move to Motown as a staff writer/producer and performer under the name of Michael Lovesmith. Lovesmith, or just plain Smith had found earlier success at the end of the '60's with a song "Little Girl" sung by The Isley Brothers before he moved onto Stax where he was backed by The Bar Kays and where Isaac Hayes wanted to sign him to a ten years' contract. His manager declined the offer, on his behalf, and he next made the acquaintance of Holland Dozier Holland signing not only a recording contract for himself but also for his brothers as The Smith Connection.

The Smith Connection released four singles as well as the album "Under My Wings". Outside of the group Michael wrote primarily with Ronald Dunbar for Freda Payne and Laura Lee. He also became part of the staff production team under the Holland Dozier Holland banner that consisted of many creators in a collective much the same as The Corporation that had sprung up at Motown in the post- Holland Dozier Holland years.

As the team Holland Dozier Holland split up with the Holland Brothers moving to Los Angeles Smith moved with them and eventually settled into his Motown period where he forged a ten years' relationship working with The Jackson Five and Jermaine Jackson in particular on his solo debut, "My Name Is Jermaine". His work with Motown also paved the way for him to bring his brothers into the scene as Lovesmith. Michael Lovesmith absorbed much knowledge during his period with Music Merchant; Eloise Laws, on the other hand, had never been comfortable with her role at the label. It was the back end of 1971 that "Tighten Him Up" was released. The single, in the Laura Lee "Woman's Love Rights" bag only saw East Coast action. As before, Holland Dozier Holland had hit on a winning formula, perhaps by chance, remembering the reluctance at signing Laura Lee. There was no doubting now though the precious pearl they had found in Lee. Eloise Laws was a beautiful, elegant princess, born in Houston, Texas in 1949 and came from a gifted musical family of eight with brothers Hubert and Ronnie being prominent on the fledgling Jazz-Funk scene of the early seventies. At the age of ten she was a veteran of the Bell Vista Baptist Church, Houston where she would entertain the congregation with her version of grandma's favourite, "Life Is Like A Railroad Track". After cutting four sides for CBS in 1969 it was another two years before Eloise Laws released a record again. Eddie Holland had seen Eloise on a television show and saw her as the perfect replacement for Freda Payne who they were experiencing contractual problems with. Holland Dozier Holland flew out to New York from Detroit to sign her and Eloise, flattered by the attention and seeing an excellent career move, signed to Music Merchant.

Music Merchant, already lacking a commercial success, was hit by another problem when Viewlex's American Record Pressing Plant based in Owosso, Michigan, was destroyed by fire on October the 28th 1972. The company was located at 1810 West King Street in Owosso Township from 1952 until 1972 and had originally started as Vargo Record Pressing in 1951. When they moved to Owosso the following year the name was changed to the American Record Pressing. Approximately 80% of the company's business in Owosso was the pressing of Motown's record and at that time of the fire approximately 230 people were employed by ARP. Firefighters from Owosso, Corunna, Owosso Township, and Caledonia Township responded to the blaze but were unable to save the building. CBS agreed to carry on the pressing for the label and by the time the pressing was done, Music Merchant owed CBS $11,519.98.

"Tighten Him Up'" was followed in the summer of '73 by "Love Factory" with its unmistakable bass led intro and lyrics that reflected the Motor City roots with the hero, or rather villain of the piece building love affairs like GM builds cars. The reference there being to General Motors, once part of Detroit's most solid industry; but just like GM's seemingly endless announcements of layoffs showed the crumbling state of Detroit industry, Eloise Laws' own Love Factory failed to create more job prospects for the music merchants Holland Dozier Holland. Thankfully, the British collectors showed enough good sense to make it one of the Northern scene's treasures. Hidden on the 'b' side was a gem of a track, "Stay with Me" written by the golden trio. This was a beautiful mid-paced mover that had the hallmarks of that other masterpiece by Holland-Dozier, "Why Can't We Be Lovers". It was Eloise Laws' only other Music Merchant release and her experience of working with the legendary trio was less than satisfying.

As well as Eloise Laws, The Jones Girls, arguably the most successful artists ever to emerge from Holland Dozier Holland's company, albeit long after the trio's interests in them had gone, also felt that Eddie Holland, as company president, was unapproachable unlike Kenny Gamble with whom they would strike up a mutual respect in 1979 when they launched their career at Philadelphia International. Instead of grooming the young, talented sisters to be another Freda Payne or Honey Cone through the singles "Come Back", "Your Love Controls Me" and "Taster Of The Honey (Not The Keeper Of The Bee) they were left to falter. The Jones Girls, Shirley, Brenda and Valerie, released their first recording, "Learning How to Love" in 1970 on the local Detroit label GM Records as well as Jerry Butler's Memphis label before doing backgrounds for another local label Fortune. When Fortune fell upon misfortune the three sisters moved to the Music Merchant where they cut enough sides for an album that was never released plus continuing their tradition of backing others such as Freda Payne and Holland-Dozier themselves, on the "Why Can't We Be Lovers" session. Although there were no more releases on The Jones Girls through Music Merchant, they did continue to provide background vocals for Holland Dozier Holland whilst releasing their own product on Curtis Mayfield's Curtom label out of neighbouring Chicago in 1975 before touring with Diana Ross in 1976. This led them to the doors of Philadelphia

International and worldwide prominence three years later. Shirley Jones acquiring a husband along the way, McKinley Jackson.

A former Motown star, Brenda Holloway, fresh from allegedly devoting her music to the church, came to the fold for "Some Quiet Place" and "Let Love Flow" that bore the label's first catalogue number, 1001, if not the first release. Her only two sides for Music Merchant were the responsibility of William Weatherspoon and Raynard Miner. Both had been working well together on material for Laura Lee and "Let Love Grow" would have worked equally well as a follow up to "I'm Not My Brother's Keeper" by Flaming Ember. Raynard Miner's previous success, prior to working with Holland Dozier Holland, was as co-writer and piano player for Fontella Bass's evergreen Chess recording "Rescue Me" in 1965 as well as being the uncredited co-author of Jackie Wilson's "Higher and Higher". He also co-wrote Bass's 1966 stomper "Recovery" and the same year and the same label saw his credits on Sugarpie Desanto's rip-roaring "In the Basement". Sadly, "Let Love Grow", true to form for Music Merchant, never reached the chart and the success that Brenda Holloway richly deserved remained as elusive as that desperately needed by the label. Holloway had previously made her name in 1964 with "Every Little Bit Hurts" on Motown as well as making history by being the first Motown recording artist to take the label to court in 1969 regarding her financial situation. Neglected by Motown as a songwriter as well as a singer she co-wrote and recorded the classic "You Made Me So Very Happy", later a two million seller for Blood, Sweat and Tears in 1969. At Motown she had met the acquaintance of Holland Dozier Holland but was never at ease with them.

Despite those feelings of disapproval, it was Eddie Holland who stuck by her during her problem patch with Gordy, helping her out of her contract and paying her a salary for two years before finally signing her after the 'official' Motown statement that she had decided to "quit and sing for God". Even if this statement was a cover up, Holloway did have deep convictions and before leaving Motown cut a gospel album with Holland Dozier Holland that was never released. When Holland Dozier Holland found out that Holloway was not happy, they asked her to leave with them. They were responsible for getting her Jobete royalties and her BMI royalties, so she was not like the rest of the artists who had to sue. They made sure when they left that they pulled all of Holloway's royalties also. Holland-Dozier also took Motown to court in 1972 for Brenda Holloway. After her unsuccessful period with Music Merchant, Holloway faded from the scene until recording in 1987 for the UK based Nightmare label.

Of all the releases on Music Merchant the most popular in terms of underground success was the instrumental "Sliced Tomatoes" by Just

Brothers. The track appeared on the 'b' side of "Tears Ago" and "Things Will Be Better Tomorrow". Both tracks had been issued in the 1960's on other labels, making them outside productions for the company. "Sliced Tomatoes" was originally on the Lupine label while "Things Will Be Better Tomorrow" was on Empire. Just Brothers were Frank and Jimmy Bryant and recorded for the Empire and Lupine labels out of Detroit. Empire was John Winford Terry's own label formed in 1965. Johnny Terry had already had a fascinating history having met James Brown in Georgia Juvenile Institute where they formed a gospel group with three other inmates. Bobby Byrd visited the Institute as a Gospel singer and soon became friends with Brown. His family sponsored James Brown's parole from "Juvie" on 14th of June 1952 and he temporarily lived with the family. Byrd, Brown and Johnny Terry formed the Gospel trio the 3 Swanees and later formed The Avons who morphed into The Flames with Brown joining the line-up. Soon after, Brown fronted the group with a final change to The Famous Flames. "Please, Please, Please" was recorded by The Famous Flames on February the 4th 1956. Over 30 versions of the song have been recorded to date. By the time the follow up, "Try Me" came out in 1958 only Brown, Byrd and Terry remained from the original line-up. "No, No, No, No", also cut in 1956 was written with James Brown and Bobby Byrd and was later cut by Johnny & Bill on the Try Me label. Between 1962 and 1964 Terry recorded Betty Green, first on Clara with "He's Down On Me" and "He Put Me Down" on Cracker in '64. Up until 1968 Johnny Terry would wander in and out of the Famous Flames and that year he cut "Here Is My Everything" on Bobby Byrd and his wife Vicki Anderson for ABC when they took a step away from Mr Brown. From 1963 to 1966 he was also a member of The Drifters, alongside Johnny Moore, Charles Thomas, Rudy Lewis and Gene Pearson. He joined as a bass singer and contributed to such classic hits as 'Under The Boardwalk" and "Saturday Night At The Movies" amongst many others, before leaving the group to concentrate on his own productions starting with the forming of his own Empire label in 1965. In 1966 he was responsible for Johnny Daye's Northern sounding "Good Time", released on Johnny Nash's Jomada label.

On Empire in 1967 Taurus & Leo released "I Ain't Playing Baby" backed by "Going Out The World Backwards". However, his most enduring work was with the duo, Just Brothers. The brothers in the title were Frank and Jimmy Bryant and recorded for the Empire and Lupine labels out of Detroit. Empire roster included not only Just Brothers, The Honey Bees and Jack Montgomery who started life as Marvin Jones. Jones was a draughtsman by trade and was signed to the Barracuda label, owned by Don Mancha. Mancha and his business partner Don Montgomery wanted major label budgets for a couple of songs and Jones was the man

126

who he wanted to sing them but he needed a name change. Mancha came up with the name Jack Montgomery. Mancha flew to New York and met up with Johnny Terry who had connections there through his time with The Drifters. Through Terry he met with Scepter and recorded three tracks. Although Johnny Terry's name appears in the production credits Mancha claimed that he did the producing and arranging by himself. Mancha recorded three tracks at Scepter and returned to Detroit to carry on with other projects, leaving Johnny Terry to deal with the finances from the New York end but the partnership soon turned bitter and was ended.

After Jimmy Bryant's return from military service, the Bryant Brothers were recruited into a session group for Terry by the group's drummer, Funk Brother Richard 'Pistol' Allen. The session was intended to record a song called "Honey" plus its 'b' side. The musical tracks were completed when the hired vocalist was considered not of a high enough standard to record the song. Frank took the opportunity to point out Jimmy's vocal talent. Convinced by Bryant, Terry agreed to give them a stab at recording the two songs. At the subsequent session the Bryant Brothers sang on "Honey" and their songs "Things Will Be Better Tomorrow" and "She Broke His Heart." The track recorded as the B-side was titled "Sliced Tomatoes" and released in 1965 backed with "Things Will Get Better", on the Lupine label. The instruments on the track were amply played by the legendary Benny Benjamin on drums, Joe Hunter on keyboard and Frank Bryant on bass. The tune was 'borrowed a year later by Ray Charles for his song, "I Don't Need No Doctor". Bryant also co-wrote "Deeper In Love" with Don Davis recorded by J.J. Barnes in August 1966 for Ric Tic, produced by Don Davis. He later toured with Junior Walker & The All Stars. Later that year a pairing of "She Broke His Heart" and "Things Will Get Better" was released on the Empire Record Label while "Carlena" was released on the Garrison label. None of the tracks were successful and the Bryant Brothers returned to session work.

In 1969, with new member Willie Kendrick, the Just Brothers negotiated a deal at Johnny Nash's Jomada label. They recorded one unreleased track before being dropped by the label. John Winford Terry was also married to Carole Holland, sister of Brian and Eddie and he helped the Just Brothers again by organising the re-release of "Sliced Tomatoes" on Holland Dozier Holland's Music Merchant label in 1972. Terry, under the name of Winford Terry, also co-wrote "Try It You'll Like It" with brother-in-law Brian Holland and Raynard Miner for The Barrino Brothers on Invictus in 1972. He also responsible for Raynel Wynglas's "Bar-B-Q Ribs" the final single from Music Merchant. The infectious funky little number deserved to do better and leaned heavily on the popularity of the Geraldine character created by comedian Flip Wilson.

The Flip Wilson Show being the first successful network variety series with an African American star. In 1968, NBC signed him to a five-year development deal. Wilson made guest appearances on shows like Rowan and Martin's Laugh-In and on the 22nd of September 1969, he appeared with 20 up and coming comics in a Bob Hope special, which was followed by a Flip Wilson Show special, a pilot for the series to come. The special introduced many distinctive elements that would be part of the series and when Wilson donned a contemporary stewardess' outfit, loud print miniskirt and puffy cap, Geraldine Jones was born. The Flip Wilson Show joined the fall line-up on 17th of September 1970 and turned out to be one of the last successful variety shows. NBC put Flip Wilson's show to rest, airing its last episode on 24 June 1974. Raynard Wynglass turned out to be Raynard Miner. Elsewhere on the label, One single by Sweet Rock, "Big Train", an up-tempo Rock laden track, gave a rare production opportunity to Lawrence T. Horn. It too never left the station.

So, what went wrong with Music Merchant? Judging from what their artists had to say about them the trio at the helm were not exactly the best of bosses, keeping themselves distanced from their employees and not allowing the talent that had been brought together to breathe; or maybe it was down to either bad timing, a lack of originality or simply that the sounds and the times were changing rapidly. Was it fair of Holland Dozier Holland to hope to emulate either their Motown heyday or the impact that both Invictus and Hot Wax had had on their respective launches? As a year 1971 had ended relatively poorly for the labels.

The Blues & Soul Review of 1971 showed the following figures. Top selling singles artists had the Chairmen Of The Board at Number 8 followed at Number 12 by Honey Cone. In the USA Honey Cone had led the Holland Dozier Holland field with a 5th position followed by the 8th Day at 14. Freda Payne at 20 and the Chairmen bringing up the rear guard at 33. As the label's premier group, the Chairmen Of The Board would find a firmer following overseas. In an alarming statistic no albums featured at all in the best sellers for home or abroad.

New US product included the third and weaker single from the 8th Day "If I Could See The Light" and "The Road We Didn't Take", another album track from Freda Payne. The stunning debut album by Laura Lee entered the Soul chart at number 42 finally rising to number 3. "Love And Liberty" was doing the business for her in the singles market and Lee remained in denial about the liberation path she seemed to be treading. What she was doing, however, was clearing the way for artists like Millie Jackson to make a far more commercial living out of this formula with her 1974-77 outings "Caught Up", "Still Caught Up" and "Feelin' Bitchy" for the Spring label.

"Men Are Getting Scarce" finally surfaced as a single for the Chairmen with "All We Need Is Understanding" being released as a General Johnson solo single. Not only did the company appear to be making one and the same group compete with itself but also showed poor business sense. "All We Need Is Understanding" was, in fact, an unaltered album track from "In Session" by the Chairmen. Poor business sense seemed to be the order of the day with Britain re-issuing Flaming Ember's "Westbound Number 9".

In an attempt to recapture falling sales Brian Holland and Lamont Dozier took the fatal decision to record themselves. "Don't Leave Me", while being an outstanding single and the strongest Invictus release for a long, long time, fell short of the mark despite having all the right ingredients for a hit. It entered the singles chart at Number 83 only to peak at 72 before disappearing for good. Singles by Glass House, "Playing Games", "Something New About You" by Silent Majority and Chairman Harrison Kennedy's solo effort, the Honey Cone album track "Sunday Morning People", all followed the path to obscurity. Time dictated a change and so the next single from Honey Cone was a gentle ballad that probably sold more on the strength of the group than on the material itself, although "The Day I Found Myself" did remain a most beautiful ballad and as such a departure from the more rhythmic material the regular punter had come to expect from the girls. The main criticism was the one being aimed at the labels generally and that was that the material was becoming warmed over. The track had appeared on "Sweet Replies" as well as in its new adaptation on "Soulful Tapestry".

Just when the company seemed to be going nowhere 100 Proof supplied the goods with "Everything Good Is Bad" their most sophisticated sound to date ably arranged by McKinley Jackson and written by Johnson, Perry and Bond. Their second album, simply called "100 Proof" highlighted this new sophistication with the bulk of the material belonging to the writing talents of Clyde Wilson. If observers wished to criticise the company's lack of progress you only had to compare the two albums by 100 Proof. A much more laidback outing with only the current single and the follow up "Don't Scratch Where It Don't Itch" coming close to up-tempo. Two outside compositions, The Bee Gees "Words" and "Never My Love", The Addrissi Brothers Pop classic with a rare lead vocal by Don Hatcher were given the definitive Soul treatment. Despite the quality the album sank along with the second Glass House long player and Lucifer's "Bloodshot Eyes" remained closed to the chart.

Laura Lee's next single from the "Women's Love Rights" set was, to many, her greatest moment; her emotive handling of the standard "Since I Fell For You". This was a change of pace for Hot Wax's leading lady but unlike "The Day I Found Myself" by Honey Cone Laura responded magnificently launching a successful attack on the singles chart reaching the Soul Top Ten. Creatively it was a magnificent track, the album version lasting some ten minutes as Lee told us about the day she met 'him' and the relationship that blossomed only to die. When she led in with her singing the grip on your emotions was so tight that you could almost scream along with her, a moment only equalled by and comparable to the feeling you get from Linda Jones' handling of "Your Precious Love", The Impressions' classic. At the same time as Lee was making it big in the secular field her old Gospel outfit The Meditation Singers were benefiting from three tracks sung and written by her, a side of her talent never pursued at Hot Wax. Chess released the album. Laura felt that she was being played, believing that some men thought that a beautiful woman could not have a brain. She was as feisty in life as she was on her records and after a while they found out that Laura Lee was no fool but that came after they had already taken her for the ride. Laura felt that she was doing good, helping with a few lines here and there and coming up with a melody. She thought that she would get credit for this and it was not until later that she heard someone say that they had received a royalty cheque for writing or producing that she started to question why she hadn't got any money. She was told that she had to sign up and felt that she had been educated after the fact.

The next group member to try and make it solo was Melvin Davis of the 8th Day who bowed with "I'm Worried" backed by "Just As Long". Both had previously been recorded as The 8th Day. Again, the single failed to chart. After a seven month's break that had seen them down to three, the Chairmen Of The Board were back. Harrison Kennedy had gone back to school for a while and Johnson had concentrated on his writing and producing alongside his creative partner Greg Perry. The new sets from Honey Cone and 100 Proof all had Johnson's stamp on them. "Men Are Getting Scarce" had changed to "Bittersweet" and was due for an imminent release. Johnson's solo career had not been the anticipated success with his first and second singles bombing.

A solo album, "Generally Speaking" was slated for a March release alongside "Bittersweet". More inter-group competition that made no sense at all. He was eager to get back to Europe where the group had proved far more popular, as soon as they were happy with the way things were in their own 'backyard.' After a relatively poor third single The 8th Day hit back with the stronger "Eeny-Meeny-Miny-Mo" backed by the less commercial Holland Dozier Holland composition "Rocks In My Head" a guitar laden driving classic. The lead single from the Chairmen was the title track of their forthcoming album, "Bittersweet", a most beautiful ballad that had a mid-way rhythm pace change that put the group back in its early dance style before returning to the ballad section. An unusually structured recording that nevertheless worked. It was supported on the 'b' side by the track that General Johnson had regarded so highly, "Elmore James". With April came announcements that Chairman Danny Woods was due a solo album, "Aries" while Glass House product Scherrie Payne was also being groomed for a solo career after allegations that Freda had been signed to Motown. A highly unlikely event considering the blinkered approach to other female artists outside of Ms Ross by Berry Gordy.

Despite being overlooked and containing the Chairmen tracks that he had sung lead on, "Aries" was a far more accomplished album than sales suggested. As the second lead singer the charismatic Danny Woods' energy had no bounds, jumping chairs and doing back flips. He had all this energy and people went crazy. Danny Woods was born and raised in Atlanta and at the age of 19 moved to Detroit with the band The Tears hoping to be successful in the City that was leading the way not only in the car industry but in Soul music.

"At that particular time weren't nothing happening in Atlanta, Motown was hot so I basically went up to Detroit and after a month I started singing as a single artist ...went to Motown, auditioned for Motown and they told me I sounded a lot like Jackie Wilson and when they had a project or a song like that, they would let Eddie Holland do it."

Danny Woods

When you know that Danny Woods was influenced by the late, great Jackie Wilson you will also know the direction that this Board member was coming from.

"As a young child I heard Jackie Wilson and I thought he had one of the most fantastic voices I had ever heard. And I would sing a lot of his songs and got a lot of inspiration from him and after so many years had the pleasure of performing with him at the Apollo Theatre in New York. That was great."

The Apollo would be home to the Chairmen on more than one occasion.

"Going to the Apollo Theatre you see that was always a dream of everybody; if you got to the Apollo then you knew you were on your way. We went three times and the next time we went we headlined...that was a great compliment."

131

The Tears dried up but Woods had a successful solo act playing with David Ruffin, with whom he shared a house and performed with in New York, Eddie Kendricks, Walter Jackson, and a band called the Sunliners, later Rare Earth. For Correc-tone he cut one single, "You Had Me Fooled" in 1962 and later two singles for Smash, "90 Days In The County Jail written by Woods along with M. Campbell, R. Monnette, and R. Kreiner backed by "Sweet Darling" written by Woods along with McKinley Jackson. The second Smash (or not as the case may be) single was "Come On And Dance part 1" backed by "I Want To Thank You (For Love And Devotion)" written by Jackson and Woods with B Slater and one Bob Babbitt, ace Bass player for Detroit's recording industry. Some six or seven years passed then Danny was introduced to General Johnson who, through Jeffrey Bowen, made him a permanent fixture within the Chairmen of the Board.

Like Harrison Kennedy before him Danny Woods released his own solo album, "Aries"; and, again, his set included group tracks, "Everybody's Got A Song To Sing", "Try On My Love For Size" and "Working On A Building Of Love". Around the time of the third Chairmen album there seemed to be a more spiritual influence creeping into some of the songs with the aforementioned ""Everybody's Got A Song To Sing", "Working On A Building Of Love" and "I'm On My Way To A Better Place".

"I had a Gospel background and I love that music because it's very positive and everybody's got a song to sing no matter what your conditions are."

If Harrison Kennedy had tried to go for a more personal approach with some of his own compositions on show: Danny Woods seemed more than happy to have the full weight of his bosses behind him. Therefore, most of the tracks were either written or partly written by the top men themselves, Holland Dozier and Holland and among them were some gems that on second listening should have brought Woods far more acclaim.

"At that particular time, I was just learning about how to write songs and things like that. It was quite exciting because the musicians that we used, they were all friends of mine and it was amazing to me to hear them play."

Instead, the album was lost in the company's sea of despair. Most of the tracks were up-tempo and sat comfortably in the Joe Tex method of delivery. "Funny How Time Slips Away" the classic Willie Nelson song and "I've Been Loving You Too Long" written and performed at separate times by both Otis Redding and Jerry Butler were selected by Danny and were equal to any other version. The most unusual offering had to be the album's closing track, a Soulful rendition of "Danny Boy", previously cut by his hero Jackie Wilson.

"I chose that song because I admired him so much and I had sung that song for many years. People loved it and I wanted to do it again."

Harrison Kennedy recalled that one night in England the audience wouldn't let Danny leave the stage and he ended up doing "Danny Boy" three times, he was in tears. To me the standout track is the Holland Dozier and Angelo Bond song, "Two Can Be As Lonely As One". Classic Invictus from the opening guitar riff through to the background harmonies and Woods impassioned vocal delivery. "Let Me Ride" backed by "It Didn't Take Long", both Holland Dozier compositions failed to consolidate a chart position for Woods and a follow up "Everybody's Tippin'" a non-album track backed by "Roller Coaster" also failed to do the job for Danny Woods. If there was anything Woods felt strongly about the album it was the fact that Holland Dozier Holland couldn't seem to get the best out of his vocal skills,

"General, he could write for me 'cos he and I were close and we always have been close all these years and he could get inside of my feeling and that was no problem. A lot of things that Holland Dozier Holland done, a lot of those songs I sang high, real high and it was forceful but I have another style that they never captured and it was mellow."

Danny Woods was not the first artist to have complained about Holland Dozier Holland's direction. Marvin Gaye was a prime example, often complaining that both he and Levi Stubbs of The Four Tops were cut unnaturally high. It was only when Gaye started to produce himself that his vocal style began to show more depth and creativity.

After Eddie Custis had left the group Danny Woods, of the three remaining Chairmen, had the crispest, clearest and most commercial voice. Despite this he was unable to achieve solo success.

"I guess every artist hopes that he will get a chance to have a solo album and I was happy about mine but I wish it had been promoted more."

The Politicians self-titled album got a release but more interestingly was the record industry's sudden interest in the Holland Dozier Holland back catalogue.

Over the next few months there was a flood of Holland Dozier Holland songs, either originals on the re-issue merry-go-round in England or in the

United States new recordings by Jackie Moore, "Darling Baby", Donny Elbert, "Where Did Our Love Go", "This Old Heart Of Mine" and "I Can't Help Myself", The Continental 4 "Heaven Must Have Sent You", Rueben Bell "Baby Love" and "Baby I Need Your Loving" by Geraldine Hunt. If only the record buyers had shown as much interest in Holland Dozier Holland's contemporary work.

While everybody was plundering the team's back catalogue, Invictus was hard at work on others with Ty Hunter releasing a carbon copy of Eddie Holman's classic "Hey There Lonely Girl" in May, the same month as fellow group member Scherrie Payne released her version of Honey Cone's "V.I.P.". Laura Lee's second album, "The Two Sides Of Laura Lee" hit the charts at the end of June 1972 and the covers continued with "Every Little Bit Hurts", "When A Man Loves A Woman", "At Last" and "Guess Who I Saw Today" appearing. Laura Lee was able to create her own designs into the existing fabric of these standards and interweave them with new material; one being her most recent single "Rip Off". Laura came up the idea of the two sides of Laura Lee because she could sing 'Chitlin' or ballads. "Rip Off" reached Number 5 on the Soul Chart, Lee continuing to prove the early doubters wrong once again and along the way becoming the company's most consistent artist both in terms of chart success and quality of material. Ironically, the very night she went into the studio to record that song someone broke into her home. This it happened on two occasions. She declared that the song was bad luck to her but loved singing it to people because of its popularity.

"Everybody's Got A Song To Sing" failed for the Chairmen as did the final single for the company by Parliament, the powerful "Come In Out Of The Rain" supplied by the writers Ruth Copeland and Clyde Wilson and as with the earlier "Breakdown" Wilson as Steve Mancha was the featured vocalist. What was also interesting was the fact that the ringmaster for the circus known as Parliament, George Clinton, wasn't on the session.

"George wasn't even there when we cut the track, sure he was there when we were mixing it but not when we cut it. I had three groups of musicians working on "Come In Out Of The Rain".

Steve Mancha

For the sentiments alone the track deserved to do better. Copeland's career was still on the up despite a lack of commercial success and she opened for David Bowie on his Ziggy Stardust US tour. Her personal life was changing though and having left Jeffrey Bowen she left the label and moved on to RCA where she released "Going Back To Baltimore" in 1976 before disappearing from the record industry forever. Parliament remained inactive until 1974 when Casablanca issued the "Up For The Down Stroke" set. Inactive is probably not the right word, though, because, as Funkadelic, the same band of players had released their self-title debut album and its follow up, "Free Your Mind And Your Ass Will Follow" in 1970, "Maggot Brain" in 1971, "America Eats Its Young" in 1972 and "Cosmic Slop" in 1973. With "Up For The Down Stroke" Clinton began to explore the more danceable side of his music; still remaining experimental but tighter with former James Brown sidekick Bootsy Collins coming in along with uncredited horn players who would turn out to be The JB horn section. The Casablanca debut set relied heavily on revivals of earlier Parliament material, "Testify", "The Goose", and "All Your Goodies Are Gone" but newer material such as the title track and "I Can Move You" showed the direction that Parliament would continue to go in well into the 80's and through to the Rapping generation of the 90's. This generation would sample Clinton's P-Funk, as it was tagged in 1976, mercilessly.

As July heated up, Honey Cone came through with the first release heralding their fourth and final set, "Love, Peace And Soul". "Sittin' On A Time Bomb" complete with sound effects and a stunning flipside, "It's Better To Have Loved And Lost" was pure unadulterated Detroit magic and if Holland Dozier's first single together as recording artists had failed, the second one hit the target. As with "Don't Leave Me" Lamont Dozier took the lead on "Why Can't We Be Lovers" leading it eventually to a top Forty position on the British Pop chart, a Number 12 position in the American Soul chart and, in doing so igniting a spark inside Dozier that would eventually lead him away from the Holland Brothers and onto a solo career. August saw Brian Holland and Lamont Dozier supply The Barrino Brothers with the most beautiful ballad "I Had It All". The song had everything from a first-class production, sympathetic strings adding to the overall pathos as the lead singer, Perry Barrino, half cried his way through the lyrics of love that was lost. Love wasn't the only thing lost as the record failed to chart. So why was even the new product failing? Sure, there was every reason for old album tracks to fail, if people had already bought the album but these were Holland Dozier Holland. Failure had never been a part of the equation.

They had tackled the Motown machine and won, at least partially. Had the ongoing battle with Gordy paid its toll? Had Gordy's pursuit of the team intentionally been set up to confuse their business plans? The Motown exodus was well and truly on with The Spinners firmly ensconced at Atlantic, The Four Tops due to sign for ABC/Dunhill, Martha Reeves ready to go solo with sister Louis joining Quiet Elegance down in Memphis and the company itself preparing to uproot the whole show and relocate to Los Angeles. Holland Dozier Holland should have gone for the killer punch, signed up the refugees as they had done before with great success and made Detroit their own. Instead, the product seemed to be weakening. Freda Payne had "Through The Memory Of My Mind", from 1969, released, 100 Proof followed "Everything Good Is Bad" with a carbon copy in "Don't Scratch Where It Don't Itch" and just like a carbon copy had some of the original's features but also lost something in the copying it too was a bit more faded, although it did feature Chairman Harrison Kennedy blowing a mean harmonica. Two new Clyde Wilson, aka Steve Mancha ballads graced the album and reminded us not just what an outstanding vocalist he was but what an incredible songwriter too and more the pity that other artists hadn't prospered from his input. "I Don't Care If I Never Get over You" and "Don't You Wake Me" were the epitome of Detroit Soul ballads with lyrics that were ever present in that dream world of lost love.

Laura Lee continued to show the way with her album at Number 6 and the new single, "If You Can Beat Me Rockin'" a Holland Dozier Holland composition, about to dent the chart with the additional treat of a non-album 'b' side, "If I'm Good Enough To Love, I'm Good Enough To Marry" courtesy of HDH as well. She would sing this live on stage and the audience would love it. Predating Millie Jackson's later output, Laura would stop in the middle of the song and rap to the female members of the audience about how tough she was with her man and asking that if anyone was 'badder' than her, then step up. Laura had a very personal relationship with her audience and some night the pimps would bring their girls in and she would take their point of view and tell the pimps how the girls wanted to be treated.

The Glass House tried again to assault the chart with "Thanks, I Needed That" but to no avail. Maybe we all took for granted that Holland Dozier Holland would be like one of their company's straplines, Forever Gold and that Invictus would simply grow from the seeds that Motown had planted in Detroit those many years earlier. If that were true, then maybe we overlooked the richness that propagated from within the Glass House and let it die. Honey Cone were more successful with their fourth and final album, "Love, Peace & Soul". England was about a release behind on every group when EMI chose to issue anything and The 8th Day could no longer be assured of a chart place even though their product was still sounding good. "I Gotta Get Home" was pure Holland Dozier Holland but didn't make it home. Their second album was interesting to say the least. A mixture of traditional Soul like the title and Melvin Davis' reworking of his own Mala recording "Faith" alongside such jazz workouts as "Cheba" written by Lyman Woodard but when Holland Dozier Holland moved to Los Angeles Melvin Davis stayed loyal to Detroit and formed his own Rock Mill label. On this label he recorded and wrote for himself under the abbreviated name of Mel Davis releasing "Double Or Nothin'" as well as Charisma's "Let Love In Your Life "in 1983.

After the explosive "Time Bomb" Honey Cone followed with the weak imitation of former glory "Innocent Til Proven Guilty" and the Chairmen followed the pattern with their "Let Me Down Easy" harking back to their very first release in sound. Harrison Kennedy, of the Chairmen, had his "Hypnotic Music" album issued in October and despite being a commercial failure it did contain some interesting material outside of the scattering of Chairmen cast-offs.

"They had this image of me as this wild child which was funny because I actually thought of myself quite differently."

Harrison Kennedy

I remember seeing the Chairmen Of The Board on Top Of The Pops, British Television's equivalent of American Bandstand, when Harrison Kennedy blew a mean harmonica on the track "Chairman Of The Board" and I was in awe at the enormity of his Afro and Harrison still has a photograph of himself outside Buckingham Palace with his hair being compared to a Guard's Busby. Kennedy had a voice like dry tinder waiting to ignite. A voice so brittle, nervous and yet powerful that at times you could feel that raw power just waiting to erupt. When it was unleashed his contribution to the Chairmen's repertoire was usually of the least commercial kind. Still, that also meant that it was often the more interesting. Kennedy was born in Hamilton, Ontario, Canada. His father was a black Sicilian while his mother was of Irish descent. Prior to leaving Canada, for Detroit, he had been across the border as a kid to buy beer and blues records in Buffalo but the Blues and booze trips were his only visits to the United States Of America. While at University, and Majoring in English, Kennedy was beginning to work with a thirteen-piece Rhythm and Blues band and one of the female singers was due to travel to Detroit to audition for Holland Dozier Holland.

It was during the summer vacation and so Harrison went along for the fun of it but was still intending on going back to University. When they arrived in Detroit the girl got the jitters. At this point the group was in a bar and to help them relax and get themselves together Kennedy asked if anyone had an acoustic guitar. Someone did and so Harrison Kennedy took to the stage and started singing songs to the owner's seven years' old daughter. By coincidence, Holland Dozier Holland were sitting silently watchful in the audience. After this non-eventful trip to the Motor City Harrison Kennedy returned to Canada determined to get some money together to go back to University when he received a phone call inviting him to join a group that Holland Dozier Holland were putting together. He refused at first, not wishing to become a member of a group or going into the music business in that way. He was more interested in concentrating on his schooling. A week later he received a second call and this time, with no job to support his schooling he accepted. He was invited down to Detroit but before joining the group he had never done any recording, never been in a studio. Everybody else had miles and miles of experience in the industry but he had always written poetry and protest songs but never thought about it in a commercial vein. The thought of his songs being a money-making possibility had never entered his head.

"When I got to Detroit it was entirely different to that. They were serious gentlemen deeply into the science of writing; the whole way of looking at it was a revelation to me."

Harrison Kennedy

It was at the suggestion of Eddie Holland that Harrison recorded his solo effort. Holland bought him an acoustic guitar and proposed that he write some new songs, protest songs, songs of significance that Holland knew Kennedy had always had an interest in.

"Edward Holland bought me a guitar and he said, "I know you've written some tunes I want you to do an album." It was fun, I just loved it because he was showing faith in me. It was wonderful, it was fun to have someone put faith in you in that way and I've never forgotten that. I've always been indebted to Edward Holland for that. I had everything here I had all the resources. I had good writers, I had the studio, it was great."

At the time Kennedy wanted the project to reflect the personal side of his music and so there was a mixture of Rock, Folk and Soul within the fabric. Holland also put Kennedy together with Lamont Dozier, to help him construct his songs.

"I was basically green, man, I felt like a baby, I had no idea what I was doing, I'd just get up in the morning and be there and do the best I could."

He was hanging out in Dearborne, outside of Detroit and asked a band there to play on his album. A lot of the tracks were done in one take and Kennedy felt that some of these should have remained as out takes but Holland said they were fine and had them released. Despite Kennedy's gratitude to Holland for giving him the opportunity there did still seem a suggestion that maybe some contractual obligation between Invictus and the distributor, Capitol had been fulfilled. Although the album was a commercial failure "Hypnotic Music" did contain some interesting material outside of the scattering of Chairmen tracks lifted from earlier group albums and in many ways was superior to the General's own offering. Harrison Kennedy's only single release was his version of the Honey Cone's album track "Sunday Morning People". Invictus tried twice with this song, firstly backed by "Up The Organization", a rousing harmonica blowing instrumental and secondly with The Beatles "Come Together", originally from the very first Chairmen Of The Board album. Kennedy showed a daring rarely seen in the majority of Invictus material with songs about the ecology in "You Hurt Your Mother Again" and homosexuality in "Closet Queen" showing a direction that Holland Dozier Holland would have been wise to exploit. Not only were these subjects taking Holland Dozier Holland out of the safety of the sanitised Motown sound but were treading the same ground as Marvin Gaye and Curtis Mayfield in their own personal musical revolutions. Harrison Kennedy was a talent that was sadly lost in all of the problems that eventually destroyed Invictus Records and should have been given more freedom to explore his own writing skills.

"I definitely could have contributed more given time ... I felt I was playing catch up with everyone in the band. You see, number one the band was getting comfortable with the writing and the living; I was still basically trying to learn to live in the United States. I was just getting comfortable with my life outside of the band, trying to struggle with that and trying to live in Detroit and I voiced that opinion. They said, "You've gotta get over it." I said, "I'm going to get over it but you've got to give me time, I'm re-adjusting my whole psyche here and I have, like, no time to do it; plus, I'm trying to be creative and it's tough to be creative when you're getting uptight."

Harrison Kennedy

The album was produced by the ever-reliable Ronald Dunbar. As time showed that things at Invictus were never going to get better Harrison Kennedy went the way of the anti-Vietnam draft board dodgers in escaping to Canada until the war was over. This war, however, was raging within Invictus and the board he was running from was The Chairmen. He laid low until his contract became null and void but unlike Danny Woods never returned to the Chairmen Of The Board. Another failed long player was The Glass House's final release, "Thanks, I Needed That".

In an attempt to explain why the labels weren't seeing the same chart action as had once gone without saying, General Johnson made a bizarre statement. He suggested that trends changed and that for the moment the Invictus sound was not what the public was rushing out to buy. He then went on to say that Brian Holland and Lamont Dozier had taken a rest for a while, too, as they were tired of setting all the trends and needed a break. Hence the emphasis had switched somewhere else for a while. He then went on to say that with the tremendous talent that they had that they would be back in front whenever they want to be. The statement seemed to suggest a certain amount of naiveté on the part of Holland Dozier Holland. If it was true, then it simply went to emphasise the poor management of the company. No business could afford to allow the opposition to take over for a while because its owners chose to rest.

Outside of Detroit where the city was in danger of losing its sound and in turn an integral part of Soul music, the sound that was about to dominate was coming from Philadelphia courtesy of Kenny Gamble and Leon Huff who's stable of stars was about to overshadow any one company from Detroit to as far south as Memphis where the Stax empire was finding financial difficulties too much to be able to continue. On the other hand, we had Gamble and Huff who were climbing slowly and becoming respected writers and producers on their way, also to becoming highly successful label owners. Their story began in 1965 when Leon Huff first worked with Kenny Gamble. Both had begun working in Philadelphia as songwriters, Leon also as a session pianist. After working on the same session, Candy & The Kisses "The 81" a carbon copy of the Motown sound of Martha & The Vandellas, the two started to talk and soon realised that they shared a common belief, that although they hadn't been treated poorly, as Holland Dozier Holland had always believed themselves to have been, their own potential could be better realised. By 1966 the duo decided to launch their own label, Excel and released The Intruders "Gonna Be Strong". Excel soon became the Gamble label, following in Berry Gordy's Motown footsteps naming the Gordy label after himself. Again, The Intruders supplied the label with its first release, "United". By 1968 Gamble & Huff were creating interest throughout the Soul world and it was now the turn of Detroit's neighbouring City, Illinois' Chicago to play a major role in their development.

The Soul scene in Chicago, Illinois was in full bloom long before Berry Gordy created his empire in Detroit. In fact, without the Chicago connection Motown could have been a different proposition. As well as being the adopted home of the acknowledged father of Soul, Sam Cooke, the Chess label of Chicago would be responsible for early distribution of Motown productions by amongst others, The Miracles, whilst native Detroiter,

Jackie Wilson more recognised as a product of Chicago Soul would give Gordy early success as a writer with "Reet Petite" (1957) and "Lonely Teardrops" (1958). Throughout their histories artists and producers had crossed the state line to create individual yet related sounds: a fourteen years' old Detroiter named Aretha Franklin recorded early tracks for Chess in 1956 and The Four Tops signed for the Chess Brothers prior to signing for Motown. Whilst Etta James, one of the stalwarts of Chess Records through original cuts like "I'd Rather Go Blind " had reached Number One in 1960 with "All I Could Do Was Cry " written by Berry Gordy along with his sister Gwen and Billy Davis. VeeJay, owned by Ewart Abner who would later become President of Motown, was fundamental in forming the ever-growing Soul scene and the label was home to The Impressions who boasted Curtis Mayfield and Jerry Butler amongst its members who, again, would serve the City well. Sadly, VeeJay slid into bankruptcy in 1965 but there was still an important player to emerge from the Windy City the Okeh label.

Like VeeJay before it Okeh was not simply a Soul label but was responsible for many classic Soul sides. Behind the success of Okeh was one man who may have been without the muscle of Berry Gordy but who would remain from the earliest stages in Chicago Soul's development until the curtain came down on its sound, Carl Davis. Davis was offered an A&R job at Columbia Records after it became common knowledge that he had been the uncredited producer of Gene Chandler's 1962 smash "Duke Of Earl" for VeeJay. At Columbia he took over the creative handling of one of the recording industry's oldest labels, Okeh; a dormant label previously regarded as a 'Race music' label but soon to reach legendary status. Ignoring the fact that Davis had failed to sign The Jackson Five, Kenny Gamble (who would later team up with Leon Huff to conceive The Philly Sound after Chicago's Chess label agreed to distribute a new Gamble & Huff label, Neptune) and the team of Isaac Hayes and David Porter (who would find fame at Stax) Davis was able to sign many young artists to keep his reputation intact. Political changes within Columbia meant that the new, improved Okeh label sank at a time when it should have sailed along smoothly. Okeh's allegiance was shifted within the Columbia Corporation and Davis's new team leader didn't share his vision, consequently Davis resigned and created his own production company, DAKAR. Davis planned to create a Chicago sound on par with Gordy's Motown intending to develop a Curtis Mayfield, Johnny Pate (noted arranger) Carl Davis Sound. You only have to take a listen to the Holland Dozier Holland influenced "You've Been Cheatin'" by The Impressions in 1965 to get a feel of what might have been.

The year 1968 saw the death of Leonard Chess affecting the whole Chess empire. During its short life Gamble & Huff's Neptune did connect The Three Degrees and The O'Jays to the duo and of all the groups the two worked with The O'Jays arguably remain the most prolific and synonymous with them. With Gamble & Huff, The O'Jays had an astounding run of hits beginning in 1972 with "Backstabbers" and culminating with three Gold singles, five Gold Albums, two Platinum singles and four Platinum albums. The individual artist who benefited most from the creative team was Chicago's adopted son Jerry Butler. Gamble & Huff became a trio with respected Philly arranger/producer/writer Thom Bell joining the team. Bell was already making waves doing creative chores for Philadelphia's premiere group The Delfonics and would work in and out of the G&H company throughout the '70's with The Stylistics and the aforementioned Spinners, fresh from Motown reaping the greatest rewards from the alliance. In the Blues & Soul Poll for 1972 the previous years' accolades went to Gamble & Huff. They topped both the Top Composer and Top Producer lists whilst their composition "If You Don't Know Me By Now" was voted top single. After more outside work that involved giving a new lease of life to some established artists, Wilson Pickett and Joe Simon, the team made perhaps the biggest decision of their creative life.

In 1971 they proudly announced the birth of Philadelphia International. Having failed to get picked up by Columbia in the 60's Kenny Gamble, now with partner Leon Huff, approached the huge corporation who were beginning to see black music as a lucrative market. The duo themselves believed that if they were to progress then they too had to go with the big company. The Ebonys "You're The Reason Why" became the label's first relatively modest hit but the next two years would show Gamble & Huff's faith in themselves and in their growing roster of stars and supporting musicians paying dividends. The O'Jays struck Gold with "Backstabbers "and "Love Train" in 1972, the same year that Harold Melvin & The Bluenotes unleashed both the monstrously deep "I Miss You" and "If You Don't Know Me By Now" coupled with the monster voice of Teddy Pendegrass as lead singer. Along with these acknowledged classics Billy Paul's "Me & Mrs Jones" was destined to be a part of this vintage period closing 1972 on a high note and an even higher chart position.

Another new group for Hot Wax, Satisfaction Unlimited, was due to have a single released called "Bright City Lights" but it was never issued. Outside of the rumours that Dionne Warwick was recording in Detroit with Holland Dozier Holland and that another mellow offering from 100 Proof, "Nothing Sweeter Than Love" was surfacing Soul was dominated by Philadelphia and the final Holland-Dozier single for '72 sounded more like a plea to the punters than anything else, "Don't Leave Me Starvin'". If 1972 was the beginning of 'The Philly Sound' taking off, then 1973 and 1974 consolidated Gamble & Huff's position at the top. Again, they took top writing and producing honours for 1973 with The O'Jays receiving 5th and 8th top album awards. Three out of the top six singles were Philly cuts. In the same interview that heard General Johnson defending and trying to rationalise Holland Dozier Holland business dealings and suggesting that they were simply 'resting' he was also quick to deny any truth to the rumours that Holland Dozier Holland were returning to Motown and pointed out that they were working on more projects for Invictus than ever before with Freda Payne having returned to the fold. On the suggestion of whether Holland -Dozier would be seen on stage following the success of "Why Can't We Be Lovers" he said that there was only Lamont Dozier on the record and that he might do it. Prophetic words indeed.

At the beginning of 1973, the only artist doing anything chart wise for Holland Dozier Holland was Laura Lee. On Music Merchant Smith Connection appeared with an album of pleasant ballads, "Under My Wings" mostly written by Ronald Dunbar with group leader Michael Smith. From the album came "I've Been A Winner", more subliminal messages from Holland Dozier Holland. The second album by The 8th Day, "I've Gotta Get Home" and "Livin' High Off The Goodness Of Your Love" by The Barrino Brothers made no impression whatsoever and "Don't Leave Me Starvin'" failed to emulate its predecessor for Holland-Dozier, this time the lead singer had been Brian Holland. Light years behind, EMI in England issued a double delight with "Wedlock Is A Padlock" and "Since I Fell For You", her first ever Hot Wax single coupled with her most successful. Sadly, the pulse was long gone for the company and "The Best Of Laura Lee" was issued in March along with the final Honey Cone release. The group that had previously reached the dizzy heights fell to earth when "If I Can't Fly" failed to take off. The three girls who had been so important to Holland Dozier Holland returned to their background work while Gamble & Huff's Three Degrees out of Philadelphia took up the girl group mantel for a while. The vitality that seemed boundless in Philly could not be matched in a City that had lost its heart.

Despite the one non-single release, in 1973 Holland Dozier Holland gambled on a relatively unknown group, one that had not had a single release on which to mount an album attack releasing "Think Of The Children" by Satisfaction Unlimited on Hot Wax. This would prove to be the final album to be issued by the failing label but just like the label's Silent Majority before them Satisfaction Unlimited were no newcomers to the music industry. The group had started life as The Marvels in 1954 in the 12th and Potomac section of Washington DC. The group consisted of Sam Gilbert (lead), James "Junior" Isom (second tenor), Ronald Boyd

143

(baritone), and James Mitchell (bass). Washington, like many other cities in America had a wealth of street corner groups but no major labels at this time so groups migrated to other places in search of fame, fortune and a recording contract. In the late spring of '58, the Marvels set their sights on New York and struck a deal first time, signing to Gene Schwartz's Laurie records with July's "I Shed So Many Tears" backed by "So Young, So Sweet" being released.

Despite a promising start the single failed and the group was three years without another record. When the initial record did nothing, they abandoned recording for those three years and returned to DC to play live gigs. In September 1961 they went back into the recording studio, this time for John Dickerson's Winn label in Washington. This was to cut a remake of the Brown Dots' "For Sentimental Reasons". By this time, they faced group name competition from the Mar-Vels, the Marvelettes and the Marvellos and so took a new name, The Senators, named after the local major league baseball franchise. Winn went on to release "Wedding Bells" in April 1962, but again the single failed to give the guys the break they so desperately craved and so with morale reaching a low they disbanded with James Isom joined up with another Winn act, The Gales. This venture only lasted a month before he joined The Satisfactions. In September 1966, the group released "Give Me Your Love". Despite, yet another failed attempt at recording success the group did begin to pick up more work on the strength of it and they found themselves travelling to Ohio, Toronto and Montreal. In June of 1967 "Take It Or Leave It" was released on Smash, followed by November's "Use Me". Conway Twitty's studios in Oklahoma in 1970 found The Satisfactions recording material which was released on the Lionel label run by Dallas Smith and former Motown songwriter Jimmy Webb and distributed by MGM Records. The Satisfactions first single was also the first release for the label: "This Bitter Earth" backed by their version of the standard "Ol' Man River" released in May 1970. This was the breakthrough they had longed for, reaching Number 36 on the R&B Charts. Lionel followed this with "One Light Two Lights" in August. "One Light Two Lights" fared even better than its predecessor and reached Number 21 on the R&B charts. Their last Lionel single was "God, I'm Losing My Baby" issued in February of '71.

After this they extended the name to Satisfaction Unlimited, a year later signing to Hot Wax. The group now consisted of Lorenzo Hines (lead tenor), James Isom (second tenor), Earl Jones (baritone) and Fletcher Lee (bass) with production by Winford "Johnny" Terry, who co-wrote all the tracks on a solid album. The album opened with the planned single, "Bright City Lights" with Lorenzo Hines singing lead. The track was a departure for the label sound wise and should have been not just a single but a hit single. Sparse instrumentation allowed the warm, summer feel to shine through. "I Know It's Love" followed, giving Lorenzo Hines the opportunity to share lead vocals with James Isom while the rest of the group augmented the sound with polished group harmonies. Track 3, "Spread Your Love Around" was almost funky but held back enough to let the strong lyrics have their say. This made way for "Let's Change The Subject", again, as with all the tracks it was the lyrics that were clearly defined and, in this case verging on comedic. That wasn't to say that it wasn't a strong track and again the vocal interplay helped to make the playful lyrics come to life. Then came the heart wrenching title track.

Again, as with all the production by Winford Terry the instrumentation was stripped to a minimum so that the song of separation hit hard. "Think Of The Children" had the husband pleading with his wife to think about the devastating affect her departure would have on their kids. "Time For Us" opened side two in high spirits with the funkier "Somebody Else's Woman" showing a harder edge than some of the other songs. "Why" composed by Raynel Wynglass and Winford Terry returned to the same composers' playful lyrics as heard on "Let's Change The Subject" before the rhythmical "Seeing You Through The Eyes Of A Blind Man" once again had the group sparring with the backing track. "Don't Call Me, I'll Call You" had almost a Parliament groove and was more Pop than Soul while the final track, "Come on Back" closed the set in an upbeat groove. It had to be said though that none of the faster tracks were aimed at the dance floor as earlier Invictus, Hot Wax or Music Merchant material had been which is possibly why there were no more singles pulled from the album. This was no lightweight album. It was a labour of love; intelligently executed and one that has been a sleeper for far too long.

There had been a definite maturing of style surfacing within the HDH organisation, seen in later work by Honey Cone and 100 Proof but time was running out. Cecil Holmes, Vice President of Buddha Records, Hot Wax's USA distributors had previously stated that Hot Wax was a bit quiet but promised that they would be back. Around 1971 Hot Wax had begun to default on payments to CBS and the money owed was becoming a substantial amount. The label's financial state was partly due to Buddha failing to pay Hot Wax money owed to them, thus causing a domino effect.

That year, Buddha was authorised to pay the money owed by Hot Wax directly to CBS with Buddha taking on the responsibility for future pressing costs. A letter from CBS was sent to Hot Wax stating this but Buddha Records went belly up and Holland Dozier Holland were left with only one national distributor, Capitol and although hit singles kept coming, album sales through the Capitol distribution system were disappointing. Record companies made the majority of their profits through albums, not singles.

Holland Dozier Holland began feeling that Capitol would never get the kind of album sales that they knew were possible with their black artists. The team knew that they would never have a completely successful record company unless something was done to get better album sales; "Think Of The Children" should have been such an album.

April promised a new lease of life when Invictus switched distribution from Capitol to CBS, the major company behind Gamble & Huff's growing Philadelphia empire. They had previously gone with two different national companies so that they could not be exclusively under the control of any one company. Then Clive Davis called.

Clive Davis was the CEO of CBS Records (Columbia/Epic labels) and was now the biggest major record company in the world and wanted to make its mark in the black music segment of the industry. Because it didn't have the in-house staff to create this type of music, they wanted associations with independent black labels. CBS told Holland Dozier Holland that they could, with their superior distribution, sell three to four times the records that Capitol could. After switching to CBS with 100 Proof's "My Piece Of The Rock, with a new line-up, being the first Hot Wax issued single through CBS, the problems really intensified. Report of records doing well on radio but without product in the stores began to surface. Sales dropped for albums and even for the main product of Holland Dozier Holland, the hit singles. CBS had not only gone after distribution of Holland Dozier Holland product but the distribution of every major black independent record label and once critical deals were made, all of the black labels being distributed by CBS suffered from reduced sales. CBS began to offer the black artists on those labels new deals to have the artists abandon their independent label and contract directly with CBS as artists. The same type of argument was used to convince the artists to switch.

"You can sell more records through us." When the Jackson Five and Michael Jackson switched from the Motown Label to the CBS Epic Label in 1975, the "raiding" was all but complete. The Jackson Five announced their departure from Motown but because of legal restrictions they would be known simply as The Jacksons from then on.

Although there was an element of truth in this political manoeuvring there was one other difference. Freshness. The vitality that seemed boundless in Philly could not be matched in a City that was on its knees. Detroit had seen its lifeblood sucked out of it, an ailing car industry, the abandonment of Berry Gordy Jr and Motown to LA. Even the 1967 riot was still showing the scars.

"It really did sound the death knell. People were still just as active but, you know, no sales, no promotion."

Steve Mancha

Despite all of this there still seemed hope. New albums were announced on Holland-Dozier entitled "The Pen Is Mightier Than The Sword", Freda Payne and the Chairmen Of The Board along with singles from the Chairmen and General Johnson whilst Hot Wax had Laura Lee's latest single to survive on for a little longer, "Remember Me", a Holland Dozier Holland composition that for once was not an album track. Greg Perry had done his last work for the company and Jeffery Bowen was about to take over the vacant space as Johnson's writing and producing partner. Although he had not officially worked for the label prior to this he had been responsible for the early Parliament productions while still contracted to Motown where he had debuted with The Temptations "In A Mellow Mood" set. The new Johnson / Bowen material was "Finders Keepers" by the Chairmen Of The Board and "Only Time Will Tell" by General Johnson. Both, though, were somewhat derivative of current trends. In the case of "Finders Keepers" Bowen was developing a Stevie Wonder "Superstition" type groove, whereas "Only Time Will Tell" was picked from Willie Mitchell's Al Green production draw.

Again, another new Chairmen track, "Let's Have Some Fun" was an Isley Brothers style tune thrown in for good measure, none of which suited the General. He felt that Jeffrey Bowen was in love with Parliament-Funkadelic and Sly & The Family Stone. He had Billy Bass Nelson, Bernie Worrell, Tiki Fullwood and Eddie Hazel on the tracks but to Johnson it was like when Phillipe Wynne from the [Detroit] Spinners joined Funkadelic, it didn't work. That was how he felt about "Skin I'm In." He remembered when the Chairmen Of The Board played with Funkadelic backing them and felt that the experience was horrible. Horrible as it may have seemed to the General the album has remained as the most sought-after Chairmen record and could have so easily heralded a new direction for Holland Dozier Holland, if producer Jeffrey Bowen had had his way. The epic "White Rose / Life And Death" and the single "Everybody Party All Night", with its Jimi Hendrix style intro were worth the price of the album but then you had the politically charged title track and two outstanding ballads.

In 1970 Bootsy Collins moved to Detroit where Mallia Franklin, a friend of George Clinton, decided after seeing his group The House Guests that they should hook up with the similar Funkadelic who were seemingly running neck and neck in the acid test. The two bands had kept missing each other, every gig The House Guests went to Funkadelic had just left but finally Mallia Franklin who literally had the group as house guests at her mother's place took Bootsy over to Clinton's house. The lightning struck and a friendship was forged. The House Guests joined Funkadelic as musicians with Phillipe Wynne, their lead singer choosing to take up The Spinners offer to become their lead vocalist. Musically, creatively and historically both parties made the correct decision for themselves at that moment. Wynne would later reunite with Bootsy under the flag of Uncle Jam taking up the role of 'Thrill Instructor' as well as cutting a solo album for Clinton's Uncle Jam label under the guidance of Ronald Dunbar. Bootsy Collins' first creative input in the camp appeared on Funkadelic's "America Eats Its Young" album in 1972 when material he had prepared during his House Guests period began to filter into the equally experimental work of Clinton. However, one year later the threesome chose to break away from the madness that was Clinton's world to become The Complete Strangers back in Cincinnati. The non-stop touring with a crazy, drug taking band of musicians who had outfreaked them saw them heading towards a collective mental and physical collapse. George Clinton had been long gone from Holland Dozier Holland's Invictus label and had established Parliament at Neil Bogart's Casablanca label. Meanwhile Bootsy was sitting in Holland Dozier Holland's Invictus Records office waiting for a major deal. Bootsy's Early Sun, as the group was to be christened originally, had their demo material ready to go. 'I'd Rather Be With You' and 'Together', originally entitled 'Together In Heaven', a track that was recut by Parliament (1975) for their Chocolate City set, were among the tracks up for grabs.

There had always existed a rivalry between Jeffrey Bowen and George Clinton and now he was helping the embryonic group put things together with a view to signing for Holland Dozier Holland. He wasn't prepared to play the rotating label games that his own group had had to endure back in the 60's. By now, Holland Dozier Holland had moved to Los Angeles where Bowen and Bootsy were staying when Clinton got wind of what was happening. He stepped up his interest, got Bootsy to come to Detroit with his demos and a star was born. Bootsy came bouncing back the following year, though, initially as a session musician and songwriter, appearing on Parliament's initial outing on Casablanca, "Up For The Down Stroke", performing and co-writing the title track. From now on Bootsy and Clinton would remain creatively inseparable as P-Funk in the form of Parliament / Funkadelic / Fred Wesley & The Horny Horns / Parlet / The Brides Of Funkenstein and last but most definitely not least the newly named Bootsy's Rubber Band prepared to take the musical world by storm. For next to the main body of Parliament and Funkadelic, or the Parliafunkadelicment Thang, it would be Bootsy and his Rubber Band who would shine the brightest in the Funk Galaxy. Holland Dozier Holland had lost out.

148

On Music Merchant Eloise Laws' second release was failing despite gaining a strong following on the Northern Soul scene in England. The far stronger mix of "Rip Off" was replaced for the British buyer by the album mix and Freda Payne was on a British tour. A lukewarm affair that, despite having the legendary Earl Van Dyke as musical director and pianist, was aimed at cabaret audiences instead of hard-core soul followers. A new album "Reaching Out" was imminent but had been held up because of the previous contractual problems and also because of the Dionne Warwick set on Warner Brothers, "Just Being Myself". Diplomatically Freda Payne played down the fact that some of the material for the Warwick set was probably intended for her. Warwick herself was less than enthusiastic about the product and working with Holland Dozier Holland was different to what she was used to and was like a whole new thing to her. Warwick was not personally satisfied with the finished product, or her own part in it. What she felt let the project down was not having the right amount of time to do a great job. She also felt that the material was good for the Invictus artists but just wasn't right for her.

The Chairmen Of The Board's Greatest Hits was released in England with the inclusion of the never UK released "Let Me Down Easy" and the relatively poor sales for Honey Cone's "Love, Peace & Soul" set suggested that the Holland Dozier Holland sound was beginning to wane. "Finders Keepers", the latest record from the Chairmen was at Number 9 in the Soul Chart and Holland-Dozier saw their fourth release living up to its name as "Slipping Away" went from Number 93 to 96 up to 58 and down to 64. Outside productions brought in Lee Charles from Chicago, who had previously recorded for Gene Chandler's Bamboo label, Brunswick and most successfully Revue on which he had reached Number 41 in the Soul Chart of 1968 with "Standing On The Outside". On Hot Wax he had his second biggest success with the Jerry Butler style "I Just Want To Be Loved" with an arrangement by the legendary Tom Tom. Despite being a mellow, soul ballad it was a complete outside hope and as such didn't give the company anything other than a minor hit and Lee Charles almost another bite of the cherry.

Before we knew it August was upon us, the month of great change. Holland Dozier Holland scored the soundtrack to "Motown 9000" through Motown with Laura Lee contributing the title track but the project never saw the light of day and the final Smith Connection release on Music Merchant, "I'm Bugging Your Phone" was a "Finders Keepers" cum "Superstition" cash-in and as such failed to score. Holland Dozier quickly followed their "Slipping Away" with "New Breed Kinda Woman" fronted by Lamont Dozier. If Michael Smith was fading out of the picture with Smith Connection on Music Merchant his writing chores with Ronald

Dunbar were proving successful as Laura Lee continued her streak of singles success with another non-album recording, the ballad, "I'll Catch You When You Fall" backed by "I Can't Hold On Much Longer" originally cut by the aforementioned Smith Connection. New material appeared from Freda Payne but "Two Wrongs Don't Make A Right" was out of time and so added to the growing list of failures. Then came the dramatic announcement that ABC had signed Lamont Dozier.

The Holland Brothers sued ABC over the allegation but the headlines were true. The Chairmen Of The Board were over in England for another tour while America overlooked the superb "Born On The Wild" by the underrated Barrino Brothers produced by Ronald Dunbar and composed by Dunbar alongside Michael Smith. They faded into obscurity soon after. CBS took over European handling of the Invictus label whilst one of the funkiest tracks ever to come out of the company, "Everybody Party All Night" by the Chairmen. Raynel Wynglas's "Bar-B-Q-Ribs was failing on Music Merchant. In September, the label folded with Eloise Laws being retained and moving across to the main Invictus label. EMI's final releases were "Everybody's Tippin'" by Danny Woods, a re-issue of "Band Of Gold" and 100 Proof's handling of "Never My Love".

Back in The States "Reaching Out", Freda Payne's final set was issued at long last but paled in comparison to "Contact". Having been sued as well as suing HDH over a failure to pay her for work done on Invictus Freda Payne had relented and agreed to what would be her final offering for the trio. Most of the material was supplied by Ronald Dunbar and Michael Smith along with three Holland Dozier Holland compositions and two cabaret numbers. "Mother Misery's Favourite Child" was the most creative track courtesy of Holland Dozier Holland. Payne herself considered it a stronger set than its predecessor but was quick to point out that a lot more love had gone into "Contact". The musical arrangements had become dull and obvious, played by numbers. The sparkle that was so obvious in Contact had faded. Even the track, "Right Back Where I Started From" lifted its opening bars directly from "Someday We'll Be Together", Diana Ross's farewell song to The Supremes whilst the verse echoed "I Can't Help Myself".

In the USA Holland Dozier's final single was the Brian Holland led warning "I'm Gonna Hijack Ya, Kidnap Ya, Take What I Want". Despite being one of their strongest releases it too failed. On ABC Lamont Dozier had his first solo single, "Trying To Hold On To My Woman" written and produced by McKinley Jackson formerly of The Politicians and main arranger for Invictus. The album "Out Here On My Own" was soon to follow. All the tracks were co-written by Jackson but remarkably no Lamont Dozier compositions were on show. Tony Newton was on bass alongside many respected Detroit session men. The sound of Invictus/Hot Wax was being kept alive even if the labels themselves had all but died. Basically 1973 was the year that the legend of Invictus and Hot Wax came to an end along with the collective names of Holland Dozier Holland, with most of the people who had made the company what it was either trying to leave or already succeeding in doing so. He felt that more and more of his time was needed in the office, behind a desk. It got so he didn't see a recording studio from one week to the next and had always wanted to stay close to the music, to write, produce, be involved, but a lot more of his time now went into administration. Their company employed staff producers and composers and bit by bit he became less physically involved. Although the company was doing well he began to feel that the team of Holland Dozier Holland had run the gamut and he started to think that it would be a good thing to make a move back to recording himself as an artist. Ever since The Romeos he had always been something of a frustrated singer and after the success of "Why Can't We Be Lovers", the idea was firmly planted in his head that he wanted to move out in that direction again. It was difficult to pinpoint the exact reason why he had to split from Brian and Eddie. One thing he felt was that when you team up with brothers they stay very close together.

General Johnson was less than diplomatic. He felt that Invictus had fallen to pieces and that if the situation had been resolved that Harrison would be back in the group. He wasn't out of the group but was suffering from frustration. The group was in litigation with the label and they were not recording. In fact, Johnson admitted that they hadn't recorded in over two years and suggested that their last album "Skin I'm In" was just some unreleased tapes that the company had stored away. He also added that when people were treated properly that they don't drift away, According to General Johnson there was only Eddie and Brian Holland left and that everyone else had gone or were trying to leave. The Chairmen had recorded their last session for them. Despite this bitterness he conceded that it was sad because he believed in what they were doing but in his mind the concept at Invictus was simple, two hit singles and clean out the can with whatever is there and you've got an album. There was some truth in that statement but there had been some magnificent stand-alone albums that came first. Maybe then they were milked for as many singles as possible. This wasn't just common to Holland Dozier Holland though, when The Stylistics debut album arrived from Philadelphia, every track would eventually end up as an 'a' side or 'b' side of a single.

Laura Lee was out of contract and Eddie Holland made a personal visit to her home to ask her to come back so she returned to cut her third and final album, "I Can't Make It Alone. She found herself switched to Invictus as Hot Wax had 'temporarily retired' but there was talk that Motown was close to making a distribution deal for the label, about a decade too late. Music Merchant was also rumoured to be signed to a distribution deal with another major company. Neither happened and in April 1974 Hot Wax was officially closed and Laura Lee's first Invictus single was released. "I Need It Just As Bad As You" was written by Holland, Holland and Wylie. Richard 'Popcorn' Wylie had been a longstanding Detroit singer/writer/producer label owner, Soul Hawk, and may have been the injection needed by Holland and Holland after the departure of Lamont Dozier. Unfortunately, the magic didn't work this time around although the record was up to Laura Lee's expected excellence. Her final album for the company, "I Can't Make It Alone" failed to reach the same heights as its predecessors, despite Lee's stunning handling of the tracks. One problem was the inclusion of previous tracks, "Crumbs Off The Table" and "Every Little Bit Hurts" from "Two Sides Of Laura Lee" plus three tracks that had already sold well as singles. The new tracks came courtesy of Holland and Holland with the title track and "We've Come Too Far To Walk Away" reflecting the mood of the day. Lee cut the Barbara Streisand vehicle "The Way We Were" in her own inimitable style for the album but sadly it was not included and instead remains a lost masterpiece.

At the height of her success with Hot Wax, the City of Detroit designated July the 20th 1974 as "Laura Lee Day" and 36,000 people turned out to a festival on the riverfront to celebrate. Lee Charles fared worse after "Love Ain't Gonna Run Away" had failed to be issued on Hot Wax and he was moved to Invictus. His only Invictus release was the unexploded "Sittin' On A Timebomb" and a man who had had underground praise heaped on him faded from the scene. The 'b' side was an instrumental version of the 8th Day's "Eeny-Meeny-Miny-Mo" produced by Ronald Dunbar under the title "Get Your House In Order". Whose house and what was he trying to say?

With the collapse of the Holland Dozier Holland labels, Dunbar turned to independent production projects including Betty LaVette's Invictus sounding "You're A Man Of Words, I'm A Woman Of Action" on Epic in 1975 and three sides for ABC records on Ruby Andrews between 1976 to 1977, "I Don't Know How To Love You", "Little Fixin' Up" and "I Wanna Be Near You". In 1978 he joined forces with George Clinton working primarily with the female groups attached to P-Funk. George Clinton had wanted General Johnson to join up with him but he had declined. Instead, he suggested Ronald Dunbar who went on to have a successful run within the P-Funk organisation. For The Brides Of Funkenstein he wrote "When You're Gone" in 1978 that would have suited Honey Cone down to the ground while "Never Buy Texas From A Cowboy" was pure P-Funk

152

indulgence. Bruce Nazarian of The 8th Day played guitar on this album incidentally. With George Clinton's Uncle Jam Records, he again became the A&R director, co-ordinating the 150 hours of production done each week by George & company for two years until the label folded in 1980. When George Clinton chose to issue five volumes of never before released material, more Ronald Dunbar productions and compositions for The Brides came to light as well as "To Care" by The Four Tops. Staying momentarily with the Four Tops Lamont Dozier was also reunited with them in 1974 with their ABC single "Midnight Flower". Ronald Dunbar also co-produced Parlet and when Clinton created his own Uncle Jam label in 1980 it appeared as though Detroit Soul was going to survive with Ronald Dunbar on staff. Sadly, the label died a death after three album releases. The same year Tony Hester's brilliant career ended abruptly when he was robbed and gunned down on the streets of Detroit. Hester was a drug addict, which is ironic, since he wrote two anti-dope songs for The Dramatics, "The Devil Is Dope" and "Beware of the Man With the Candy in His Hands."

Laura Lee's final single for the label was sadly her weakest. Her handling of Holland Dozier's "Don't Leave Me Starving For Your Love" was a poor finale for a singer of such class and ability. Laura Lee finally left the company around 1974 but label mate Greg Perry was soon on the phone. Although they didn't work much together at Hot Wax they were friends. He called her and said that he had written a tune for her, so she flew out to California because there was the chance of a deal with Ariola. They waited outside the president of Ariola's office and as she decided that she'd had enough and was heading for the door they were playing "Love's Got Me Tired". The president stopped her, said he wanted the record and signed them up. She recorded several tracks with Greg Perry at Ike and Tina Turner's studio while Greg and Ike put the musicians together. The only tracks released were "Love's Barking Up The Wrong Tree" and "Love's Got Me Tired" and in 1976 she moved to Fantasy and then returned to Church. Her former Beau, The Reverend Al Green, benefited from Laura Lee's mighty lungs on their rendition of Curtis Mayfield's "People Get Ready" on his "Higher Plane" set and in 1983 she had "Jesus Is The Light Of My Life" released on Myrrh Records, with co-production honours going to Al Green. Laura Lee preferred to remain within the Church and in 1985 released "All Power" on Circle City Records.

In May, the company's other leading lady Freda Payne signed to ABC where she had once recorded prior to her Holland Dozier Holland days with her debut set "Payne And Pleasure" being released at the latter end of the year. As with Lamont Dozier production went to McKinley Jackson but sadly the album continued Payne's inability to regain the glory she had found at the beginning of her Invictus days. After a lack of success, she moved to Capitol in 1976, where she reunited with Tony Camillo who had worked with her way back on her debut Invictus set. Taking up a career in acting Payne appeared on television shows like "Police Story" before returning to recording in 1982 for the Sutra label. In 1986 two versions of "Band Of Gold" emerged by Bonnie Tyler and Belinda Carlisle: Freda sang harmony on Carlisle's version.

Despite having not recorded any new material the Chairmen Of The Board followed "Finders Keepers" with "Let's Have Some Fun" and "Everybody Party All Night Long" before the "Skin I'm In" album was issued in December 1974 long after the group had left the company. Described by Black Music magazine as one of the best albums of the year the set was certainly an unexpected delight after General Johnson had described it as old tracks thrown together or "a trampled flower". Bowen continued to show his eclectic nature in these tracks combining the musicianship of Funkadelic's Billy 'Bass' Nelson, Tiki Fullwood on drums, Eddie Hazel on guitar and Bernie Worrell on keyboards alongside Donald Baldwin giving a harder edge to the up-tempo material. Johnson's handling of the ballads, "Love At First Sight" one of the most climactic ballads you could ever wish to experience and "Only Love Can Break A Heart", a Bacharach and David composition complimented the up-tempo tracks perfectly. "Only Love Can Break A Heart" once again saw Johnson entrenched in Al Green territory. Green's definitive re-working of the Bee Gees "How Can You Mend A Broken Heart" 1971, being the perfect partner to this. Even the rap in the Chairmen track tells us that the singer is 'tired of being alone'. The partnership between Johnson and Bowen was most definitely different than his earlier coupling with Greg Perry,

"Well, Jeffrey came in when the label was going out of business. He was trying to do something constructive but was taking the Chairmen into a different direction. We'd cut the tracks and then he'd start adding synthesisers to it. We'd just look and think, what! Synthesisers!"

General Johnson

Brian Holland released the first of his two solo efforts "I'm So Glad" with moderate success and would later re-work the song with Junior Walker & The All-Stars upon the Holland Brothers return to Motown. New names appeared but Natural High, Tyrone Edwards, Earl English and The Hi-Lites never got beyond initial releases. That wasn't to say that the material wasn't good enough. Natural High's "Bump Your Lady" was as infectious a record as you could hope to hear and was every bit as good as other group's around during this golden period of funk but maybe there were too many 'Bump' records around. "Can't Get Enough", the one release by Tyrone Edwards was a rousing piece of Invictus magic which was rumoured to be none other than Edward Holland himself. The 'b' side had appeared earlier as the 'b' side of "I'm Gonna Hijack Ya" by Holland Dozier but this was a different arrangement and vocal performance. Little was known about the outside-produced "Wanting You" by Earl English except that the critics enjoyed it but the public didn't. "That's Love", the single release by The Hi-Lites was written by Keith Barrow best remembered for his Top 30 hit, "You Know You Wanna Be Loved." Born in Chicago on September the 27th 1954, he was dead at 29 through complications brought on by the AIDS virus. Barrow was the only son of civil rights and human activist, Rev. Willie T. Barrow of the Rev. Jesse Jackson led Operation Push organization. Barrow signed to CBS records in 1978, where he worked with producer Michael Stokes but in 1974 his magic touch should have given The Hi-Lites a hit.

Lamont Dozier sued the Holland Brothers for money he claimed they owed him from the Invictus days while America prepared for the release of his second album "Black Bach" in May of 1975. Outside of the single "Let Me Start Tonite" most observers felt that the stronger set was the one that Invictus released in an attempt to garner sales on the strength of Dozier's newfound solo popularity. "Love And Beauty" was tagged "The New Lamont Dozier Album" when in fact it was simply the Dozier led Holland-Dozier tracks plus two unreleased numbers. It was "Black Bach" that reached the chart.

Invictus counter-attacked just as Holland Dozier Holland had done to Motown back in 1968, suing ABC for conspiracy to drive it out of business by enticing its producers, writers and artists away.

Although the fact remained that Dozier, McKinley Jackson, Freda Payne, Tony Newton and Angelo Bond were all doing work for ABC the case was deemed not to be strong enough. It seemed ironic that the one thing that had pushed Holland Dozier Holland away from the clutches of Motown was now blowing their own empire apart, money owed. Artists such as Freda Payne, Melvin Davis and Steve Mancha who had contributed so much to Holland Dozier Holland's post-Motown successes never saw their just rewards.

"It was a big thing, people were suing each other, everybody was getting suspicious of everybody else ... back in those days that was the climate. Artists didn't know anything and they weren't allowed to use their own lawyers. I don't think anybody did any good except Holland Dozier Holland."

Steve Mancha

Outside of an attempt in 1976/77 to rebuild the Invictus/Hot Wax labels with newly formed Chairmen releasing "You've Got Extra Added Power In Your Love" lead by Prince Harold nothing happened. Holland Dozier Holland had gambled that the name of the Chairmen could do better business than the relatively unknown Prince Harold, a name that almost implied a snub to the General. As Harold Beatty he had recorded for Mercury back in 1966 releasing "Forget About Me". Prince Harold would figure prominently in future Holland-Holland developments in much the same way as General Johnson had, by writing and producing other acts in the new stable but not to the same degree of success. The company had relocated to Los Angeles just like Motown had done and in so doing given many artists a tough choice to make.

Clyde Wilson (Steve Mancha) chose to remain in Detroit where he became a gospel singer for the Heavy Faith label. As well as this he wrote for other local gospel acts on the same label most notably on Ed Henry's superb album "The Doorman". He also took up a more active role within the church. Both Mancha and fellow 100 Proof member Joe Stubbs returned to secular singing in the 80's; Stubbs in 1982 on Atkins All Star with "Got To Make A Move" with The Falcons as well as becoming involved in Ian Levine's Motortown Operation as did Mancha with "It's All Over The Grapevine" and "Hopelessly".

100 Proof released "I'm Mad As Hell" featuring Greg Massengale after Steve Mancha's departure and a new line-up of Honey Cone fronted by Sharon Cash issued a single release "Somebody's Always Messing Up A Good Thing" backed by "The Truth Will Come Out". The product bombed and the labels all but shattered in the explosion. Like so many times before the team had tried to conjure up their special alchemy to create gold. They had tried it first at Motown and then on leaving brought in General Johnson to recreate Levi Stubb's voice. Most obvious had been the cloning of Freda Payne and when Laura Lee was accepted into the fold Eloise Laws came along to "Tighten Him Up". With Sharon Cash Holland and Holland seemed determined that their new direction was going to be down the street where Laura Lee and Eloise Laws hung out. Her voice was remarkably like Laws but the new Honey Cone never made it beyond the initial release.

Eloise Laws remained uncomfortable with the label and her failure to achieve success had led her away from Holland Dozier Holland. The company had by now relocated to Los Angeles just like Motown had done and in so doing had given many of its artists a tough choice to make, move with the company or stay behind in Detroit. In the case of Eloise Laws her choice had already been made and besides, Holland and Holland were not Holland Dozier Holland and Los Angeles wasn't Detroit.

156

The three dimensions that made up HDH became two dimensional. The recognisable City sounds of Soul had already started to be attacked by the growing threat of Disco and with the exception of Philadelphia that had become the nearest acceptable Soul to the Disco boom Detroit, Chicago and Memphis all suffered. The migration from Detroit in two waves to LA's coast had all but left a depleted Detroit floundering.

Meanwhile, after performing around different States to raise money that hadn't come forward from her recording contract Eloise Laws briefly joined The Fifth Dimension, brief meaning one appearance on The Johnny Carson Show. Artistic integrity won over the need for comfort. She was working at The Playboy Club in Lake Geneva. Mark Gordon, manager of the Fifth was in the audience and he was looking for a replacement for Marilyn McCoo who had left the group along with husband Billy Davis to pursue a new direction. Mark Gordon told Eloise that he had auditioned over 200 women throughout the country but that she was the one. After much soul searching and taking into account problems she was experiencing with her ex-manager and other contributing factors she stepped down from the opportunity even though she could have made lots of money. Instead, she slept on a floor for nine months. She found her way to Los Angeles where she hooked up again with Eddie and Brian Holland. This time Eloise signed to the revived Invictus label in a move that promised much but delivered about the same as before.

This time around, though, the facts appeared also to be true not only of Eloise Laws' relationship with Invictus but also Invictus' relationship with its new distributor CBS whose promise of support never came through. She was disappointed in working with the Holland brothers because she felt that they were very domineering and not willing to bend in terms of the artist. They did things a certain way and they didn't want to change it. Her debut single was the previously released 'b' side "Stay With Me" backed by a Holland-Holland composition, "Touch Me". The difference in the two sides emphasised the difference between the old and the new sound. The melody so strong on the top side gave way to sheer infectious power as Brian Holland attempted to redesign the company's sound without the Dozier dimension. The single was followed, though, by an outstanding album, "Ain't It Good Feeling Good". Despite Laws' criticism the album showed that the Holland Brothers could still work their magic, the most poignant and melodic track being "Where Did We Go Wrong" a duet with Brian Holland. The music for the album was supplied by New York Port Authority and the final album for the label belonged to this new house band but NYPA's "3000 Miles From Home" was electronically charged pop funk that could have been recorded by any number of bands playing by numbers.

As you would expect from the name the new house band for Invictus originated from the East Coast and had started out in 1969 as Moonshadow building up a strong following on the Eastern coastline of America before trying their luck across the other side in Los Angeles where the Holland Dozier Holland organisation, as the new company was named, was now entrenched. Holland Dozier Holland's operation was not the destination they had planned out but once in LA they tried to touch base. Nothing came from this first non-event of a meeting and so the group disappeared back to New York. Then in 1975 part of the group found their way to LA again and were this time intent on meeting what was now the two Holland brothers only.

By 1976 the group members had signed up and changed their name to keep a little piece of home with them. The group was made up of Reginald A. Brown on bass and lead vocals, Rodney J. Brown on trumpet and percussion, Stafford M. Floyd keyboards and trombone, John O. Hargrove on Alto Saxophone, Monwell E. Lowndes drums and Melvin Miller Jr on lead and rhythm guitar. Miller had previously played in the Motown Snake Pit Band and signed to Holland Dozier Holland as a Staff songwriter along with Harold Beatty and Richard Davis. He co-wrote four songs with Brian and Edward Holland, Harold Beatty and Richard Davis on Eloise Laws "Ain't it Good Feeling Good" album and would go on to co-write songs for The Supremes Albums "High Energy" and" Mary, Scherrie & Susaye" on Motown Records. On their own album Eloise Laws supplied background vocals for the single "I Got It" and "I Used To Hate It (Till I Ate It)" while new lead singer for the re-formed 100 Proof Aged In Soul, Greg Massengale, assisted on "Guess I'm Gonna Cry" and "Home On A Rainy Day". A new era had started. and with it, new musicians to lay the unstable foundations for Eddie and Brian Holland that could allow the brothers to continue. The Politicians who NYPA replaced remained around Detroit where they worked individually. "How 'Bout a Little Hand For The Boys In The Band" remained an unissued track, originally recorded by McKinley Jackson & The Politicians at United Sound Recording Studios in Detroit but re-mixed at Stax Records in Memphis. Group bassist Rodney 'Peanut' Chandler cut sides with George Clinton and Clay Robinson showed up as a writer on The Dells 1974 album "The Mighty Mighty Dells" with the track "Bonafide Fool". The group would later turn to funk as Morning. Noon and Night on United Artists releasing an album as well as the quaintly titled "Bite Your Granny" single. Sadly, Chandler would become yet another victim of Detroit's violent lifestyle when, in October 1994 he repaired a guitar and set off to collect his payment. The man whose guitar he had fixed had other ideas and shot Peanut Chandler several times thus ending the life and career of one of Detroit's lesser known but highly respected musicians.

Tony Camillo formed a band Bazuka who succeeded in 1975 on A&M with "Dynomite" based on comedian Jimmy Smith's famous catchphrase. Incidentally, Bob Babbit, company bass man was on the bottom line. Dennis Coffey had already made a successful career for himself as a performer for Westbound Records and keyboard player Johnny Griffiths had "Grand Central Shuttle" RCA Records with Johnny Griffith, Inc as well as hitting "The Scene" on Geneva Records.

The whole palette that had painted such a glorious picture for Detroit's soul scene was being washed clean and the musicians being diffused throughout the wider musical spectrum. Creators like George Clinton who had painted so abstractly still tried to show that, like any Pablo Picasso or David Hockney you had to be an accomplished draughtsman and so in 1980 brought together the following line-up to support Detroit Spinner Philipe Wynne's "Wynne Jammin'" on his short-lived Uncle Jam label. So, Bruce Nazarian, Dennis Coffey and Willie "Preacher" Hampton were on guitars. Bernie Worrell, Rudy Robinson supplied keyboards while Bruce Nazarian and Frank Bryant played bass with background vocals by Brandye (Telma Hopkins and Joyce Vincent). The Horn background arrangements were supplied by Ronald Dunbar and Rhythm arrangements by Rudy Robinson and Bernie Worrell. Finally, the String & Horn Arrangements were supplied by Tony Camillo and the strings themselves, who else but Gordon Staples and The Detroit Symphony Orchestra could have performed them?

While Holland and Holland attempted to rekindle the fire, Edna Wright released a solo album on RCA "Oops! Here I Go Again" with the single "You Can't See The Forest For The Trees" written by her husband Greg Perry and former Hot Wax and Invictus lyricist Angelo Bond. The whole project was a direct continuation of the Honey Cone sound and deserved to reap rewards. Wright continued working in Los Angeles on backgrounds and commercials. Carolyn Willis remained in demand for supporting vocal work while Shellie Clark faded away from the limelight, having married Verdine White, bass player for Earth, Wind & Fire on December the 31st 1980. Interviewed by Paul Williams in 1984 Edna Wright put the group's failing down to bad timing, although at the time that wasn't apparent for how can a pioneer know if what you are doing is right or wrong? What do you have to be judged on or judge yourself by? Edna Wright felt that had they had hits at the beginning of the '80's instead of the '70's, that they would all have been filthy rich. Greg Perry who was undoubtedly one of Holland Dozier Holland's most prolific and gifted creators left the fold and released "One For The Road" on Casablanca in 1975 using a predominantly family unit to supply the music; brothers Zachery and Jeff proving to be equally talented while Edna Wright was the album's executive producer. Along the way he had married Edna Wright who had performed background

159

duties for him on his Casablanca debut as well as on its follow up the 1977 RCA album "Smokin'". Two tracks were co-written by T.S.Wynn, remember "A Touch Of Venus" by Sandy Wynn, alias Edna Wright?

By 1975 the Chairmen had been touring Europe extensively under that name, unable to use it in their homeland. The touring had started to take its toll and so Johnson folded things up and pursued a solo career with Arista Records, He released one self-titled album in 1975 cut in New York which left him cold. He felt that the label was trying to make him into something he wasn't, however, the one good thing to come out of the relationship was Arista's ability to have its executives dissuade Holland Dozier Holland from filing a lawsuit against Johnson. After this he was able to retain the name of the Chairmen Of The Board and along with group member Danny Woods became part of the new wave of Surfing Soul that allowed many of the older Soul artists the chance to remain untouched and unspoiled in the timeless Beach scene of Carolina. The Tams of "Hey Girl Don't Bother Me" and "Be Young, Be Foolish Be, Happy" fame, had remained in steady work there for twenty-five years when Johnson was interviewed in 1987. To be fair to Johnson he had been one of the greatest talents unearthed by Holland Dozier Holland and now he had found a niche in the Music industry that proved that recording wasn't all the industry was about. In Carolina records served as an advertisement for live appearances with shows 275 to 300 days a year. According to Johnson, Beach Music as pioneered by The Drifters, Kings of Beach, was as much a part of America as Jazz. On the recording front the Chairmen came closest to their former glories with the 1986 recording "Lover Boy" on Surfside, re-issued a year later with re-mixes by Ian Levine. Previous re-mix duties had fallen to Paul Weller. In England, the material had been issued through EMI's Syncopate label. 1989 saw "Gone Fishin'" released on Surfside, not to be confused with Bing Crosby.

Angelo Bond, one of the company's finest lyricists, had gone to ABC where he also cut a solo album, "Bondage" in 1975. As expected, the set was lyrically strong with the single "Reach For The Moon" exemplifying the positive aspects of the album. In the single "Reach For The Moon" Bond was cutting his own "Patches", basing it in Detroit and using the City's plight and a blend of sensitive lyrics around the more personal problems surrounding many a family to tell a poem set in front of a musical score. This would have done the Holland Dozier Holland company proud, had it remained a company. The set was produced by Bond along with McKinley Jackson. Additional background vocals included the contribution of Mrs McKinley Jackson, Shirley Jones from The Jones Girls whilst the musicians were made up from former members of The Politicians and supplemented

160

with top Detroit session players Melvin 'Wah Wah' Watson on guitar, Eddie 'Bongo' Brown on percussion and on bass, Tony Newton formerly of The 8th Day.

Brian Holland and brother Eddie began to work for Motown again as did Lamont Dozier, albeit on separate projects.

The Road We Didn't Take

post-Invictus

That was it then, well, for now at least. A label that was born from the mixed roots of Detroit's past and one that had been elevated to becoming possibly the city's last real chance to retain its International identity in the future had gone. General Johnson was particularly upset about the Invictus failure as he felt that it could have been avoided. As he said, somebody was obviously doing something wrong for a company with that much success going for it to end up in that state. Despite his own personal issues with the trio he still had the greatest respect for what they had achieved and the talent that they had. It was recognised, not only by the General, that the three were stronger as a unit than as the individuals they had sadly become.

Lamont Dozier and the Holland brothers all returned to the new Motown for various projects. For the Originals Lamont Dozier created a companion piece to his own "Black Bach" album, utilising the same array of musicians and, once again, collaborating with arranger McKinley Jackson. Ty Hunter once more joined the group from The Glass House in 1971 although due to contractual complications with Invictus his name was not to be found credited until 1973. The group relocated to California in 1974 and a year later under the writing and production skills of Lamont Dozier with arrangements by Jackson, recorded what was one of their finest albums, "California Sunset". By 1978 and after a move to Fantasy Records Hunter was able to flex his writing muscles on "Another Time, Another Place". Sadly, on the 24th of February 1981 at the age of 38, Ty Hunter died from cancer.

The Holland brothers involved themselves deeper with their former company from 1975 with a return to The Supremes, albeit a new look group. In 1973 Mary Wilson had asked Shellie Clarke of The Honey Cone to join the group but she declined the offer, citing that she didn't want to do the group thing again. Mary ended up hiring Clarke's label mate Scherrie Payne, formerly of The Glass House. Two tracks appeared on their self-titled album in '75, "Early Morning Love" and "Where Do I Go From Here". The Jackson 5's "Moving Violation" album from 1975 pitched the brothers in with the group that one could well have imagined them working with had things worked out differently for Holland Dozier Holland at Motown the first time around. The Jackson brothers were contracted to deliver one final album for Gordy before they moved on and remarkably, considering the recent history between the parties Motown asked the Holland brothers to oversee the project, ironically entitled "Moving Violation". It was felt that despite the bad blood there was unity amongst those labels who were angered by the CBS move to destroy the independent

Black owned companies. Brian and Eddie Holland were now West Coasters and although Motown had its own engineers, they insisted that their former mastering engineer Robert Dennis be involved in cutting the original masters for their part of the project. Under other producers the brothers had dipped into the HDH catalogue, most notably, "Reflections" produced by James Carmichael on the "Get It Together" set. On "Moving Violation" five out of the nine tracks on show were produced by Brian Holland including the lead track, their update of Diana Ross & The Supremes "Forever Came Today" written by Holland Dozier Holland. One has to wonder whether or not the Holland boys were trying it on to see if it fit.

Despite the view that the Holland brothers and Lamont Dozier by himself were not the heavyweights of years gone by Brian Holland was championed by the British publication Black Music in a new column called "A Splice Of History" in which a specific track was deified. The first such track was "Forever Came Today" by The Jackson 5 as produced by Holland. Although the decade was only half done the track was described as 'arguably the most important dance creation of the seventies' Holland would have relished the fact that the author had compared the Disco movement and here the invention shown in his contribution to it with French Impressionism and poets. The track was seen as a fusion made up from the best of Holland's 60's productions, meshed with Motown's 70's instrumental contributors such as Melvin 'Wah Wah' Ragin on guitar. The innovation, however, came in the use of the bass guitar as pioneered by Larry Graham, who had started out as Sly & The Family Stone's bass man before fronting his highly successful Graham Central Station. His walking bass moved effortlessly from funk to disco and in the hands of Holland was turned into an art form. The article closed with the statement that Brian Holland had never been adequately recognised the revolutionary work that he had been doing in the mid-seventies.

Robert Dennis described the session as a marvel of the then current 16 track recording technology of the day, something that only the best recording facilities of the time could pull off. The session took place at the Mowest studios in Los Angeles. Brian Holland overdubbed the string section of the songs in one studio while in another studio Edward Holland overdubbed Michael Jackson's lead vocals. The engineers would then synchronise the two reels together for a 32 track mixdown. Nothing out of the ordinary there, however, this was a Michael Jackson session and directly or indirectly the unusual was bound to be lurking somewhere. In the vocal studio instead of there being just Jackson there was a Japanese girl standing next to him wearing headphones. Apparently, Holland was not allowed to talk directly to Jackson and so had to communicate through the girl. Michael Jackson was at that tender age where strange things can happen to a growing boy's voice and if he couldn't reach the notes then the girl could. Because there was no line of vision between the producer and the vocal booth Holland could not tell who was hitting the notes at any given time. Also, in 1975 former Temptation front man Eddie Kendricks cut "Get The Cream Off The Top", a Holland-Holland composition for his set "The Hit Man". Holland Dozier Holland Productions Inc. was being given more production scope at Motown and The Dynamic Superiors benefitted with their "Give & Take" set. It was apparent that the brothers were still willing to make a go of it and were not the isolated unit that General Johnson had led people to believe. The songs were collaborations between Brian and Eddie Holland and other writers for their company. Reginald A. Brown and Stafford M. Floyd from New York Port Authority collaborated with Richard Davis, later President for the Holland Group, and as with The Jackson 5 Brian Holland dipped into their own songbook to produce the old Supremes hit, "Forever Came Today" at breakneck speed. Incidentally, the arrangements were again by McKinley Jackson.

Another year passed and Holland and Holland wrote "Keep Holding On" for The Temptations for their disastrous "House Party" set as well as the majority of Junior Walker & The All Stars "Hot Shot" album. Walker was fed two tracks previously recorded by Brian Holland during their Invictus days, "You Ain't No Ordinary Woman" and "I'm So Glad" as well as his version of "Why Can't We Be Lovers". The best was yet to come though, with Brian Holland producing the best two Supremes albums to come out of their post-Diana Ross days. "High Energy" and "Mary, Scherrie and Susaye" both in 1976. For once the magic really worked. The production of Brian Holland sparkled and the three girls sang their hearts and souls out. "High Energy" mixed upbeat rhythms with captivating ballads perfected in the medley of "Til The Boat Sails Away" and "I Don't Want To Lose You". "Mary, Scherrie and Susaye" could well have been recorded at the same session because it was the natural successor.

Scherrie Payne joined up with Mary Wilson and Cindy Birdsong in the latest incarnation of The Supremes but by 1976 Birdsong had left the line-up to be replaced by former Stevie Wonder backing singer Susaye Greene. The trio of Wilson, Payne and Green separated after the two classic albums but in 1979 Motown issued "Partners" by Payne and Greene. Single releases by Scherrie Payne appeared during the 80's on Record Shack and Megatone. In 1984 the partners reunited as backing singers for James Ingram's "Party Animal" track from his "It's Your Night" set on Qwest. Former Supremes Lynda Lawrence and Jean Terrell joined Scherrie Payne becoming The Flos, Former Ladies Of The Supremes and perhaps a subconscious tribute to the fallen Supreme Florence Ballard, to hit the night-club scene. Her 1987 debut with Philip Ingram on the Superstar

International Label, "Incredible" was met with a positive critical reaction and as a solo artist she continued to have moderate success all the way up to the late 80's with Ian Levine's Nightmare Records releasing "Chase Me Into Somebody Else's Arms" as well as reviving "Stoned Love" alongside Terrell and Lawrence for Levine's Motor City label.

With the temporary departure of The Temptations to Atlantic Records in 1977 their second set away from home was given to the renamed Holland Group Productions Inc. to produce. "Bareback" released in 1978 proved a moderate success but it wasn't long before The Temptations returned to Motown. In 1979, a major project jointly supported by Jobete and Gold Forever (Motown and Invictus' publishing companies respectively) was on the cards. The project, "Yesterday, Today and Forever" was to be an overview of Holland Dozier Holland's catalogue stretching throughout their Motown career and culminating in their Invictus work. In 1980 the special promotional package was recorded by the Holland brothers, a combination of new arrangements on their old standards as well as fresh material. Although there was no material from the Invictus period. The project included involvement from The Commodores ex-vocalist Lionel Richie, Motown's latest girl group High Energy as well as Eddie Holland and Deborah Holland, Eloise Laws and relatively new name Sterling Harrison.

When he was eight years old Sterling Harrison began his stage career and was lucky enough to share the limelight with an array of top Soul artist. Two promoters took him under their wing and put him on all the big shows. In the '60s and '70s, Harrison shared the spotlight with James Brown, Jackie Wilson, Sam Cooke, and Otis Redding, Jimi Hendrix even appeared as a sideman in Harrison's band at a Nashville club. Then a bandleader who worked out of Connecticut, Buddy Lucas, asked if he could go to New York where he cut his first record, "The Devil's Got a Spell on Me" on Vim Records, in the mid 50's. He went back to Richmond and finally back to New York City. During this time, Harrison cut two singles for Smash and then the tiny 4V label. The idea was to come up with a new dance craze. He did a song called 'The Wobble,' and they billed him in New York City as the 'King of the Wobble.' From there he went to All-Platinum in 1972 where he released "Ps & Qs" on the Astroscope, imprint written and produced by former member of The Rimshots, Joe 'Groundhog' Richardson. Producer Gene Redd encouraged Harrison to move to the West Coast in 1977 where he met Harold Beatty, by now the assistant A & R director of Holland Dozier Holland Productions. Harrison, whose lifelong dream had been to work with the legendary song writing, record producing team convinced Beatty that he was perfect for HDH. Holland Dozier Holland saw him at the First and Western and from that he went on to record the hideous 12-inch single "Roll Her-Skate Her" in 1979 for Motown under the guidance of the Hollands but it failed to sell. In 1980 Angelo Bond co-produced "Power" by The Temptations alongside Berry Gordy and again McKinley Jackson was on hand to help with the arrangements. Co-production and writing chores also went to William Weatherspoon returning to Motown after his successful spell at Invictus and Hot Wax. "How Can I Resist Your Love", "Struck By Lightning Twice" and the ballad "Go For It" reflected the type of song structure Bond and Weatherspoon had developed during their stay with Holland Dozier Holland. After that William Henry Weatherspoon devoted himself to gospel music and continued to produce and publish through his own company, God Touch Publishing. In 2005 and despite failing health he finished producing an album on his former first lady of soul Laura Lee, staying up and working on the project until the early hours of the morning, as if he knew that time was of an essence and that it was quickly running out for him. William Henry Weatherspoon died on Sunday, July 17th, 2005 in Lathrup Village. He was 69 years old. His former partner in rhyme, Angelo Bond, said that he enjoyed every stage of his life of music and that he was a genius.

A brief period of collaboration between Lamont Dozier and his former colleagues then came about that spawned two albums for the Atlantic distributed Real-World Records. The self-titled Sterling Harrison and, again, the self-titled Margo Michaels & Nitelite set, produced and mostly written by Holland Dozier Holland. The first three tracks on the Harrison album "One More Time For Love", "Back Tracking" and "Love I'm Coming Home Again" moved along in a funky groove with Sterling Harrison sounding uncannily like Lamont Dozier. These were the highlights of what was still an above average set. Yet something was missing. The soul that seemed to disappear on Freda Payne's final Invictus offering, "Reaching Out" never seemed to fully show itself again in the work of HDH. Maybe the ingredients missing were the fantastic musicians assembled in Detroit who hadn't travelled to the coast. The only ballad on the album was a strange mix that seemed to want to be a Gospel song, right down to the title, "Because You Are Love (Of Thee I Sing)", but when Harrison sang, "Thank you, baby" one wondered if his relationship with God was a little too personal. Margo Michaels' album was a far more solid set, kicking off with the horn led "Common Ground", the whole album was strictly for the movers and groovers of the '80's. The single "Take My Everything" wasn't the strongest track but the 'b' side "Thank You For The Love" was more in keeping with the type of song Holland Dozier Holland were doing at Invictus. In fact, it would have served Freda Payne well as a follow up to "Band Of Gold" but as with Sterling Harrison's material there was a hollowness where the soul should have lay. Margo Michaels' voice seemed to run the gamut of Holland Dozier Holland females from Diana Ross, Freda Payne and, mostly, Eloise Laws. The whole album was aimed at the dance floor without being disco but, again, was out of step with the developments of the new decade. Still, it was well produced and arranged and should have fared better and probably will when time allows us to make decisions not based on current trends. Lamont Dozier continued to develop as a solo artist launching his own Wheel label towards the end of 1980 to be distributed by 20th Century Fox Records.

Sterling Harrison's 1981 album on Phono, "One Size Fits All" became a much sought-after release and the production belonged to Holland Dozier Holland Productions. Inc. The first side was co-produced by Harold Beatty (Prince Harold of later Chairmen fame) while the more together second side belonged to Brian Holland. "You've Got That Thing" written by Beatty and the Holland brothers proved to be a gem of a track and "Jump In The Middle Of Love" was reminiscent of the later Invictus material. Lamont Dozier moved from label to label as a performer and the next stop was Arista Records where he recorded what he considered to be his best solo work but when his A&R man switched labels for Columbia, taking with him the album, the project got lost. At this point Dozier decided to take a break from releasing albums and concentrated on the area he had longed to get into way back in the days of Motown, cinema and television soundtracks. He moved to England with his wife and children where he worked with some of the UK's top 80's talent including Alison Moyet, writing "Invisible" and Simply Red including the Platinum selling "You've Got It" "Infidelity" and "Suffer" from Simply Red's "Men And Women" album.

Collectively Holland Dozier Holland combined once more and wrote and produced the first side of The Four Tops 1983 album "Back Where I Belong", the Tops first album after returning to Motown and fittingly shared with Holland Dozier Holland, the team that had given them their first successes for the label. It had been fifteen years since the Tops and Holland Dozier Holland had worked together and the sound had progressed into a new electronic age where the music was more reliant on programming than before. There was no return to the Snake Pit and many of the musicians who had been an integral part of the team's product where a distant memory. Again, as a period piece it stands up but lacks the passion that real musicians had been able to add to the earlier blend. Rumours of a reconciliation with Motown were unfounded and in the same year Eddie Holland claimed that they had received more money in 1983 through royalties than when they had worked for Motown. In the same year Norman Whitfield returned to The Temptations co-writing five tracks for their "Back to Basics" set. "Miss Busy Body (Get Your Body Busy)", "Sail

Away", "Outlaw", "Stop the World Right Here", "Make Me Believe in Love Again" were all co-written with Angelo Bond.

The news broke on April the 1st 1984 of the death of Marvin Gaye at the hands of his father and the world mourned the passing of this fractured, flawed genius. The following year, In Los Angeles Lamont Dozier met Phil Collins backstage at one of Collin's shows. He had already had a massive hit with his version of "You Can't Hurry Love", and the two of them became good friends. Collin's later started to work on co-producing the "August" album for Eric Clapton and Dozier was contacted. He wrote two songs for Clapton, "Hung Up On Your Love Again" and "Run". Collins was also beginning to get into films, not necessarily from the musical perspective alone, and in 1988 he began working on "Buster" both as actor and performer. He returned to Dozier to write and produce some songs for the soundtrack. He flew down to Acapulco, where filming was taking place and when he heard the songs he was impressed, as well he should have been. Between them they composed three songs for "Buster", including the Grammy-winning "Two Hearts", which also received a Golden Globe, BPI Award, Oscar Nomination, and Ivor Novello Award.

One year later Brian Holland signed an interesting affidavit in defence of the late James Jamerson, the bass playing superstar of Motown's Snake Pit. When Allan Slutsky began writing his book, 'Standing In The Shadows Of Motown' in 1987 he contacted a lady by the name of Carol Kaye. The point of the contact was to make sure that he didn't cite Jamerson as the player on any tracks cut by Kaye. Unfortunately, by doing so he opened up a can of worms with Carol Kaye laying claim to some of Motown's greatest hits, "Bernadette", "Reach Out, I'll Be There", "Baby Love", "I Was Made to Love Her", "Ain't No Mountain High Enough", "Dancing In the Streets" and "I Can't Help Myself" to name a few.

Brian Holland attested to the fact that James Jamerson played on almost every one of their productions. Brian Holland signed the notarised affidavit categorically stating that "Bernadette", "Reach Out", "Can't Help Myself", "Keep Me Hanging On", "Standing in the Shadows of Love", "Reflections", "Baby Love", "Back In My Arms Again", "Come See About Me", and "Can't Hurry Love", were in fact, played by James Jamerson. Holland went as far as to say that he had never even heard of Carol Kaye. The Union contract from the "Reach Out" session, dated July 6, 1966 listed James Jamerson as the bassist for which he earned $61.00 and Detroit's Hitsville studio as the place where it was recorded.

Around this time this wasn't the only controversy surrounding former Motown employees, as Brian Holland's sound engineer and mentor Lawrence T. Horn was making headlines. During the 1960's and 70's the engineers didn't have the same amount of console automation and endless effects units to work with and blood, sweat and tears had to be readily available to get the sound done to the satisfaction of the companies. When console automation came along, 65% of the reason for multitrack pre-mastering vanished. Another 20% had become unnecessary because of the multiple and inexpensive processing devices becoming more readily available. This led to the old stagers being replaced by new technology. Harrison Kennedy said that L.T. Horn was a genius in the studio but completely crazy and by the 90's he was about to show just how crazy he had become.

By this time Horn was divorced from his wife Mildred. The two of them had had a child with a disability who was now 8 years of age and being looked after by Mildred Horn. Trevor had been born prematurely and had suffered health problems. To add to this, the hospital had been negligent and failed to see that his tracheotomy tube had become dislodged during a routine hospital check-up. This resulted in eight minutes of oxygen deprivation and severe brain damage. The family sued the hospital and received a large settlement. Lawrence T. Horn, by now down on his luck in these progressive times, desired this money badly. He was to inherit the money if his child died and he just couldn't wait for that. Horn hired James Edward Perry to murder his ex-wife and child and on March the 3rd 1993 Perry entered Mildred Horn's home, shot both her and Janice Saunders, the child's nurse and used a pillow to smother Trevor. Horn and Perry were subsequently found guilty and Perry was sentenced to death on three counts of first-degree murder and one count of conspiracy. L.T. Horn was given life imprisonment. Sadly, the other engineer associated with Detroit Soul and co-writer of the Honey Cone's "Want Ads", Barney Perkins, died on the 15th of December in Los Angeles in the same year. "Tell It To My Heart" Taylor Dane's 1988 debut album had included her re-working of "Want Ads" The debut album sold over 1 million copies worldwide and hit number 1 in five countries.

There had also been fresh interest shown in the trio's work with cover versions of "How Sweet It Is To Be Loved By You" by James Taylor, and "Standing In The Shadows Of Love" appearing on Barbara Streisand's latest album. In March 1983 the Holland brothers re-formed The 8th Day as a four-piece vocal group using their old trick of retaining the name and replacing the membership for A&M Records. Their debut single "Call Me Up" was followed by an album but neither promised a return to greatness for the brothers or the group. The set was arranged by McKinley Jackson and recorded at the Hitsville Recording Studio in Hollywood while the group consisted of Tyrone Douglas, Virginia McDonald, Denzil Broomfield and Barrington Henderson. In 1998 Barrington Henderson joined the Temptations and debuted on the album "Phoenix Rising" which went double platinum and featured him as the lead vocalist. Even if they weren't making headway themselves, they were still capable of recognising talent.

New short-lived Holland Dozier Holland projects faded away without any success and the trio went their own ways yet again, Eddie and Brian Holland staying as a team whilst Lamont Dozier remained a solo performer. New group Heavy Traffic Starring V was a group that was being supervised by Eddie and Brian Holland in 1986 but the group failed to materialise into anything beyond a luke-warm album. The single from the set, "Coming Down With Love" did garner some interest amongst soul collectors though.

On November the 21st 1987 the National Academy Of Songwriters (NAS) in their third annual salute to the American Songwriter presented Holland Dozier Holland with a Lifetime Achievement Award and at the ceremony Lamont Dozier performed a nine song Holland Dozier Holland medley. Speaking further about the award noted author Nelson George was quick to point out the importance of such an honour. Holland Dozier Holland had been background boys to Gordy and although Gordy had created the Motown legend it was the genius of Holland Dozier Holland that had helped the legend grow. Both Smokey Robinson and Stevie Wonder had received more acclaim because they were seen equally as performers but the work of Holland Dozier Holland would stay the course because they were masterful examples of the craft of song writing.

In 1988, Fantasy Records signed a Worldwide distribution deal with the Hollands to handle Music Merchant and the HDH label. Groups were to include The Boyz (not to be confused with the Motown Boys being produced by LA and Babyface) who bowed in with "I've Got Female Trouble", the trouble being the lead singer's dealing with his girl's menstruation. A strange subject to start a new venture off with and one that failed to grip the imagination of the record buyers.

Meanwhile Bill Warner formed his own entertainment management company and teamed with Brian Holland and Eddie Holland. This collaboration resulted in one CD and several singles by a very talented singer/songwriter named Cassandra Jordan on HDH. This collaboration was a critical success, however due to poor marketing and promotion the project was a commercial failure. Teamwork and Liquid Heat also appeared on HDH. The Music Merchant label was to be re-activated along with a sister label, Shanty Town. The initial release on Shanty Town was to be "Do You Care" by Hard Cover whilst Music Merchant offered "Spotlight" by Team Work in 1989 and "Intensive Care" again by the newly named Boyz From Detroit (1989). Further releases were "It's A Tight Fit" and "Rain Song" by Lipstick as well as "Who Put The X In Sex" by Brim Rock, a group, according to the label, 'starring' Angelo Bond arranged by

McKinley Jackson and written by Eddie and Brian Holland, Richard Davis and Angelo Bond. The new deal didn't work and once more the trio split with the same feeling of Deja vu.

In January 1990, Holland Dozier Holland were inducted into America's Rock And Roll Hall Of Fame but the new decade would be an even more exceptional one than any of the three partners could ever have imagined. A year later and Lamont Dozier again began composing songs with an eye towards landing another record deal for himself. He met with Atlantic Records who signed him up to release the album, "Inside Seduction". Although the album featured guest appearances by Eric Clapton and Phil Collins it failed commercially and so once again Dozier had to make another decision about where his career was moving. There was no getting away from it, the end had seemingly come and after so many separations and reconciliation's the marriage to Brian and Eddie Holland seemed over.

As the decade grew to a close 1998 was to prove another revolutionary one in their long and winding history. They won a Trustees Award for lifetime achievement by non-performers at the Grammy Awards and began to work on a musical together; their first collaboration in many a year. The biggest news, however, was a ground-breaking $40 million deal with bonds being sold against their future royalties. Other composers also planned to tap into the burgeoning market for intellectual property-backed investments by staging bond issues, notably Bernie Taupin, the lyricist for many of Elton John's hits including "Crocodile Rock", "Daniel", "Rocket Man" and "Candle in the Wind." The Holland Dozier Holland deal, which was arranged by the Pullman Group, the New York-based finance House, was the second bond issue backed by intellectual property. The first was the "Bowie Bond" followed by Rod Stewart who clinched a $15.4m securitised loan from Nomura Capital which was backed by revenues from his music publishing catalogue. The Holland Dozier Holland bond consisted of a 300-strong catalogue of songs which had remained steady royalty earners since the 1960s. Investors were to be repaid from the royalties earned by the songs over 15 years and these royalties were made payable every time a song was played by a radio or television station, sold on a recording or featured in a film soundtrack or a television commercial. David Pullman, managing director of the Pullman Group, said that musicians and composers were becoming more comfortable with the idea of raising capital in the form of securitised loans as an alternative to negotiating advances from record companies or music publishers. The successful completion of the Holland Dozier Holland issue suggested investors' appetite for such transactions was still strong.

Also, in 1998 the Holland Group, formed by Edward Holland, began a re-organisation to re-launch the Holland-Dozier-Holland record labels as a

172

new hit making company. Holland planned releases on nine acts to launch the label but quickly ran into problems co-ordinating production. He knew who he wanted and called Ronald Dunbar to help get the productions done in a regular, well-organised manner. Dunbar had been out of the Recording industry for a while selling perfume and lingerie with his wife. Between them Holland and Dunbar shaved the initial plans down and decided to release material on four artists, three of which, although not gaining National Pop status did reach specialist charts in 1999. Because of the success credited to Ronald Dunbar he was given the official title of 'Assistant to the President'.

As they entered a new millennium and a new phase the Holland Group had its first valid national hit in over 20 years with "Dream A Little" by Eloise Laws' brother Ronnie Laws. Again, the Project Manager was Ronald Dunbar. The CD reached Number 1 on The Wave, one of the biggest smooth jazz/adult contemporary radio stations in America based in Los Angeles. Eloise Laws performed some of the backing as well as singing lead on the track "Old Days Old Ways." produced again by Ronald Dunbar.

More old links were suddenly being re-forged in unlikely places. The Brianbert Music Company back in Detroit was back in business and Robert Bateman, the Motown veteran from the very early days was back, joined by another early associate Barret Strong. Both Bateman and Strong, had platinum hits in the 60's with Motown, and both knew the "Motown" process that it took to create that success.

The Motown hit making process began with the backing track with producers working out a rhythm, chord changes and bass line and record it with little or no idea of the melody or lyrics that would eventually be applied to that track. After the track was completed, songwriters would compose melody and lyric content to that track. The newest Brianbert recording artists were now Rappers like Estilo and the 'freestyling' to the tracks was a direct descendant of the Motown formula from the 60's. On October the 15th 1999 Estilo signed a six years' exclusive artist contract to Motortown Internet Records and on March the 6th 2000 the recording contract was picked up by Brianbert Music Co. Further production was ongoing and the group "GifTvS" had a commitment from the Holland Group to nationally press, promote and distribute the release, providing it tested well in Michigan. In Eddie Holland's mind sampling was a form of respect and wished that the Rappers would sample the hell out of his music., going on to say that if they were all in their twenties today, they'd be rappin' their asses. Lamont Dozier felt that Rap was an art form, entertaining and enlightening. He felt that it was quite interesting what the kids were thinking about nowadays and that they had a lot more to deal with than they did growing up.

In 2000 two British releases sparked a row between companies issuing the material. 'The ABC Years And Lost Sessions' along with 'Going Back To My Roots' both had unreleased material but arguments ensued between Lamont Dozier and the labels releasing the tracks. On October the 4th 2000 Lamont Dozier was due to play at the Jazz Café in Camden in London but the show had to be cancelled because of 'differences between the record companies involved'. Elsewhere, Ronald Dunbar and Holland Dozier Holland were not the only members of the old team who were getting recognised. In 2001 General Johnson was about to have a most unusual accolade bestowed upon him. The years had not mellowed the General's anger and frustration at Holland Dozier Holland and yet without that period of creativity what came next would never have happened. Johnson seemed hesitant in his gratitude.

"I have no problem with anyone from those days, what happened back then is history. If you are still living in what happened 26 years ago, then you have a problem. I was thankful for the opportunity to work with Holland Dozier Holland, I learned a lot but now if I see anyone from then it's like, whoa, we still feel awkward talking about it."

General Johnson

HOUSE JOINT RESOLUTION NO. 32
Offered April 26, 2001

Designating June 9, 2001, as General Johnson Day in Virginia.
Patrons-- Jones, J.C., Christian, Crittenden and Day

Unanimous consent to introduce

Referred to Committee on Rules

WHEREAS, General Johnson and the Chairmen Of The Board remains one of the most enduringly popular rhythm and blues bands in the nation; and

WHEREAS, for nearly 40 years, General Johnson, who began singing in Norfolk churches as a seven-year-old boy, has entertained fans of R&B music from Detroit to London, from New York to the beaches of North Carolina; and

WHEREAS, during a career that has taken him from Norfolk to New York City to Detroit during the height of the Motown sound to extensive touring across the country and around the world, General Johnson has excelled as a performer, songwriter, and producer; and

WHEREAS, among General Johnson's more recognizable hits are "Give Me Just a Little More Time," "Somebody's Been Sleepin' in My Bed," and "Pay to the Piper"; and

WHEREAS, General Johnson won a Grammy award for writing the top-ten hit "Patches," recorded by Clarence Carter, and won BMI's Songwriter of the Year Award for his work with partner Greg Perry on many million-selling songs; and

WHEREAS, General Johnson and the Chairmen Of The Board have performed on "The Tonight Show" with Johnny Carson, on "Soul Train" and "American Bandstand," and in such renowned venues as the Apollo Theater and Avery Fisher Hall in New York and the Hammersmith Odeon in London; and

WHEREAS, General Johnson remains a popular musician, primarily playing in beachfront communities in North Carolina, where his unique sound combines with the enduring popularity of his songs to attract audiences of all ages; now, therefore, be it

RESOLVED by the House of Delegates, the Senate concurring, That the General Assembly hereby designate June 9, 2001, as General Johnson Day in Virginia, in recognition of the manifold contributions of General Johnson to American popular music.

Like they say what goes around comes around. Some records cause revolutions, others simply revolve. With Holland Dozier Holland we had some of each category and the mere fact that all three have remained active for well over forty years individually or collectively deserves more than just a passing mention. Dozier decided to start his own record label Hithouse Records with his wife and business partner, Barbara Ullman Dozier to market and distribute his own recordings. The first release was to be "Lamont Dozier...An American Original", The album received a Grammy Nomination in 2002 for Best Traditional R&B Vocal Album. Dozier re-arranged classic tracks such as "This Old Heart Of Mine", "I Hear A Symphony", "Reflections", and "My World Is Empty Without You" into stripped down ballad form. He felt that it was finally time to give this music a new face. Everybody in the business had done these songs at one time or another but no one had ever heard how they were originally created. He said that most of them had started out as ballads and he suggested that they would have a more of a melancholy feeling, soft and sweet.

This was not necessarily true. "My World Is Empty Without You" was cut as a ballad on the Smith Connection's Music Merchant album in 1972 whilst elsewhere Tami Lynn's "Love Is Here And Now You're Gone" set of '72 took the record to an almost stand still position in its sombre delivery and at Stax Margie Joseph did a similar job on "Stop In The Name Of Love". Dozier continued on a roll creating a series of educational audiotapes, "The Lamont Dozier School of Music," based on lectures he had given to music classes over the years as well as developing new artists and creating a story, music and lyrics for a solo musical entitled, "Angels".

In 2001 he appeared in a Motown Revue at the Royal Festival Hall in London and also that year Berry Gordy Jr sued Edward Holland Jr for 'malicious prosecution'. Some wounds just don't heal. The lawsuit stretched way back to 1968 since when, sixty-four of the claims, in three lawsuits had been dismissed. The 1968 litigation was ultimately settled but in 1987 Holland filed another lawsuit making the same claims as the '68 one. This was dismissed in 1980 but in 1992, Holland filed a third lawsuit with the same claims.

Although the complaint didn't specify damages Berry Gordy had allegedly spent over $2 million in legal fees. A spokesperson for Gordy said, that for Mr. Gordy, it wasn't about money, it was about setting the record straight and that Berry Gordy felt that he had an obligation to the countless people who together created the Motown legacy and that this action is part of that responsibility."

On Sunday September 28th, 2003 at the Beverly Hills Hotel, In Los Angeles, The "original Supremes" Diana Ross, Mary Wilson and Florence Ballad, as well as Cindy Birdsong received the "Heroes and Legends Award" organised by Janie Bradford who had worked with both Lamont Dozier and Brian way back in 1962 on Stevie Wonder's "Contract On Love". Former Debonnaires and Invictus session singer Joyce Vincent and her former boss Brian Holland formed part of a musical tribute to The Supremes. Ex-Glass House and Supremes member Scherrie Payne performed the Heroes and Legends theme song and sister Freda Payne presented one of the evenings awards as well as doing an impromptu version of "Band of Gold." Mary Wilson also introduced Berry Gordy and as the evening came to a close sang "Someday We'll Be Together" as Cindy Birdsong, Jean Terrell and Scherrie Payne joined her on stage. Brenda Holloway, Kim Weston, Pete Moore and Claudette Robinson of the Miracles were also there. Not just a Motown legacy but Holland Dozier

Holland's own history was paraded to a hungry audience some forty years after their first hit with "Come And Get These Memories" Eddie Holland, Lamont Dozier & Brian Holland were awarded the BMI's 2003 Icon Award as part of the 51st annual BMI Pop Awards on Tuesday the 9th of December 2003.

The following year on Thursday May 27th the team were awarded the coveted Ivor Novello International Song writing Award in London. Despite this renewed interest in the team, the skeletons were rattling to get out of Eddie Holland's closet. The tax bill grew after he was involved in a $15 million deal in 1998 involving bonds backed by future song royalties. Holland received $8.4 million while another $1.7 million was spent on debt, mostly federal taxes, according to court files. The next year, the deal was refinanced, The Royal Bank of Scotland loaning one of Holland's companies $14.6 million, a loan backed by song royalties. The government sued Holland in 2013, alleging he owed $18.4 million in delinquent taxes, interest and penalties. The taxes dated to 1991.

Between 2005 and 2009 Martha Reeves became a councilwoman for Detroit before returning to full-time performing and there were still glimmers of financial hope for Eddie Holland with a new generation sampling their material. In 2006 Sleepy Brown had taken the Holland Dozier track, "Don't Leave Me Starvin' For Your Love" and used it for the track "I Can't Wait" featuring Outkast but by 2014, Holland's company had defaulted on the loan and owed the bank approximately $8 million, according to court records. Separately, lawyers claimed Holland owed $6 million for representing him in state court lawsuits in the 1980s and 1990s, according to court records. In 2015, a year after the default, Holland's company sold a catalogue of songs to a private equity fund for $21 million. The money went into a pot and Holland's creditors, including the government, the bank and the lawyers spent two years fighting to be first to tap the fund.

By the end of 2016, the government said Holland's tax bill had grown to more than $19.9 million. In December 2017 it was reported that Eddie Holland was trying to prevent the IRS (Inland Revenue Service) from taking his Social Security benefits to clear a $20 million tax debt and his lawyer filed a Federal lawsuit on his behalf to hold onto Holland's last remaining assets, Eddie Holland, by now 78 years old, no longer received royalties for his back catalogue, having pledged his money in a series of business ventures. Song royalties went to a bank until the bonds were repaid. Holland's only current source of income was Social Security and a series of tax levies had left him temporarily penniless, according to the lawyer. Holland had requested a payment plan for delinquent taxes but the government had denied the request, the lawyer wrote. It was possible some of Holland's tax debt would be paid out of the fund. His lawyer made the statement that his client put $21 million into the fund to cover his tax liability and that he didn't intend to go back and make more money in the music business as soon as these issues are resolved.

On October the 17th 2008 came the news that Levi Stubbs had passed away after a long fight with cancer. Eddie and Brian Holland said that working with Levi was one of the most inspirational aspects of the time that they had spent at Motown and just listening to the way he was able to deliver the Holland Dozier Holland songs brought more beauty to them than they could have imagined, adding that he was an inspiration to them as songwriters and producers. Sadly, more of the greats were leaving us, General Johnson, who had done so much for Holland Dozier Holland, passed away on October the 13th 2010 also from cancer and three months later Gladys Horton of The Marvelettes died in a nursing home on January the 26th 2011 after years of ill health and a series of strokes aged 65. Fellow Marvelettes member Georgia Dobbins joined her on September the 18th 2020 following a cardiac arrest at the age of 78.

Further interest in their Invictus and Hot Wax material reappeared in 2016 when The Avalanches, an Australian group, sampled Honey Cone's "Want Ads" for the track "Because I'm Me". On September the 18th of that year, Edna Wright along with Shellie Clarke were honoured with the 2016 National Rhythm and Blues Music Society Unsung Heroine Awards, Caroline Willis, who was not in attendance, also received an award. The following September they were honoured with the Heroes and Legends Award (HAL).

Then, on a sadder note, on the 13th of January 2018 Danny Woods, former Chairman of The Board member, passed away at the age of 75. Ronald Dunbar followed on the 4th of April at the age of 77. On September 12, 2020, Wright died suddenly, at age 75 after suffering a heart attack at a hospital in Encino, California. She suffered from chronic obstructive pulmonary disease. On the 8th of January 2021, her group Honey Cone was inducted into the Soul Music Hall Of Fame Class of 2020, then the following month came the news that Mary Wilson had died in her sleep on February the 8th at the age of 76 from a cardiovascular disease. Berry Gordy said he was "extremely shocked and saddened" by the news of her death and said that she was "quite a star in her own right and over the years continued to work hard to boost the legacy of the Supremes. Diana Ross sent her condolences to the family. To the many fans and people whose life she changed throughout her 76 years, she will always be unforgettable, ever present and forever supreme.

"I was so down when Smokey Robinson called and told me that Mary had just passed, it's taken me three days and I still can't got over Mary not being here...because the fact of the matter is that I was supposed to have called Mary four or five days before they said she had passed and I kept putting it off. So that bothers me too."

Eddie Holland

Thankfully, the music doesn't stop because the musicians have. We grow old, that's nature. Some of us hope that what we do in life and what we leave behind can in some way make us immortal. Holland Dozier Holland released "Don't Stop Playing Our Song" back in 1974 on their Invictus label and their songs have never stopped being played. they are with us wherever we go. Turn on the TV and they are advertising chicken or burgers, go to the fair and they are there with us on the Waltzer and have you been to a party where they don't play at least one of their mini masterpieces? Two years ago, I went to see Martha Reeves live at a local venue, I was going with some trepidation, wondering if she could still perform that magic. Somewhere, in my mind I could hear her whisper, "Come And Get These Memories". I did and she could.

It may be a cliché to say that something is life's soundtrack but remember this, before the cliché there is the original, or in this case three.

Let The Record Show

Thanks to Keith Hughes, Roger Green, Chris Jenner, John Lester, Andy Ricks. Reg Bartlette, Pete Gregory, Bob Cattaneo, Tony Cox, Mark Harley, Jim Moorehouse, Jim Stewart and John Manship

Recordings by Brian Holland		
Title	Label	Year
Where's The Joy?) In Nature Boy / Shock	Kudo	1958
Recordings by Eddie Holland		
Title	Label	Year
You (You, You, You, You) / Little Miss Ruby	Mercury	1959
Merry Go-Round / It Moves Me	United Artists	1959
Because I Love Her / Everybody's Going	United Artists	1960
Magic Mirror / Will You Love Me	United Artists	1960
The Last Laugh / Do You Want To Let Me Go	United Artists	1960
Jamie / Take A Chance On Me	Motown	1962
Jamie version 2 / Take A Chance On Me	Motown	1962
You Deserve What You Get / Last Night I Had A Vision	Motown	1962
If Cleopatra Took A Chance / What About Me	Motown	1962
If It's Love / It's Not Too Late	Motown	1962
Darling, I Hum Our Song / Just A Few More Days	Motown	1962
Baby Shake / Brenda	Motown	1963
I'm On The Outside Looking In / I Could Cry If I Wanted To	Motown	1963
Leaving Here/ Brenda	Motown	1963
Just Ain't Enough Love / Last Night I Had A Vision	Motown	1964
Candy To Me / If You Don't Want My Love	Motown	1964

What Goes Up Must Come Down / Come On Home	Motown	1964*

* credited to Holland Dozier with the Four Tops and The Andantes

Eddie Holland Motown acetates

I Like Everything About you
Love Is What You Make It
Welcome Back
Twin Brother

Holland/Dozier Acetate

In The Neighbourhood aka 'On The Avenue'

Recordings by Lamont Dozier aka Lamont Anthony

Title	Label	Year
Let's Talk It Over / Popeye The Sailor Man*	Anna	1960
Let's Talk It Over / Benny The Skinny Man	Anna	1960
Just To Be Loved / I Didn't Know	Checkmate	1961
Dearest One / Fortune Teller Tell Me	Melody	1962

*This version was withdrawn under pressure from King Features who owned the copyright of George Segal's famous character

Also of interest

Hitsville U.S.A. Greetings To Tamla Motown Appreciation Society - 1964
This single was limited to 300 Copies.
Artists included The Miracles, Stevie Wonder, Marvin Gaye, The Marvelettes, The Temptations, Martha & The Vandellas, The Contours, Kim Weston, The Supremes and Eddie Holland

The Romeos
Lamont Dozier, Tyrone (Ty) Hunter, Gene Dyer, Ken Johnson, Leon Ware and Don Davenport

Gone, Gone, Get Away / Let's Be Partners	Fox	1957
Moments To Remember You By / Fine, Fine Baby	Fox	1957
Moments To Remember You By / Fine, Fine Baby	Atco	1958

The Satintones
Charles "Chico" Leverette, Freddie Gorman, **Brian Holland**, James Ellis, Sonny Sanders, Robert Bateman, Vernon Williams, Sammy Mack and Joe Charles

Motor City / Going To The Hop	Tamla	1960
My Beloved / Sugar Daddy	Motown	1960
Tomorrow And Always / A Love That Can Never Be	Motown	1961
Angel / A Love That Can Never Be	Motown	1961
I Know How It Feels / My Kind Of Love	Motown	1961
Zing Went The Strings Of My Heart / Faded Letter	Motown	1962
The Voice Masters Ty Hunter, C.P. Spencer, **Lamont Dozier**, David Ruffin and Freddie Gorman		
Hope And Pray / Oops I'm Sorry	Anna	1959
Needed / Needed (For Lovers Only)	Anna	1959
In Love In Vain / Two Lovers	Frisco	1960

An A to Z of Holland Dozier Holland

Please note that this covers the period from 1959 to 1977

A Bad Case Of Love [Brian Holland, Lamont Dozier, Eddie Holland] The Marvelettes - no known pressing [1965]

A Bird In The Hand (Is Worth Two In The Bush) [Eddie Holland, Norman Whitfield] The Velvelettes [1965]

A Gift Of Me [Ruth Copeland, Brian Holland, Lamont Dozier, Eddie Holland] Ruth Copeland [1971]

A Little Bit Of Lovin' [Brian Holland, Lamont Dozier, Henry Cosby] Eddie Holland no known pressing [1962]

A Little Bit Of Sympathy, A Little Bit Of Love [Lamont Dozier, Brian Holland, Anthony Hester] The Marvelettes [1963]

A Little More [Brian Holland, Lamont Dozier, Eddie Holland] Honey Cone [1971]

A Love Like Yours (Don't Come Knocking Everyday) [Brian Holland, Lamont Dozier, Eddie Holland] Martha & the Vandellas [1965]

A Need For Love [Eddie Holland] The Marvelettes [1964]

A Tear For The Girl [Eddie Holland] Martha & the Vandellas [1964]

A Tear From A Woman's Eyes [Brian Holland, Lamont Dozier, Eddie Holland] acetate The Temptations [1964]

Ain't It Good Feeling Good [Brian Holland Eddie Holland Richard Davis M Miller] Eloise Laws [1977]

Ain't Love Wonderful [Brian Holland, Lamont Dozier, Eddie Holland] Eddie Holland - no known pressing [1964]

Ain't Too Proud To Beg [Norman Whitfield, Eddie Holland]
The Temptations [1965]

All I Do Is Think Of You [Michael L. Smith Brian Holland] Jackson 5
[1975]

All I Know About You [Frank DeVol, Brian Holland, Lamont Dozier,
Eddie Holland] The Supremes [1967]

All I Need [Eddie Holland, Frank Wilson, R. Dean Taylor]
The Temptations [1967]

All That Glitters Isn't Gold [Brian Holland, Lamont Dozier, Billy
Gordon] acetate Martha & the Vandellas [1962]

All The Love I've Got [Berry Gordy Jr, Brian Holland, Janie Bradford]
Marv Johnson [1960]

All We Need Is Understanding [Brian Holland, Lamont Dozier, Eddie
Holland] Chairmen Of The Board [1971]

All You Can Do With Love [Harold Beatty Brian Holland Eddie Holland]
Dynamic Superiors [1977]

Any Girl In Love (Knows What I'm Going Through) [Brian Holland,
Lamont Dozier, Eddie Holland] The Supremes [1965]

Are You Man Enough, Are You Strong Enough? [Brian Holland,
Lamont Dozier, Eddie Holland] Honey Cone [1970]

Ask Any Girl [Brian Holland, Lamont Dozier, Eddie Holland]
The Supremes [1964]

Baby Don't You Do It [Brian Holland, Lamont Dozier, Eddie Holland]
Marvin Gaye [1964]

Baby I Need Your Loving [Brian Holland, Lamont Dozier, Eddie Holland]
Four Tops [1964]

Baby Love [Brian Holland, Lamont Dozier, Eddie Holland] The Supremes
[1964]

Back In My Arms Again [Brian Holland, Lamont Dozier, Eddie Holland]
The Supremes [1964]

Band Of Gold [Brian Holland, Lamont Dozier, Eddie Holland] Freda
Payne [1969]

Beach Ball [Brian Holland, Lamont Dozier, Eddie Holland]
The Supremes [1964]

Beauty Is Only Skin Deep [Norman Whitfield, Eddie Holland]
The Temptations [1966]

Because I Love You [Brian Holland, Robert Bateman, Vernon Williams,
Chester Scott]

Bernadette [Brian Holland, Lamont Dozier, Eddie Holland]
Four Tops [1966]

Big Joe Moe [Brian Holland, William Stevenson]
Singin' Sammy Ward [1962]

Bikini Party [Brian Holland, Lamont Dozier, Eddie Holland]
The Supremes no known pressing [1964]

Brenda [Eddie Holland] Eddie Holland [1963]

Bright Lights Big City [Eddie Holland, Norman Whitfield]
no known pressing Edwin Starr

Bring Back The Love [James Dean, William Weatherspoon, Jack Goga,
Eddie Holland] The Monitors [1967]

Build Him Up [Brian Holland, Lamont Dozier, Eddie Holland]
Martha & the Vandellas no known pressing [1962]

California Sunset [Lamont Dozier] The Originals Motown [1975]

Camouflage [M Miller Brian Richard Davis Holland Brian Holland]
Eloise Laws [1977]

Call On Me [Brian Holland, Lamont Dozier, Eddie Holland]
Four Tops [1964]

Can I Get A Witness [Brian Holland, Lamont Dozier, Eddie Holland]
Marvin Gaye [1963]
Can You Fix It (My Broken Heart) [Brian Holland, Lamont Dozier,
Eddie Holland] Mary Wells [1963]

Candy To Me [Brian Holland, Lamont Dozier, Eddie Holland]
Eddie Holland [1964]

Can't Break The Habit [Brian Holland, Lamont Dozier, Eddie Holland]
Martha & the Vandellas acetate [1965]

Can't Get Enough (Instrumental) [Holland Dozier Holland] Holland-
Dozier [1973]

Can't Get Enough Of You [Eddie Holland Brian Holland Angelo Bond]
Tyrone Edwards [1974]

Chairman Of The Board [Holland Dozier] Chairmen Of The [1970]

Cherish What Is Dear To You [Holland Dozier] Freda Payne Invictus
[1971]

Coca Cola commercial (Baby Love) [Brian Holland, Lamont Dozier,
Eddie Holland] The Supremes [1965]

Coca Cola commercial (When the lovelight) [Brian Holland, Lamont
Dozier, Eddie Holland] The Supremes no known pressing [1965]

Come And Get These Memories [Brian Holland, Lamont Dozier, Eddie
Holland] Martha & the Vandellas [1963]

Come Back [Holland Dozier] Jones Girls [1972]

Come Into My Life [Brian Holland Eddie Holland Richard Davis] The
Supremes [1976]

Come Into My Palace [Wm. Stevenson, Lee Moore, Brian Holland]
Lee & the Leopards [1962]

(Come 'Round Here) I'm The One You Need [Brian Holland, Lamont
Dozier, Eddie Holland] The Miracles [1966]

Come Together [Brian Holland] Brian Holland previously unissued Invictus CD

Come On Home [Brian Holland, Lamont Dozier, Eddie Holland, Janie Bradford] Holland & Dozier [1963]

Come See About Me [Brian Holland, Lamont Dozier, Eddie Holland] The Supremes [1964]

Continental Strut [Brian Holland, Robert Bateman, William Mitchell] The Satintones acetate [1960]

Contract On Love [Brian Holland, Janie Bradford, Lamont Dozier] Little Stevie Wonder [1962]

Crumbs Off The Table [Brian Holland, Lamont Dozier, Eddie Holland Scherrie Payne] Glass House [1969]

Dance A While, Cry A While [Eddie Holland, Norman Whitfield] The Marvelettes Acetate [1963]

Darling Baby [Brian Holland, Lamont Dozier, Eddie Holland] The Elgins [1965]

Darling, I Hum Our Song [Brian Holland, Lamont Dozier, Eddie Holland] Eddie Holland [1962]

Day Dreamer [Lamont Dozier, Fran Heard, Eddie Holland] no known pressing Eddie Holland [1962]

Dearest One [Brian Holland, Lamont Dozier, Eddie Holland] Lamont Dozier [1962]

Deeper And Deeper [Norma Toney Brian Holland, Lamont Dozier, Eddie Holland] Freda Payne [1970]

Detroit Is Happening [Brian Holland, Lamont Dozier, Eddie Holland, Frank DeVol] Willie Horton [1967]

Don't Blame Me [Brian Holland, Freddie Gorman, Robert Bateman] Freddie Gorman no known pressing [1961]

Don't Burn The Bridge (That Took You Across) [Eddie Holland Lamont Dozier Brian Holland] Dionne Warwick [1973]

Don't Compare Me With Her [Eddie Holland, Janie Bradford, Lamont Dozier] Kim Weston [1965]

Don't Fool Around [R. Dean Taylor, Eddie Holland] R. Dean Taylor [1967]

Don't Go Looking For Something (You Don't Want To See) [Holland Dozier] Glass House [1972]

Don't Leave Me [Brian Holland, Robt. Bateman, Wm. Sanders, Berry Gordy Jr] Marv Johnson [1959]

Don't Leave Me [Holland Dozier Holland] Holland-Dozier [1972]

Don't Leave Me Starving For Your [Holland Dozier Holland] Holland-Dozier [1972]

Don't Lose What You Got (Trying to Get Back What You Had) [Brian Holland Eddie Holland] Jr. Walker & All Stars [1976]

Don't Tear Down What Took So Long To Build [Harold Beatty Brian Holland Eddie Holland Lawrence T. Horn] G.C. Cameron [1977]

Don't Let It Rain On Me [Holland Dozier Scherrie Payne] Glass House [1972]

Don't Let My Teardrops Bother You [Eddie Holland Lamont Dozier Brian Holland Richard Wylie] Dionne Warwick [1973]

Don't Let True Love Die [Brian Holland, Lamont Dozier, Eddie Holland, James Dean] The Supremes [1965]

Don't Stop Playing Our Song [Brian Holland, Lamont Dozier, Eddie Holland] Holland Dozier [1974]

Don't Turn The Lights Off [Lamont Dozier] The Originals [1975]

Early Morning Love [Eddie Holland Brian Holland] The Supremes [1975]

Everybody's Got A Song To Sing [Holland Dozier Holland] Chairmen Of The Board [1972]

Everybody Needs Love [Eddie Holland, Norman Whitfield] Jimmy Ruffin [1965]

Everybody's Tippin' [William Weatherspoon Angelo Bond Brian Holland, Lamont Dozier, Raynard Miner] Danny Woods [1972]

Everything's Tuesday [Brian Holland, Lamont Dozier, Eddie Holland, D Dumas] Chairmen Of The Board [1970]

Everything Is Good About You [James Dean, Eddie Holland] The Supremes [1965]

Faded Letter [Vernon Williams, Robt. Bateman, Sammy Mack, Brian Holland] The Satintones [1961]

Fifty Years [Lamont Dozier] The Originals [1975]

Financial Affair [Lamont Dozier] The Originals [1975]

Finders Keepers Losers Weepers [Brian Holland, Lamont Dozier, Eddie Holland] The Marvelettes [1964]

Filet De Soul [Brian Holland, Lamont Dozier, Eddie Holland] Flaming Ember (1969)

Fire [Brian Holland, William Stevenson, Andre Williams] Gino Parks [1961]

Flashbacks And Reruns [Brian Holland, Lamont Dozier, Eddie Holland, General Johnson] Flaming Ember [1970]

Forever Came Today [Brian Holland, Lamont Dozier, Eddie Holland] The Supremes [1967]

Forever [Brian Holland, Freddie Gorman, Lamont Dozier] The Marvelettes [1962]

Fortune Teller (Tell Me) [Lamont Dozier, Freddie Gorman, Elizabeth Dozier] Lamont Dozier [1962]

189

Free Your Mind [Brian Holland, Lamont Dozier, Eddie Holland] The Politicians featuring McKinley Jackson [1972]

Function At The Junction [Frederick Long, Eddie Holland] Shorty Long [1966]

Funky Toes [Brian Holland, Lamont Dozier McKinley Jackson] The Politicians featuring McKinley Jackson [1972]

Gee Whiz, I Give [Eddie Holland, Robt. Bateman, Freddie Gorman] Henry Lumpkin no known pressing [1961]

Get The Cream Off The Top [Eddie Holland Brian Holland] Eddie Kendricks [1975]

Girl (Why You Wanna Make Me Blue) [Eddie Holland, Norman Whitfield] The Temptations [1964]

Girls It Ain't Easy [Brian Holland, Lamont Dozier, Eddie Holland] Honey Cone [1969]

Giving Up The Ring [Holland Dozier Ty Hunter] Glass House [1972]

Give It All Up [Eddie Holland Brian Holland Janie Bradford]] Dynamic Superiors [1977]

Give Me Just A Little More Time [Brian Holland, Lamont Dozier, Eddie Holland] Chairmen Of The Board [1970]

Goddess Of Love [Brian Holland, Lamont Dozier] The Marvelettes [1962]

Going Down For The Third Time [Brian Holland, Lamont Dozier, Eddie Holland] The Supremes [1966]

Good Lovin' Is Just A Dime Away [Lamont Dozier] The Originals [1975]

Gotta Have Your Love [Brian Holland, Janie Bradford] Eddie Holland [1962]

Gotta Say It, Gonna Tell It Like It Is [Brian Holland, Lamont Dozier, Eddie Holland] Four Tops no known pressing [1963]

Gotta See Jane [Eddie Holland, Ronald Miller, R. Dean Taylor] R. Dean Taylor [1968]

Grass Seems Greener (On The Other Side) [Lamont Dozier, Robert Hamilton] The Marvelettes acetate [1963]

Greetings (This Is Uncle Sam) [Robert Bateman, Lawrence Horn, Ronald Dunbar] The Valadiers [1961]

Growing Pains [Brian Holland, Lamont Dozier, Eddie Holland] Brotherly Love [1972]

Guarantee (For A Lifetime) [Brian Holland, Lamont Dozier, Eddie Holland] Mary Wells [1966]

Hanging On To A Memory [Brian Holland, Lamont Dozier, Eddie Holland, D Dumas] Chairmen Of The Board [1971]

Happy Go Lucky [Norman Whitfield, Eddie Holland] Eddie Holland acetate [1963]

He Gave Me You [William Stevenson, Brian Holland, Marv Johnson] Marv Johnson [1961]

He Holds His Own [Brian Holland, Lamont Dozier, Eddie Holland] Mary Wells [1964]

He Was Really Sayin' Somethin' [Norman Whitfield, Wm. Stevenson, Eddie Holland] The Velvelettes [1964]

He Who Picks A Rose [Norman Whitfield, Eddie Holland] The Temptations [1968]

He Won't Be True (Little Girl Blue) [Brian Holland, Lamont Dozier, Eddie Holland] The Marvelettes [1963]

Heart Broken, Heart Breaker (And The Clock) [Eddie Holland, Norman Whitfield] Eddie Holland no known pressing [1963]

Heart On (Loving You) [Brian Holland, Lamont Dozier, Eddie Holland]
Flaming Ember [1970]

Heaven Is There To Guide Us [Holland Dozier Scherrie Payne] Glass
House [1971]

Heaven Must Have Sent You [Brian Holland, Lamont Dozier, Eddie
Holland] The Elgins [1965]

Helpless [Brian Holland, Lamont Dozier, Eddie Holland]
Four Tops [1965]

He's All I Got [Brian Holland, Lamont Dozier, Eddie Holland, James
Dean] The Supremes [1966]

He's in My Life [Brian Holland, Lamont Dozier, Eddie Holland] Glass
House [1970]

Here Comes That Feeling Again [Brian Holland Eddie Holland Harold
Beatty M Woods] Dynamic Superiors [1977]

High Energy [Harold Beatty Brian Holland Eddie Holland] The Supremes
[1976]

Honey Boy [Brian Holland, Lamont Dozier, Eddie Holland] The Supremes
[1965]

Honey Love [Michael L. Smith Eddie Holland Brian Holland] Jackson 5
[1975]

Horse And Rider [Holland Dozier Scherrie Payne] Glass House [1972]

How Can I Live Without My Life [[Holland Dozier] Freda Payne [1972]

How Does It Feel [Brian Holland Lamont Dozier Eddie Holland] Honey
Cone [1971]

How Sweet It Is (To Be Loved By You) [Brian Holland, Lamont Dozier,
Eddie Holland] Marvin Gaye [1964]

I Believe In You Baby [Brian Holland Eddie Holland Angelo Bond]
Eloise Laws [1977]

I Can't Get Along Without You [Brian Holland, Lamont Dozier, Eddie Holland, Barrett Strong] Martha & the Vandellas [1969]

I Can't Give Back The Love I Feel For You [Nickolas Ashford, Valerie Simpson, Eddie Holland] Rita Wright [1967]

I Can't Go On Sharing Your Love [Brian Holland, Lamont Dozier, Eddie Holland] Chuck Jackson [1968]

I Can't Help Myself (Sugar Pie, Honey Bunch) [Brian Holland, Lamont Dozier, Eddie Holland] Four Tops [1965]

I Can't Make It Alone [Brian Holland, Lamont Dozier, Eddie Holland] Diana Ross & The Supremes [1968]

I Can't Make It Alone [Brian Holland, Lamont Dozier, Eddie Holland] Laura Lee [1973]

I Couldn't Cry If I Wanted To [Norman Whitfield, Eddie Holland] The Temptations [1966]

I Couldn't Dance unidentified acetate [Eddie Holland] Freddie Gorman

I Don't See You In My Eyes Anymore [Brian Holland, Lamont Dozier, Eddie Holland, D Dumas] [1972]

I Don't Want To Be Tied Down [Brian Holland Richard Davis Eddie Holland] The Supremes [1976]

I Got A Feeling [Brian Holland, Lamont Dozier, Eddie Holland] Four Tops [1966]

I Got A Weak Heart [Brian Holland, Lamont Dozier, Eddie Holland] unidentified acetate Kim Weston

I Got Heaven Right Here On Earth [Eddie Kendricks, Eddie Holland, Norman Whitfield] The Temptations [1966]

I Got It Part [Eddie Holland, NYPA] New York Port Authority [1976]

I Gotta Dance To Keep From Crying [Brian Holland, Lamont Dozier, Eddie Holland] The Miracles [1963]

193

I Gotta Find A Way To Get You Back [Cornelius Grant, Norman Whitfield, Eddie Holland, Eddie Kendricks] Tammi Terrell [1967]

I Gotta Get Home (Can't Let My Baby Get Lonely [Holland Dozier Holland] 8th Day [1972]

I Gotta Know Now [Norman Whitfield, Eddie Holland] The Temptations [1965]

I Guess I'll Always Love You [Brian Holland, Lamont Dozier, Eddie Holland] The Isley Brothers [1966]

I Had It All [Holland Dozier] Barrino Brothers [1972]

I Hear A Symphony [Brian Holland, Lamont Dozier, Eddie Holland] The Supremes [1965]

I Hope You Have Better Luck Than I Did [Brian Holland, Lamont Dozier, Eddie Holland] Martha & the Vandellas [1969]

I Know His Name (Only His Name) [Lamont Dozier, Brian Holland, Freddie Gorman] The Velvelettes [1963]

I Know How It Feels [Janie Bradford, Robt. Bateman, Brian Holland, Richard Wylie] The Satintones [1961]

(I Know) I'm Losing You [Norman Whitfield, Eddie Holland, Cornelius Grant] The Temptations [1966]

I Like Everything About You [Brian Holland, Lamont Dozier, Eddie Holland] Four Tops [1963]

I Need It Just As Bad As You [Eddie Holland Brian Holland Richard Wylie] Laura Lee [1974]

I Need You Right Now [Brian Holland Eddie Holland] Junior Walker & All Stars (with Thelma Houston) [1976]

I Shall Not Be Moved [Holland Dozier] Barrino Brothers [1972]

I Think You Need Love [Eddie Holland Lamont Dozier Brian Holland] Dionne Warwick [1973]

I Understand My Man [Brian Holland, Lamont Dozier, Eddie Holland]
The Elgins [1966]

I Use To Hate It (Till I Ate It) [Eddie Holland, Stafford Floyd, Rodney
Brown Reginald Brown] New York Port Authority [1977]

I Want A Guy [Berry Gordy Jr, Brian Holland, Freddie Gorman] The
Supremes [1960]

I Want Her Love [Eddie Holland, Norman Whitfield]
Jimmy Ruffin [1964]

I Wanted To Tell Her [Brian Holland, Lamont Dozier, Eddie Holland)
Holland & Dozier no known pressing [1963]

If It Ain't Love, It Don't Matter [Brian Holland, Lamont Dozier, Eddie
Holland] Glass House [1971]

If I'm Good Enough To Love (I'm Good Enough To Marry) [Brian,
Lamont Dozier Angelo Bond] Laura Lee [1973]

If It's Good To You (It's Good For You) [Brian Holland, Lamont
Dozier, Eddie Holland] Flaming Ember [1971]

If It's Love (It's Alright) [William Stevenson, Brian Holland]
Eddie Holland [1962]

If You Can Beat Me Rockin' (You Can Have My Chair) (Holland
Dozier Holland) Laura Lee [1972]

If You Don't Want To Be In My Life [Holland Dozier Holland]
Holland-Dozier [1973]

If You Don't Want My Love [Brian Holland, Lamont Dozier, Eddie
Holland] Eddie Holland [1964]

If You Were Mine [Brian Holland, Lamont Dozier, Eddie Holland]
The Andantes [1964]

I'll Come Crawling [Brian Holland, Lamont Dozier, Eddie Holland]
Chairmen Of The Board [1970]

I'll Be Your Servant [Eddie Holland, Brian Holland] G.C. Cameron [1977]

I'll Love You Forever [Richard Davis, Brian Holland, Eddie Holland] G.C. Cameron [1977]

I'll Take Care Of You [Brian Holland, Lamont Dozier, Eddie Holland] Marvin Gaye [1965]

I'll Turn To Stone [Brian Holland, Lamont Dozier, Eddie Holland, R. Dean Taylor] Four Tops [1966]

(I'm A) Road Runner [Brian Holland, Lamont Dozier, Eddie Holland] Junior Walker & the All Stars [1965]

I'm Comin' Home [Brian Holland, Robert Bateman, Berry Gordy Jr, Gwendolyn Murry] Marv Johnson [1959]

I'm Giving You Your Freedom [Brian Holland, Lamont Dozier, Eddie Holland] The Supremes [1962]

I'm Gonna Let My Heart Do the Walking [Harold Beatty Eddie Holland Brian Holland] The Supremes [1976]

I'm Grateful [Cleo Drake, George Fowler, Eddie Holland] Four Tops [1965]

I'm In A Different World [Brian Holland, Lamont Dozier, Eddie Holland] Four Tops [1967]

I'm In Love Again [Brian Holland, Lamont Dozier, Eddie Holland] The Supremes [1964]

I'm Gonna Hijack Ya, Kidnap Ya, Take What I Want [Holland Dozier Holland] Holland-Dozier [1973]

I'm Mad As Hell (Ain't Gonna Take No More) [Brian Holland, Harold Beatty, Eddie Holland] 100 Proof (Aged In Soul) [1977]

I'm Not Getting Any Better [Holland Dozier] Freda Payne [1971]

I'm On The Outside Looking In [Eddie Holland] Eddie Holland [1963]

I'm Ready For Love [Brian Holland, Lamont Dozier, Eddie Holland] Martha & the Vandellas [1966]

I'm So Glad [Brian Holland] Brian Holland [1974]

(I'm So Glad) Heartaches Don't Last Always [Brian Holland, Lamont Dozier, Eddie Holland] The Supremes [1964]

In And Out Of Love [Brian Holland, Lamont Dozier, Eddie Holland] The Supremes [1967]

In His Eyes [Eddie Holland] The Supremes no known pressing [1964]

In My Lonely Room [Brian Holland, Lamont Dozier, Eddie Holland] Martha & the Vandellas [1964]

It Could Never Happen [Lamont Dozier] The Originals [1975]

It Didn't Take Long [Brian Holland, Lamont Dozier, Eddie Holland] Danny Woods [1972]

It Don't Take Much To Keep Me [Brian Holland, Lamont Dozier, Eddie Holland] [1969]

It's A Good Feeling [Brian Holland, Lamont Dozier, Eddie Holland] The Miracles [1966]

It's All Your Fault [Brian Holland, Lamont Dozier, Eddie Holland] The Supremes [1965]

It's Best To Be Sure [Eddie Holland] Eddie Holland acetate [1963]

It's Better With Two (Coca Cola Commercial) [Brian Holland, Lamont Dozier, Eddie Holland] The Supremes no known pressing

It's Instrumental To Be Free [Brian Holland, Lamont Dozier, Eddie Holland] 8th Day [1971]

It's Not What You Stand For [Holland Dozier] Laura Lee [1972]

It's The Same Old Song [Brian Holland, Lamont Dozier, Eddie Holland] Four Tops [1965]

I've Got A Notion [George Fowler, Brian Holland, Robert Bateman]
Henry Lumpkin [1961]

Jealous lover [Brian Holland, Lamont Dozier, Eddie Holland] Martha &
the Vandellas [1963]

Jimmy Mack [Brian Holland, Lamont Dozier, Eddie Holland] Martha &
the Vandellas [1964]

Just A Few More Days [Eddie Holland] Eddie Holland [1963]

Just Ain't Enough Love [Brian Holland, Lamont Dozier, Eddie Holland]
Eddie Holland [1964]

Just A Little Bit Of You [Brian Holland Eddie Holland] Michael Jackson
[1975]

Just As Long As You Need Me [Brian Holland, Lamont Dozier, Eddie
Holland] Four Tops [1965]

Just Being Myself [Eddie Holland Lamont Dozier Brian Holland Richard
Wylie Reggie Dozier] Dionne Warwick [1973]

Just Can't Get Enough [Eddie Holland Brian Holland] Junior Walker &
All Stars [1976]

Just For You [Brian Holland, Robert Bateman, Freddie Gorman, Janie
Bradford] Freddie Gorman [1961]

Just Like In The Movies [Brian Holland, Lamont Dozier, R. Dean
Taylor] R. Dean Taylor no known pressing [1964]

Just One Last Look [Brian Holland, Lamont Dozier, Eddie Holland] The
Temptations [1966]

Keep Holding On [Eddie Holland Brian Holland] The Temptations
[1975]

Kiss Me When You Want To [Richard Davis, Brian Holland, Eddie
Holland] G.C. Cameron [1977]

Knock On My Door [Brian Holland, Lamont Dozier, Eddie Holland] The Marvelettes [1963]

Lady By Day [Brian Holland] Brian Holland [1974]

Last Night I Had A Vision [Brian Holland, William Stevenson, Eddie Holland] Eddie Holland no known pressing [1962]

Lead Me And Guide Me [Brian Holland, Lamont Dozier, Eddie Holland] Holland & Dozier no known pressing [1963]

Leave It In The Hands Of Love [James Dean, Brian Holland, Lamont Dozier, Eddie Holland] Martha & the Vandellas no known pressing [1968]

Leaving Here [Brian Holland, Lamont Dozier, Eddie Holland] Eddie Holland [1963]

Let It Flow [Holland Dozier Scherrie Payne] Glass House [1972]

Let Me Live In Your Life [Lamont Dozier] The Originals [1975]

Let Me Ride [Brian Holland, Lamont Dozier, Eddie Holland] Danny Woods [1972]

Let Yourself Go [Harold Beatty, Eddie Holland, Brian Holland The Supremes [1976]

Let's Get Together [Brian Holland] Brian Holland [1974]

Let's Go Somewhere [James Dean, Eddie Holland, R. Dean Taylor] R. Dean Taylor [1965]

Let's Run Away Together [Reggie Brown Stanford Brown Brian Holland, Eddie Holland] G.C. Cameron [1977]

(Like A) Nightmare [Brian Holland, Lamont Dozier, Eddie Holland] The Andantes [1964]

Little Darling (I Need You) [Brian Holland, Lamont Dozier, Eddie Holland] Marvin Gaye [1965]

Little Things Mean More (Coca Cola commercial) [Brian Holland, Lamont Dozier, Eddie Holland] Martha & the Vandellas acetate

Livin' High Off The Goodness Of Your Love [Holland Dozier Holland Scherrie Payne Richard Stringer] Barrino Brothers [1972]

Live Wire [Brian Holland, Lamont Dozier, Eddie Holland] Martha & the Vandellas [1963]

Living In A Memory [Brian Holland, Robert Bateman, Vernon Williams, Chester Scott] The Satintones no known pressing [1961]

Locking Up My Heart [Brian Holland, Lamont Dozier, Eddie Holland] The Marvelettes [1963]

(Loneliness Made Me Realize) It's You That I Need [Norman Whitfield, Eddie Holland] The Temptations [1967]

Lonely Lonely Man (Girl) Am I [Norman Whitfield, Eddie Holland, Eddie Kendricks] Jimmy Ruffin [1964]

Lonely Lover [Brian Holland, Lamont Dozier, Eddie Holland] Marvin Gaye [1965]

Look What We've Done To Love [Brian Holland, Lamont Dozier, Eddie Holland] Glass House [1971]

Love Factory Eloise Laws [Brian Holland, Lamont Dozier, Eddie Holland, Richard Wylie] [1973]

Love Feels Like Fire [Brian Holland, Lamont Dozier, Eddie Holland] Four Tops [1965]

Love Goes Deeper Than That [Harold Beatty Brian Holland Eddie Holland] - Eloise Laws [1977]

Love Has Gone [Brian Holland, Lamont Dozier, Eddie Holland] Four Tops [1964]

Love I Never Knew You Could Feel So Good [Brian Holland, Richard Davis, Brown Stafford] The Supremes [1976]

Love Is Here And Now You're Gone [Brian Holland, Lamont Dozier, Eddie Holland] The Supremes [1966]

Love Is In Our Hearts [Brian Holland, Lamont Dozier, Eddie Holland, James Dean] The Supremes [1966]

Love Is Like A Heat Wave [Brian Holland, Lamont Dozier, Eddie Holland] Martha & the Vandellas [1963]

Love Is Like An Itching In My Heart [Brian Holland, Lamont Dozier, Eddie Holland] The Supremes [1965]

Love (Keep Us Together) [Brian Holland Eddie Holland] Junior Walker & All Stars [1976]

Love Machine [Brian Holland, Lamont Dozier, Eddie Holland] McKinley Jackson & The Politicians [1971]

Love (Makes Me Do Foolish Things) [Brian Holland, Lamont Dozier, Eddie Holland] Martha & the Vandellas [1965]

Love's Gone Bad [Brian Holland, Lamont Dozier, Eddie Holland] Chris Clark [1966]

Make It Last Forever [Brian Holland, M Miller, Eddie Holland, Harold Beatty] Eloise Laws [1977]

Mashed Potato Time [Freddie Gorman, Robert Bateman, Brian Holland] DeeDee Sharp [1962]

Meet Me Halfway [Brian Holland, Lamont Dozier] Mable John previously unreleased

Mickey's Monkey [Brian Holland, Lamont Dozier, Eddie Holland] The Miracles [1963]

Mind, Body And Soul [Brian Holland, Lamont Dozier, Eddie Holland] Flaming Ember [1970]

Mother Dear [Brian Holland, Lamont Dozier, Eddie Holland] The Supremes [1965]

Mother Misery's Favourite Child [Holland Dozier Holland] Freda Payne [1973]

Mother You, Smother You [Brian Holland, Lamont Dozier, Eddie Holland, R. Dean Taylor] The Supremes [1966]

Mr. Misery (Let Me Be) [Lamont Dozier, Freddie Gorman, Brian Holland] The Miracles [1962]

My Baby's Home [Eddie Holland, Johnny Bristol, Faye Hale] The Contours no known pressing [1964]

My Kind Of Love [Brian Holland, Robert Bateman, Chester Scott, Vernon Williams] The Satintones [1961]

My Lady Bug Stay Away From That Beatle [Brian Holland, Lamont Dozier, Eddie Holland, R. Dean Taylor] band track only acetate R. Dean Taylor [1964]

My Love For You [Brian Holland, Robert Bateman, Janie Bradford] The Satintones no known pressing [1961]

My Mind's On Leaving But My Heart Won't Let Me Go [Brian Holland, Lamont Dozier, Eddie Holland, General Johnson] Honey Cone [1970]

My Piece Of The Rock (Vocal) (Eddie Holland, Brian Holland, C Cullin) 100 Proof (Aged In Soul) [1976]

My Weakness Is You [Norman Whitfield, Eddie Holland] Edwin Starr [1967]

My World Is Empty Without You [Brian Holland, Lamont Dozier, Eddie Holland] The Supremes [1965]

New Breed Kinda Woman [Holland Dozier Holland Richard Wylie] Holland-Dozier [1973]

No Man Can Love Her Like I Do [Eddie Kendricks, Norman Whitfield, Eddie Holland] The Temptations [1968]

No Other One (Will Do) [Eddie Holland] Eddie Holland no known pressing [1963]

No Time For Tears [Norman Whitfield, Eddie Holland] The Marvelettes [1965]

Nothing But Heartaches [Brian Holland, Lamont Dozier, Eddie Holland] The Supremes [1965]

Nothing But Soul [Brian Holland, Lamont Dozier, Eddie Holland] Junior Walker & the All Stars [1966]

Nothing Can Take The Place (Of Your Love) [Lamont Dozier] The Originals [1975]

Nothing's Gonna Change It [Janie Bradford, Brian Holland] The Valadiers no known pressing [1961]

Nothing Sweeter Than Love (Clyde Wilson, Holland- Dozier] [1972]

Nowhere To Run [Brian Holland, Lamont Dozier, Eddie Holland] Martha & the Vandellas [1964]

Oh Little Boy (What Did You Do To Me) [Andre Williams, Brian Holland, William Stevenson] [1964]

Old Love (Let's Try It Again) [Brian Holland, Lamont Dozier, Eddie Holland] Mary Wells [1962]

One Block From Heaven [Brian Holland, Lamont Dozier, Eddie Holland] Mary Wells [1966]

One Way Out [Brian Holland, Lamont Dozier, Eddie Holland] Martha & the Vandellas [1966]

Only You (Can Love Me Like You Love Me) [Harold Beatty, Brian Holland, Eddie Holland] The Supremes [1976]

Pa (I Need A Car) [Brian Holland, Lamont Dozier, Freddie Gorman] The Contours [1963]

Past Time Lover [Lamont Dozier, Brian Holland, Freddie Gorman] Marvin Gaye unidentified acetate

Penny Pincher [Brian Holland, Lamont Dozier, Eddie Holland] The Supremes [1964]

Playboy [Brian Holland, Robert Bateman, Gladys Horton, William Stevenson] The Marvelettes [1961]

Playing Games [Brian Holland, Lamont Dozier, Eddie Holland] Glass House [1972]

Please Don't Go Away [Mack Green, Janie Bradford, Brian Holland, Robert Bateman] The Magnetics unidentified acetate

Please Mr. Postman [Brian Holland, Robert Bateman, Freddie Gorman] The Marvelettes [1961]

Prelude [Holland Dozier] Freda Payne (1971)

Poor Girl [Eddie Holland, R. Dean Taylor] R. Dean Taylor [1964]

Put A Little Love Into It [Harold Beatty, Brian Holland, Eddie Holland] Eloise Laws [1977]

Put Yourself In My Place [Brian Holland, Lamont Dozier, Eddie Holland, John Thornton] The Elgins [1965]

Quicksand [Brian Holland, Lamont Dozier, Eddie Holland] Martha & the Vandellas [1963]

Reach Out I'll Be There [Brian Holland, Lamont Dozier, Eddie Holland] Four Tops [1966]

Reflections [Brian Holland, Lamont Dozier, Eddie Holland] Diana Ross & The Supremes [1967]

Remember Me [Brian Holland, Lamont Dozier, Eddie Holland] Laura Lee [1973]

Remove This Doubt [Brian Holland, Lamont Dozier, Eddie Holland] The Supremes [1964]

Robot In A Robot's World [Holland Dozier] Flaming Ember [1971]

Rocks In My Head [Brian Holland, Lamont Dozier, Eddie Holland] 8th Day [1972]

Roller Coaster [Brian Holland, Lamont Dozier, Raynard Miner] Danny Woods [1972]

Run, Run, Run [Brian Holland, Lamont Dozier, Eddie Holland] The Supremes [1963]

Savannah Lady [Holland Dozier D Dumas] [1971]

Send Me No Flowers [Brian Holland, Lamont Dozier, Eddie Holland] The Supremes unidentified acetate [1964]

7 Rooms Of Gloom [Brian Holland, Lamont Dozier, Eddie Holland] Four Tops [1966]

Shades Of Green [Brian Holland, Lamont Dozier, Eddie Holland] Flaming Ember [1969]

Shake Me, Wake Me (When It's Over) [Brian Holland, Lamont Dozier, Eddie Holland] Four Tops [1965]

Since The Days Of Pigtails (& Fairy tales) [Brian Holland, Lamont Dozier, Eddie Holland] Chairmen Of The Board [1970]

Since You've Been Gone [Brian Holland, Lamont Dozier, Eddie Holland] Four Tops [1965]

Since You've Been Loving Me [Eddie Holland, Marv Johnson] The Velvelettes [1965]

Slipping Away [Holland Dozier Holland] Holland-Dozier [1973]

So Long Baby [James Young, Robert Bateman, Brian Holland] The Marvelettes [1961]

So Long [Norman Whitfield, R. Dean Taylor, Eddie Holland] Marvin Gaye [1968]

Somebody Is Always Messing Up A Good Thing [Holland, Holland, Smith] Honey Cone [1977]
[19/60]

Someday, Someway [Brian Holland, Lamont Dozier, Freddie Gorman] The Marvelettes [1962]

Someone Just Like You (Harold Beatty, Eddie Holland, Brian Holland) Chairmen Of The Board (1976]

Something About You [Brian Holland, Lamont Dozier, Eddie Holland] Four Tops [1965]

Sorry Is A Sorry Word [Ivy Jo Hunter, Eddie Holland] The Temptations [1967]

Standing At The Crossroads Of Love [Brian Holland, Lamont Dozier, Eddie Holland] The Supremes [1963]

Standing In The Shadows Of Love [Brian Holland, Lamont Dozier, Eddie Holland] Four Tops [1966]

Stay In My Lonely Arms [Brian Holland, Lamont Dozier, Eddie Holland] The Elgins [1966]

Stay With Me [Brian Holland, Lamont Dozier, Eddie Holland] Eloise Laws [1973]

Stealing Moments From Another Woman's Life [Holland Dozier] Glass House 1970]

Stop! In The Name Of Love [Brian Holland, Lamont Dozier, Eddie Holland] The Supremes [1965]

Stop The World And Let Me Off [Brian Holland, Lamont Dozier, Eddie Holland, Angelo Bond] Flaming Ember [1971]

Strange I Know [Brian Holland, Lamont Dozier, Freddie Gorman] The Marvelettes [1962]

Suddenly, It's Yesterday [Holland Dozier] Freda Payne [1971]

Sunday Morning People [Brian Holland, Lamont Dozier, Eddie Holland] Honey Cone [1969]

Superwoman (You Ain't No Ordinary Woman) [Brian Holland] Brian Holland [1974]

Surfer Boy [Brian Holland, Lamont Dozier, Eddie Holland] The Supremes [1964]

Surfer's Call [Brian Holland, Lamont Dozier, R. Dean Taylor] R. Dean Taylor no known pressing [1964]

Suspicion [Brian Holland, Lamont Dozier, Eddie Holland] The Originals no known pressing [1966]

Sweet Dream Machine [Harold Beatty, Brian Holland, Eddie Holland] The Supremes [1976]

Sweet Rhapsody [Lamont Dozier] The Originals [1975]

Take A Chance On Me [Brian Holland, Freddie Gorman, Robert Bateman] Eddie Holland [1961]

Take A Chance [Brian Holland, Robert Bateman, Marty Coleman] The Valadiers [1961]

Take Me Back [Brian Holland Eddie Holland] Michael Jackson [1975]

Take Me In Your Arms (Rock Me A Little While) [Brian Holland, Lamont Dozier, Eddie Holland] Kim Weston [1964]

Take Me With You [Brian Holland, Lamont Dozier, Eddie Holland] Honey Cone [1970]

(Talking 'bout) Nobody But My Baby [Eddie Holland, Norman Whitfield] The Miracles [1963]

Thanks I Needed That [Brian Holland, Lamont Dozier, Eddie Holland] Glass House [1972]

Thank You (For Loving Me All The Way) [Eddie Holland, Clarence Paul, William Stevenson] Little Stevie Wonder [12/61]

The Boy From Crosstown [Eddie Holland, Norman Whitfield]
The Marvelettes [1966]

The Day I Found Myself [Brian Holland, Lamont Dozier, Eddie
Holland] Honey Cone [1971]

The Empty Crowded Room [Brian Holland, Lamont Dozier, Eddie
Holland] Flaming Ember [1970]

The Easiest Way To Fall [Brian Holland, Lamont Dozier, Eddie
Holland, Scherrie Payne] Freda Payne [1969]

The Feeling's Gone [Brian Holland, Lamont Dozier, Eddie Holland]
Honey Cone [1969]

The Girl's Alright With Me [Norman Whitfield, Eddie Kendricks, Eddie
Holland] The Temptations [1964]

The Happening [Frank DeVol, Brian Holland, Lamont Dozier, Eddie
Holland] The Supremes [1967]

The Judgement Day [Holland Dozier] Warlock [1972]

The Last Laugh [Janie Bradford, Brian Holland] Eddie Holland [1960]

The Music Box [Ruth Copeland, Brian Holland, Lamont Dozier, Eddie
Holland] New Play ft. Ruth Copeland [1969]

The Only Time I'm Happy [Brian Holland, Lamont Dozier, Eddie
Holland] The Supremes [1964]

The Picture Never Changes [Brian Holland, Lamont Dozier, Eddie
Holland] Holland Dozier [1974]

The Road We Didn't Take [Holland Dozier Dumas] Freda Payne [1971]

The Truth Will Come Out [Holland Beatty Holland] Honey Cone
[1977]

The Unhooked Generation [Brian Holland, Lamont Dozier, Eddie
Holland] Freda Payne [1969]

The Wheels Of The City [Brian Holland, Lamont Dozier, Eddie Holland]
The Supremes no known pressing [1966]

The World Don't Owe You A Thing [Holland Dozier] Freda Payne
[1970]

The World We Live In [Brian Holland, Lamont Dozier, Eddie Holland,
McKinley Jackson] The Politicians featuring McKinley Jackson [1972]

There He Is (At My Door) [Eddie Holland, Freddie Gorman]
The Vells [1962]

There's A Ghost In My House [Brian Holland, Lamont Dozier, Eddie
Holland, R. Dean Taylor] R. Dean Taylor [1966]

There's No Love Left [Brian Holland, Lamont Dozier, Eddie Holland,
James Dean] The Isley Brothers [1965]

There's No Stopping Us Now [Brian Holland, Lamont Dozier, Eddie
Holland] The Supremes [1966]

There's Room at the Top [Harold Beatty, Eddie Holland, Brian Holland]
unreleased The Supremes

(They Call Me) Cupid [Brian Holland, Norman Whitfield, Berry Gordy
Jr] Mickey Woods [1961]

Third Finger, Left Hand [Brian Holland, Lamont Dozier, Eddie
Holland] Martha & the Vandellas [1964]

This Is When I Need You Most [Brian Holland, Lamont Dozier, Eddie
Holland] Martha & the Vandellas [1963]

This Little Girl [Eddie Holland, Wm. Stevenson, Henry Cosby]
Stevie Wonder [1963]

This Old Heart Of Mine (Is Weak For You) [Brian Holland, Lamont
Dozier, Eddie Holland, Sylvia Moy] The Isley Brothers [1965]

This Will Make You Dance [Harold Beatty Brian Holland] G.C.
Cameron [1977]

Three Thousand Miles From Home [Brian Holland, Stafford Floyd, Reginald Brown] NYPA [1977]

Throw A Farewell Kiss [Norman Whitfield, Eddie Holland] The Velvelettes [1964]

Tie A String Around Your Finger [Brian Holland, Lamont Dozier, Eddie Holland, Janie Bradford] The Marvelettes [1963]

Tighten Him Up [Brian Holland, Lamont Dozier, Eddie Holland] Eloise Laws [1972]

Till The Boat Sails Away [Barry Payne, Harold Beatty, Brian Holland, Eddie Holland] The Supremes High Energy [1976]

Time Changes Things [Brian Holland, Janie Bradford, Lamont Dozier] The Supremes [1962]

To Think You Would Hurt Me [Brian Holland, Robert Gordy] Martha & the Vandellas [1963]

To William In The Night [Ruth Copeland, Brian Holland, Lamont Dozier, Eddie Holland] Ruth Copeland [1971]

Too Hurt To Cry, Too Much In Love To Say Goodbye [Brian Holland, Lamont Dozier, Eddie Holland] The Darnells [1963]

Too Late To Cry [Brian Holland, Lamont Dozier, Eddie Holland] Eddie Holland no known pressing [1963]

Too Many Fish In The Sea [Norman Whitfield, Eddie Holland] The Marvelettes [1964]

Too Strong To Be Strung Along [Brian Holland, Lamont Dozier, Freddie Gorman] The Marvelettes [1962]

Touch Me [Eddie Holland Brian Holland] Eloise Laws [1974]

Touch Me Jesus [Holland Dozier Angelo Bond] Glass House [1971]

Treat Her Right [Brian Holland, Lamont Dozier, Eddie Holland] Eddie Holland; band track only acetate [1964]

Tricked and Trapped (By A Tricky Trapper) [Brian Holland, Lamont Dozier, Eddie Holland] Chairmen Of The Board [1970]

True Love Will Go A Mighty Long Way [Brian Holland, Wm. Stevenson, Eddie Holland] Eddie Holland [05/62]

True, True Loving (The World's Greatest Thing) [Eddie Holland, Norman Whitfield] Marvin Gaye [1963]

Try It You'll Like It [Brian Holland Winford Terry Raynard Miner] Barrino Brothers [1972]

Try On My Love For Size [Holland Dozier] Chairmen Of The Board [1971]

Twilight Zone [Eddie Holland - NYPA] NYPA [1977]

Twin Brother [Lamont Dozier, William Robinson, Brian Holland] Eddie Holland no known pressing [1962]

Twistin' Postman [Robert Bateman, Brian Holland, William Stevenson] The Marvelettes [1961]

Two Can Be As Lonely As One [Brian Holland, Lamont Dozier, Eddie Holland] Danny Wood [1972]

Two Wrongs Don't Make A Right [Holland Dozier Holland] Freda Payne [1973]

Two Ends Against The Middle [Eddie Holland] The Contours no known pressing [1963]

Two For The Price Of One [Brian Holland, Lamont Dozier, Eddie Holland] Holland & Dozier no known pressing [1963]

Um-Boot-Tieno (Baby I Don't Know) [Brian Holland, Lamont Dozier, Eddie Holland, Johnny Bristol] The Contours no known pressing [1964]

Unhooked Generation [Brian Holland, Lamont Dozier, Eddie Holland] Freda Payne [1969]

211

Until You Love Someone [Brian Holland, Lamont Dozier, Eddie Holland] Four Tops [1966]

Up The Organization [Brian Holland, Lamont Dozier, Eddie Holland] Harrison Kennedy [1972]

Uptight [Brian Holland, Barney Ales, Irving Biegel] Herman Griffin & Band [1962]

We Couldn't Get Along Without You [Brian Holland, Lamont Dozier, Eddie Holland] The Supremes acetate [1966]

Welcome Back [Eddie Holland] Eddie Holland [1963]

Westbound No.9 [Brian Holland, Lamont Dozier, Eddie Holland] Flaming Ember [1970]

We've Come Too Far To Walk Away Now [Brian Holland, Eddie Holland] Laura Lee [1973]

We've Got A Way Out Love [Brian Holland, Lamont Dozier, Eddie Holland] The Originals [1969]

What About Me [Janie Bradford, Brian Holland, Wm. Stevenson] Eddie Holland [1961]

What Do You Want With Him [Lamont Dozier, Mose Boone, Freddie Gorman] Marvin Gaye [1962]

What Goes Up Must Come Down [Brian Holland, Lamont Dozier, Eddie Holland] Holland & Dozier [1963]

When The Lovelight Starts Shining Through His Eyes [Brian Holland, Lamont Dozier, Eddie Holland] The Supremes [1963]

When Will It End [Brian Holland, Lamont Dozier, Eddie Holland] Honey Cone [1970]

When Will She Tell Me She Needs Me [General Johnson, Brian Holland, Lamont Dozier, Eddie Holland] Chairmen Of The Board [1971]

Where Did Our Love Go [Brian Holland, Lamont Dozier, Eddie Holland] The Supremes [1964]

Where Did You Go [Brian Holland, Lamont Dozier, Eddie Holland] Four Tops [1964]

Where's All The Joy [Brian Holland, Lamont Dozier, Eddie Holland] Flaming Ember [1970]

While You're Out Looking For Sugar [Brian Holland, Lamont Dozier, Eddie Holland] Honey Cone [1969]

Whisper You Love Me Boy [Brian Holland, Lamont Dozier, Eddie Holland] Mary Wells [1964]

White House Twist [Brian Holland, Berry Gordy Jr, Barney Ales] The Twistin' Kings [1961]

Who Could Ever Doubt My Love [Brian Holland, Lamont Dozier, Eddie Holland] The Supremes [1964]

Who Knows [James Hendrix, Brian Holland, Robert Bateman] Cornell Blakely] [1961]

We Belong Together [Brian Holland, Lamont Dozier, Eddie Holland] Honey Cone [1971]

We Should Be Closer Together [Janie Bradford Freddie Gorman William Gaines Brian Holland] The Supremes [1976]

Well Worth Waitin' For Your Love [Holland Dozier Holland Richard Wylie] Barrino Brothers [1973]

We're Almost There [Brian Holland Eddie Holland] Michael Jackson [1975]

We've Come Too Far To Walk Away [Brian Holland, Eddie Holland] Laura Lee [1973]

We've Gotta Find A Way Back To Love [Brian Holland, Lamont Dozier, Eddie Holland] Freda Payne [1973]

213

Whose It Gonna Be [Brian Holland, Lamont Dozier, Eddie Holland] Honey Cone [1971]

When Love Was A Child [Holland Dozier] Barrino Brothers [1971]

Where Did We Go Wrong [Eddie Holland, Brian Holland] Eloise Laws featuring Brian Holland [1977]

Where Do I Go From Here [Eddie Holland, Brian Holland] The Supremes [1975]

Why Can't We Be Lovers [Brian Holland, Lamont Dozier, Eddie Holland] Holland-Dozier [1972]

Why Don't You Stay [Brian Holland, Lamont Dozier, Eddie Holland] Flaming Ember [1970]

Why'd You Lie [Lamont Dozier] The Originals [1975]

With All My Heart [Brian Holland, Lamont Dozier, Eddie Holland] The Supremes no known pressing [1964]

Without The One You Love [Brian Holland, Lamont Dozier, Eddie Holland] Four Tops [1964]

Working On A Building Of Love [Brian Holland, Lamont Dozier, Eddie Holland] Chairmen Of The Board [1971]

You Ain't No Ordinary Woman [Brian Holland, Eddie Holland] Junior Walker & All Stars [1976]

You Are The Heart of Me [Michael L Smith, Eddie Holland] Dionne Warwick [1973]

You Broke My Heart [Brian Holland, Freddie Gorman, Robert Bateman] Cornell Blakely [1961]

You Brought The Joy [Holland Dozier] Freda Payne (1971)

You Can't Hurry Love [Brian Holland, Lamont Dozier, Eddie Holland] The Supremes [1966]

You Deserve What You Got [Eddie Holland, Brian Holland, William Stevenson] Eddie Holland [1962]

You Don't Know It [Brian Holland, Robert Bateman, Vernon Williams, - Scott] The Satintones no known pressing [1961]

You Got Me Loving You Again [Brian Holland, M Miller, Eddie Holland, Harold Beatty] Eloise Laws [1977]

You Keep Me Hangin' On [Brian Holland, Lamont Dozier, Eddie Holland] The Supremes [1966]

You Keep Me Moving On [Brian Holland, Eddie Holland, Richard Davis, Hugh Wyce] The Supremes [1976]

You Keep Running Away [Brian Holland, Lamont Dozier, Eddie Holland] Four Tops [1967]

You Lost The Sweetest Boy [Brian Holland, Lamont Dozier, Eddie Holland] Mary Wells [1963]

You Made Me Come To You [Brian Holland, Lamont Dozier, Eddie Holland] Honey Cone [1971]

You Made Me An Offer I Can't Refuse [Brian Holland, Lamont Dozier, Eddie Holland Raynard Miner] Eloise Laws [1972]

You Need A Strong Dose Of Love [Harold Beatty Brian Holland Eddie Holland] G.C. Cameron [1977]

You Should Know [Janie Bradford, Brian Holland, Stanley Ossman] The Marvelettes [1962]

You Took Me From A World Outside [Holland Dozier Holland] Holland-Dozier [1973]

(You Were Made) Especially For Me [Michael L. Smith Brian Holland] Jackson 5 [1975]

You'll Be Sorry Someday [Brian Holland, Robt. Bateman, Marty Coleman] The Valadiers [1963]

Your Love Is Amazing [Brian Holland, Lamont Dozier, Eddie Holland]
Four Tops no known pressing [1964]

Your Sweet Love [Harold Edwards, Brian Holland, Robert Bateman]
The Satintones no known pressing [1961]

Your Unchanging Love [Brian Holland, Lamont Dozier, Eddie Holland]
Marvin Gaye [1965]

You're A Wonderful One [Brian Holland, Lamont Dozier, Eddie
Holland] Marvin Gaye [1964]

You're Gone (But Always In My Heart) [Brian Holland, Lamont
Dozier, Eddie Holland] The Supremes [1964]

You're Gonna Need Me [Eddie Holland, Lamont Dozier, Brian Holland,
Richard Wylie] Dionne Warwick [1973]

You're My Driving Wheel [F Stafford, R Brown, Brian Holland, Harold
Beatty] The Supremes [1976]

You're Sweeter As The Days Go By [Eddie Holland]
Eddie Holland untitled acetate [1963]

You're The Only Bargain I've Got [Brian Holland, Lamont Dozier,
Eddie Holland, General Johnson] Jones Girls [1972]

You're What's Missing in My Life [Harold Beatty Eddie Holland Brian
Holland] The Supremes [1976]

Your Love Controls Me [Brian Holland, Lamont Dozier, Eddie Holland]
Jones Girls [1972]

You've Been A Long Time Coming [Brian Holland, Lamont Dozier,
Eddie Holland] Marvin Gaye [1965]

You've Been My Rock [Holland Dozier] Warlock [1972]

You've Got Extra Added Power In Your Love (Brian Holland, Harold
Beatty, Eddie Holland) Chairmen Of The Board [1976]

216

A list of some of the key Holland Dozier Holland songs from their Motown period showing a selection of the other artists who recorded versions. Thanks to Alan Warner

Baby Don't You Do It - Marvin Gaye

Other versions include:

The Band (Capitol/EMI)
The Isley Brothers (Tamla/UMG)
Nicolette Larson (Warner Bros/WSP)
The Small Faces (UK Decca/UMG)
The Steampacket
The Who (US Decca/UMG)
Delroy Wilson (Trojan)
Stevie Wonder (Tamla/UMG)

Baby I Need Your Loving - Four Tops

Other versions include:

The Fourmost (Parlophone/EMI)
Johnny Rivers (Imperial/EMI)
O.C. Smith (Columbia/Sony)
Carl Carlton (RCA/BMG)
Bobby Blue (Trojan)
Tom Clay (Mowest/UMG)
Double Exposure (Salsoul)
Lamont Dozier
Marvin Gaye & Tammi Terrell (Tamla/UMG)
The Heptones (Island/UMG)
Gladys Knight & The Pips (Soul/UMG)
Gene Pitney (Musicor)
Mitch Ryder & The Detroit Wheels (New Voice/UMG)
Sandie Shaw (Pye/Sanctuary)
Lisa Stansfield (RCA/BMG)
Joe Stubbs (Motorcity)
The Supremes (Motown/UMG)
Ruby Turner & The Four Tops (Jive/Zomba)
Was (Not Was) (Chrysalis/EMI)

Baby Love - The Supremes

Other versions include:

Honey Bane (Zonophone)
Lamont Dozier (Hit House)
Henry Jerome & His Orchestra (UA/EMI)
The Mothers Of Invention (Rykodisc)
Diana Ross (RCA)
Shalamar (Solar)
Jean, Scherrie & Lynda of The Supremes (Motorcity)

Back In My Arms Again - The Supremes

Other versions include:

Michael Bolton (Columbia/Sony)
Derek & The Diamonds (Telarc)
Donnie Elbert (All Platinum/Sugarhill)
The Forester Sisters (Warner Bros.)
Hattie Littles (Gordy/UMG)

Can I Get A Witness - Marvin Gaye

Other versions include:

Sam Brown (A&M/UMG)
The Buckinghams (Columbia/Sony)
The Commodores (Motown/UMG)
Ian Gillan & The Javelins (Purple)
Lulu (UK Decca/UMG)
Lee Michaels (A&M/UMG)
Nine Below Zero (Indigo)
Barbara Randolph (Soul/UMG)
The Steampacket w/ Rod Stewart
The Rolling Stones (UK Decca/Abkco)
Dusty Springfield (Philips/UMG)
The Supremes (Motown/UMG)
Stevie Wonder (Tamla/UMG)

Come And Get These Memories - Martha & The Vandellas

Other versions include:

Fontella Bass (Checker/UMG)
Ellen Foley (Epic/Sony)
Hattie Littles (Hot)
The Supremes (Motown/UMG)

(Come 'Round Here) I'm The One You Need - The Miracles

Other versions include:

The Cowsills (MGM/UMG)
The Jackson 5 (Motown/UMG)

Come See About Me - The Supremes

Other versions include:

Junior Walker & The All Stars (Soul/UMG)
The Afghan Whigs (Sub Pop)
Bill Black's Combo (Hi/CSM)
Lloyd Charmers (Trojan)
Dave 'Baby' Cortez (Roulette/Rhino)
The Ikettes (UA/EMI)
Lori Johnson (Orchard)
Gladys Knight & The Pips
Lord High Fixers (Sympathy)
Barbara Mason (Arctic)
Willie Mitchell (Hi/CSM)
Tracy Nelson (Flying Fish)
The Newbeats (Hickory)
The Originals (Motown/UMG)
Freda Payne (Volt/Fantasy)
Bonnie Pointer (Motown/UMG)
Mitch Ryder & The Detroit Wheels (New Voice/Rhino)
Shakin' Stevens (Epic/Sony)
The Velvelettes (Motorcity)

Darling Baby - Elgins

Other versions include:

Saundra Edwards (Motorcity)
Jackie Moore (Atlantic)

Forever Came Today - Diana Ross & The Supremes

Other versions include:

The Jackson 5 (Motown/UMG)
Lynda Lawrence (Motorcity)
Shalamar (Soul Train)

The Happening - The Supremes

Other versions include:

Herb Alpert & The Tijuana Brass (A&M/UMG)
Matt Monroe (Parlophone/Capitol)

Heatwave - Martha & The Vandellas

Other versions include:

Lamont Dozier (Hit House)
The Jam (Polydor/UMG)
Lulu & The Luvvers (UK Decca/UMG)
Shonen Knife (Virgin)
The Supremes (Motown/UMG)
The Who (US Decca/UMG)
Linda Ronstadt (Asylum/WSP)

Heaven Must Have Sent You - The Elgins

Other versions include:

Bonnie Pointer (Motown/UMG)
Marvin Gaye (Tamla/UMG)
Johnny Mathis & Deniece Williams (Columbia/Sony)
The Supremes (Motown/UMG)

Helpless - Kim Weston

Other versions include:

Tracey Ullman (Stiff)
The Four Tops (Motown/UMG)
Manhattan Transfer (Atlantic/UMG)

How Sweet It Is (To Be Loved By You) - Marvin Gaye

Other versions include:

Jr. Walker & The All Stars (Soul/UMG)
James Taylor (Warner Bros)
Long John Baldry (Pye/Sanctuary)
Dave 'Baby' Cortez (Roulette/Rhino)
Tyrone Davis (Columbia)
Lamont Dozier (Hit House)
Chris Farlowe
Jerry Garcia (Arista/BMG)
The Isley Brothers (Motown/UMG)
Liz Lands (Motorcity)
Ketty Lester (Pete)
Sam & Dave
Take 6 (Reprise/WSP)
Ruby Turner with Junior Walker (Jive)
Earl Van Dyke & The Soul Brothers (Soul/UMG)
Joe Williams with Thad Jones & Mel Lewis (Solid State/EMI)

I Can't Help Myself (Sugar Pie, Honey Bunch) - Four Tops

Other versions include:

Donnie Elbert (Avco)
Shalamar (in their "Uptown Festival" medley) (Soul Train)
Bonnie Pointer (Motown/UMG)
Phil Collins & Paul Young (A&M/UMG)
Lamont Dozier (Hit House)
Taj Mahal (Private/BMG)
Martha & The Vandellas (Gordy/BMG)
The Real Thing (Jive)
Johnny Rivers (Imperial/EMI)

The Temptations & The Four Tops (Motown)
Earl Van Dyke & The Soul Brothers (Soul/UMG)

I Gotta Dance To Keep From Crying - The Miracles

Other versions include:

Jimmy James & The Vagabonds (Pye/Sanctuary)

I Guess I'll Always Love You - The Isley Brothers

Other versions include:

The Supremes (Motown/UMG)
The Timebox (Pye/Sanctuary)
The Valadiers (Motorcity)

I Hear A Symphony – The Supremes

Other versions include:

Booker T. & The M.G.'s (Stax/Fantasy)
Derek & The Diamonds (Telarc)
Lamont Dozier (Hit House)
The Isley Brothers (Tamla/UMG)
The Jackson 5 (Motown/UMG)
Diana Ross (Motown/UMG)
The Ventures (Liberty)
Wing & A Prayer Fife & Drum Corps. (Wing & A Prayer)
Stevie Wonder (Motown/UMG)

I'll Turn To Stone – Four Tops

Other versions include:

The Supremes (Motown/UMG)

(I'm A) Road Runner - Junior Walker & The All Stars

Other versions include:

Bill Cosby (Warner Bros./WSP)
Fleetwood Mac (Warner Bros./WSP)
Peter Frampton (A&M/UMG)
Humble Pie (King Biscuit)
Dr. Feelgood (UK Grand)
Geno Washington & The Ram Jam Band (Pye/Sanctuary)

I'm In A Different World - Four Tops

Other versions include:

Dave Stewart & Barbara Gaskin (Stiff)

I'm Ready For Love - Martha & The Vandellas

Other versions include:

The Four Tops (Motown/UMG)
Betty Lavette (Motorcity)
The Pointer Sisters (Planet/BMG)
The Temptations (Gordy/UMG)

In My Lonely Room - Martha & The Vandellas

Other versions include:

The Action (Parlophone/EMI)
Diana Ross & The Supremes (Motown/UMG)

It's The Same Old Song - Four Tops

Other versions include:

Jonathan King a.k.a. The Weathermen (B&C)
Shalamar (in their "Uptown Festival" medley) (Soul Train)
KC & The Sunshine Band (T.K./Rhino)
Phil Collins & Paul Young (A&M/UMG)
KC & The Sunshine Band (T.K./Rhino)
Johnny Rivers (Imperial/EMI)
Joe Stubbs (Motorcity)
The Supremes (Motown/UMG)

Third World (Island/UMG)
Bobby Vee (Liberty/EMI)

Jimmy Mack - Martha & The Vandellas

Other versions include:

Sheena Easton (EMI America)
Betty Lavette (Motorcity)
Laura Nyro & Labelle (Columbia/Sony)
Bonnie Pointer (Motown/UMG)

Just Ain't Enough Love - Eddie Holland

Other versions include:

The Isley Brothers (Tamla/UMG)

Leaving Here - Eddie Holland

Other versions include:

The Birds (UK Decca/UMG)
The Isley Brothers (Tamla/UMG)
Motorhead (United Artists/EMI)
Pearl Jam (Epic/Sony)
The Satelliters (Dionysus)
The Who (Decca/UMG)

Little Darling (I Need You) - Marvin Gaye

Other versions include:

The Doobie Brothers (Warner Bros/WSP)

Love Is Here And Now You're Gone - The Supremes

Other versions include:

Michael Jackson (Motown)
Rare Earth (Motorcity)
Tami Lynn (Mojo/Cotillion)

Love Is Like An Itching In My Heart - The Supremes

Other versions include:

Diana Ross (Motown & EMI)
Lisa (Hot)
Shalamar (Solar)
Sherri Taylor (Motor City)
Paul Young

A Love Like Yours - Martha & The Vandellas

Other versions include:

Ike & Tina Turner (A&M/UMG)
Cher & Nilsson (Warner/Spector)
Manfred Mann (HMV/EMI)
Dusty Springfield (Philips/UMG)
Ike Turner (Resurgence)
Kim Weston (Tamla/UMG)

Love's Gone Bad - Chris Clark

Other versions include:

Michael Jackson (Motown/UMG)
The Underdogs

Mickey's Monkey - Miracles

Other versions include:

The Hollies (Imperial/EMI)
Martha & The Vandellas (Gordy/UMG)
Mother's Finest (Columbia/Sony)
Smokey Robinson (Tamla/UMG)

My World Is Empty Without You - The Supremes

Other versions include:

The Afghan Whigs (Elektra/WSP)
The Andantes (Motorcity)
Vikki Carr (Liberty/EMI)
Lamont Dozier (Hit House)
Jose Feliciano (RCA/BMG)
Marsha Hunt (Track/UMG)
Margie Joseph (Fantasy)
David McCallum (Capitol/EMI)
The Miracles (Tamla/UMG)
Sandy Nelson (Imperial/EMI)
Della Reese (ABC/UMG)
Mary Wells (Atco/WSP)
Stevie Wonder (Tamla/UMG)
The Smith Connection (Music Merchant)

Nowhere To Run - Martha & The Vandellas

Other versions include:

The Isley Brothers (Tamla/UMG)
Hattie Littles (Motor City)
Laura Nyro & Labelle (Sony)
Bonnie Pointer (Motown/UMG)
Tower Of Power (Columbia/Sony)
Ruby Turner (Jive/Zomba)
Dynamic Superiors (Motown/UMG)
As Nowhere To Run 2000
By Nu Generation (Concept: 2000)

Put Yourself In My Place - The Elgins

Other versions include:

The Isley Brothers (Tamla Motown)
Saundra Edwards (Motor City)
The Hollies (EMI/Imperial)
The Supremes (Motown/UMG)
Delroy Wilson (Trojan)

Reach Out I'll Be There - Four Tops

Other versions include:

Diana Ross (Motown/UMG)
Gloria Gaynor (MGM/UMG)
Four Tops (Motown/UMG - remix
Michael Bolton (Columbia/Sony)
Irene Cara (Network)
Petula Clark
Bill Cosby (Warner Bros/WSP)
Joey Dee & The Starliters (Roulette/Rhino)
Derek & The Diamonds (Telarc)
Lamont Dozier (Hit House)
Chris Farlowe
Genesis (Polydor/UMG)
Thelma Houston (Motown/UMG)
The Jackson 5 (Motown/UMG)
David Johansen (Blue Sky)
Hank Mobley (Blue Note/EMI)
P.J. Proby (Liberty/EMI)
Run C&W
Bobby Taylor & The Vancouvers (Motorcity)

Reflections - Diana Ross & The Supremes

Other versions include:

Lamont Dozier (Hit House)
The Four Tops (Motown/UMG)
Leo Sayer (Chrysalis/EMI)
Syreeta (Motorcity)
The Jackson 5 (Motown/UMG)

7 Rooms Of Gloom - Four Tops

Other versions include:

Pat Benatar (Chrysalis/EMI)

Shake Me Wake Me (When It's Over) - Four Tops

Other versions include:

The Satintones (Motorcity)
Barbra Streisand (Columbia/Sony)

Something About You - The Four Tops

Other versions include:

Dave Edmunds (Arista/BMG)
Sisters Love (Motor City)

Standing In The Shadows Of Love - Four Tops

Other versions include:

Rod Stewart (Warner Bros/UMG)
Barry White (20th Century/UMG)

Stop! In The Name Of Love -The Supremes

Other versions include:

Margie Joseph (Volt/Fantasy)
Shalamar (in their "Uptown Festival" medley)
(Soul Train: 1977)
Stars On 45 (Radio)
The Hollies (Atlantic)
The California Raisins (Priority)
Barbara Dickson (Columbia/Sony)
Lamont Dozier (Hit House)
The Isley Brothers (Tamla/UMG)
Gene Pitney (Musicor)
Johnny Rivers (Imperial/EMI)
Sinitta (Arista/BMG)
Jean, Scherrie & Lynda of The Supremes (Motorcity)
Kim Weston (Motown/UMG)

Take Me In Your Arms (Rock Me A Little While) - Kim Weston

Other versions include:

The Isley Brothers
The Doobie Brothers
Blood, Sweat & Tears (Columbia/Sony)
Jermaine Jackson (Motown/UMG)

There's A Ghost In My House - R. Dean Taylor

Other versions include:

The Fall (Beggars Banquet: 1987) UK #30

This Old Heart Of Mine - The Isley Brothers

Other versions include:

Tammi Terrell (Motown/UMG)
Rod Stewart (Riva: 1975)
Rod Stewart & Ronald Isley (Warner Bros)
The Contours (Motorcity)
Lamont Dozier (Hit House)
The Supremes (Motown/UMG)
Delroy Wilson (Trojan)
The Zombies (BBC)

When The Lovelight Starts Shining - By The Supremes

Other versions include:

Bonnie Pointer (Motown/UMG)
Dusty Springfield (Philips/UMG)

Where Did Our Love Go - The Supremes

Other versions include:

Dave 'Baby' Cortez (Roulette/Rhino)
Lamont Dozier (Hit House)
Sinitta (Arista/BMG)
Soft Cell
Donnie Elbert (All Platinum: 1971) US #6 R&B, #15 Pop
The J.Geils Band (Atlantic/WSP: 1976) US #68 Pop
Manhattan Transfer (Atlantic/WSP: 1978) UK #40
Tricia Penrose (RCA/BMG: 1996) UK #71

Without The One You Love – The Four Tops

Other versions include:

The Supremes & The Four Tops (Motown)

You Can't Hurry Love - The Supremes

Other versions include:

The California Raisins (Priority)
The Four Tops (Motown/UMG)
Graham Parker (Mercury/UMG)
Barbara Randolph (Motorcity)
Diana Ross (Motown/UMG)
Sinitta (Arista/BMG)
Phil Collins (Atlantic: 1983) US #10 Pop, #9 AC, UK #1

You Keep Me Hangin' On - The Supremes

Other versions include:

Vanilla Fudge (Atco/WSP: 1967) US #67 Pop, UK #8
Kim Wilde (MCA/UMG: 1987) US #1 Pop, #30 AC
Booker T. & The M.G's (Stax/Fantasy)
Sam Harris (Motown/UMG)
Tom Jones (Parrot)
Hugh Masekela (Chisa/UMG)
Reba McEntire (MCA/UMG)
Wilson Pickett (Atlantic/WSP)
Rod Stewart (Warner Bros/WSP)
Jackie Wilson (Brunswick)

You're A Wonderful One - Marvin Gaye

Other versions include:

Don Bryant (Hi/ESM)

Glossary

The following books, magazines and people have been invaluable in putting together this history of Holland Dozier Holland:

Title and author	Publisher
To Be Loved Berry Gordy Jr	Headline, 1994
The Heart Of Rock & Soul Dave Marsh	Plume, 1989
Stars Of Soul And Rhythm & Blues Lee Hildebrand	Billboard,1994
Where Did Our Love Go? Nelson George	Omnibus Press, 1986
Will You Still Love Me Tomorrow Charlotte Grieg	Virago Press, 1989
Timelines Of African-American History Tom Cowan, PHD / Jack Maguire	Perigree, 1994
Motown - The History Sharon Davis	Guinness, 1988
Motown David Morse	Studio Vista, 1971
The Pen Is Mightier Than The Sword Chris Priddle	1979
Standing In The Shadows Of Motown Dr Licks	Hal Leonard Pub. 1989
The Algiers Motel Incident John Hershey	Bantam Books, 1968
Dream Girls Mary Wilson	Cooper Square Publishers
Dancing In The Streets Martha Reeves	Hyperion Books, 1994
Remembering the Riots James Nuechterlein	Copyright © 1997 First Things
Soulful Detroit Forum Administered by Russ Terrana	Soulfuldetroit.com

Magazines Blues & Soul, Soul Express, Black Music, Black Echoes

Individuals Marcel Visser, Steve Bryant, Richard Buskin, Nat Cramp, John Lester, Lewis Dene, John Reed, Robert Dennis

A big thank you to the following artists who found time to be interviewed.
Eddie Holland, Steve Mancha, Melvin Davis, Harrison Kennedy, General Johnson, Danny Woods, Gary 'Mudbone' Cooper, Rodney J. Brown of The Holland Group

About the author

Howard Priestley has always had an equal interest in African American culture, the world of comic books, television, movies and of course, Soul music. Almost at the same time as he began his formal Art training, he became a regular contributor to the British Comics Fan scene with stories appearing in Comics Unlimited, The Alternative Headmaster's Bulletin, Graphixus and Pssst! A Halifax based 3 issue series, Shock Therapy, was also produced. The work from this period was credited in the book, Nasty Tales – A History Of The British Underground Comic Scene, 2000.

In 1984 Harrier Comics produced a new 6-part series of Shock Therapy and during its run Howard was responsible for giving work to Stephen Baskerville and Andy Lanning, two artists who went on to work for both Marvel and DC Comics. From then on in he appeared briefly in Sideshow Comics and was pencilled in to write and illustrate a P-Funk Graphic Novel for Marvel Comics in New York that would have been a culmination of science fiction and funk mythology. Just prior to the project being started Marvel closed down its music-based section leaving him disillusioned with the comic industry. He began writing and illustrating Dog Tales for the German P-Funk fanzine, The New Funk Times. The strip was later reprinted in P-Views, another P-Funk fanzine from Germany and since that time he has remained a regular writer and illustrator for a variety of music publications from Germany, Finland and England.

He has designed CD covers and art for Bootsy Collins, Mutiny, Mallia Franklin, George Clinton, Ruth Copeland Featuring Parliament and sleeve notes for CD compilations including sleevenotes for "Sweet Taste" by former Chairman of The Board Harrison Kennedy, a 2004 Juno Nominee for Best Blues Album of the Year.

He helped to launch community radio in Calderdale and hosts a regular radio show "Soul City".

Printed in the USA
CPSIA information can be obtained
at www.ICGtesting.com
LVHW011142210923
758605LV00028B/70

9 781912 587575